Presented to

_____

by

_____

_____

on

_____

_____

With Best
Wishes for
a Life of
Usefulness

FAVORITE STORIES

from the New Testament.

BY ISABEL C. BYRUM.

Author of "Beautiful Stories from the Good Old Book."

Reprinted 2000 by YBS & Co.

Original printing 1905.
Reprinted in 2000 by YBS

God's Plan.

"How came I here?
    Can some one tell?
How has it come
    I chance to dwell
Upon this earth
    So great and wide?
How does it come
    I here abide?"

My darling child,
    Just wait and see;
Perhaps we'll solve
    This mystery.
It was God's plan
    To place you here,
So do not think
    It strange or queer.

God made this earth
    Long years ago,
And then he made
    All things that grow:
He made the birds,
    The flowers, too;
And was it strange
    That he made you?

5

God loves mankind,
  Whom he has made,
And for each one
  A plan has laid:
This plan was great,
  'Twas for us all;
Yes, it includes
  E'en children small.

"What plan was that?"
  Have patience, dear;
I'll tell you all
  That you would hear.
God made man so
  That though he dies,
His soul may live
  Up in the skies.

"What is his soul?"
  I thought you'd ask,
So to explain
  Will be my task.
When from the dust
  God first formed man,
He gave him strength
  To live and plan.

Man ruled the beasts
  Which gathered near;
While in those beasts
  There rose a fear
And all obeyed
  With one accord
This man, as though
  He'd been their Lord.

Why God chose man
  We can not tell
As ruler on
  This earth to dwell;

But it was so,
  And he gave man
A thinking soul,
  To suit his plan.

This raised the man
  On higher plane
To reason, act,
  Rule and explain.
The soul within
  Now placed him where
With angels he
  Might claim a share.

A conscience with
  The soul was giv'n,
To show the man
  The way to heav'n.
You see, dear child,
  Two ways there are,
Each leading to
  A home afar.

One home is heav'n;
  The other, hell:
Both homes are where
  Men's souls will dwell.
You see, dear one,
  We all must die;
Just wait and hear
  The reason why.

In God's dear Word
  We read that all
Must die because
  Of Adam's fall.
Just how he fell
  Please turn and read
The Bible tells
  Us of the deed—

How sin was brought
　On all mankind
Because God's rules
　Man did not mind;
But in God's great
　And noble plan
Was made a way
　For fallen man.

Sin placed man on
　The way to hell,
Where Satan and
　His angels dwell.
These tried to make
　Him feel all right,
And blind him to
　His wretched plight.

God loved man so
　That he was sad
And sought a way
　To make him glad.
He promised then
　To send some day
A Savior who'd
　Take sin away.

This Savior was
　His own dear Son,
Who never had
　A wrong deed done.
Although 'twas years
　Before Christ came,
He still was in
　God's plan the same.

At last he came—
　A babe so small;
And it seemed strange
　How sin could fall

On one so young,
　But it was so:
Still, never sin
　Did this child know;

And yet the sin
　Of all mankind
Upon this child
　God was to bind.
This load he bore
　When manhood came,
And he took all
　Our grief and shame.

At last he said
　His hour was nigh;
He prayed that God
　Would glorify
His Son, and bless
　The loved ones here,
For they would need
　Much strength and cheer.

God heard that prayer.
　Christ had to die,
That all our sins
　On him might lie:
And though 'twas hard,
　Still, glad are we;
For Christ's death sets
　All sinners free.

"All sinners free?
　Then, is it true
That death is gone
　From sinners' view?"
Ah, no, dear child,
　Death's still the same;
But, then, there's life
　In Jesus' name.

Man died two deaths—
  How sad to tell!
His soul could now
  No longer dwell
In union with
  His God, the Lord,
Because he'd not
  Obeyed his word.

His body, too,
  Passed to the grave.
And thus was man
  A perfect slave
To sin and death;
  But God's great love
Now found a way
  His love to prove.

Yes, Jesus came,
  Who knew no sin.
God saw then what
  Man might have been,
And now he sees
  Us in his Son;
For when Christ died,
  Our life was won.

God loves all those
  Who care to live
As he designs,
  And strength he'll give.
In this we find
  God's noble plan,
And what he's done
  For sinful man.

And you can see
  There's much to do
For ev'ry one,
  And for you, too;

All do not know
  Or understand
About God's love
  And plan so grand.

So go and tell
  Of God's great love,
How Jesus left
  His home above,
And say, "I know
  God placed me here;
I'm glad I see
  His plan so clear."

Then God will bless
  And use you too.
He has much work
  For you to do;
For God would love
  To see all where
They'd be prepared
  His home to share.

'Tis much to be
  A Christian true;
To teach men what
  They ought to do;
To bring the news
  To fallen man,
Of Christ and God's
  Redemption plan.

Do all you can
  In ev'ry way;
God will reward
  You in the day
Of judgment, when
  All men will see
Where they must spend
  Eternity.

CONTENTS

10 *FAVORITE STORIES*

List of Illustrations

※ ※ ※

16   *FAVORITE STORIES*

FROM THE NEW TESTAMENT 17

The Need of a Savior.

—:—

Gᴏᴅ sent his Son to this earth many years ago, and I want to tell you, dear children, why it was that he did this. There was need for God to do this, or he would never have sent his dear Son down to this cruel world.

God's Son was to be a Savior of the people. That means that he was to save them from something. To find out what this was, let us go back to the beginning, and see what God did.

Here we find out just how God made the earth and everything upon it. And there was the sun to shine by day and give light, and the moon and stars to shine at night. Then, there were all the animals, the birds, the fishes, the trees, the grass, and the flowers.

And God formed a man of the dust of the ground, and breathed into his nostrils the breath of life; and man became a living soul. This man was called Adam.

God planted a beautiful garden for him to live in. Within this garden God placed everything Adam would need, and then gave him a wife. Adam called his wife's name Eve. They were very happy in the beautiful garden God had made for them.

And God said that if these two people would always do right and obey him, they should never die.

God wanted this man and woman to serve him because they had

19

a desire to do so; and this was why he told them something they must not do.   He told them that they must not eat any fruit from a certain tree in the garden.   And God showed them the place where it grew, so that they would not forget it nor take any fruit off it through mistake.

Now, Satan came into the garden to see whether he could not get Adam and Eve to do what God had told them not to do.

Satan wanders around upon the earth, and tries to get people to do wrong and disobey God.

He saw that Adam and Eve were very happy, and he does not like to see any one happy; so he whispered to Eve.   He told her that God did not mean just what he said about the tree in the midst of the garden, and that they would not die if they ate of its fruit. And Satan said God knew that the day they ate thereof their eyes would be opened; that is, they would know the difference between good and evil.

Eve thought much about what Satan had told her; and the more she thought about his words, that the tree would make her wise, the more beautiful it seemed to her.

At last she desired some of the fruit so much that she took some from the tree and ate it.   And then she gave some to her husband, and he ate.   So they both disobeyed God, and sinned; for when we disobey, or do not mind God, that is sin.

God was grieved with them when they disobeyed him, and he Said that they could not live in the beautiful garden any longer.   So he drove them out, and placed an angel at the gate of the garden, that they might not again enter.

God told them that now they would have to work very hard for the food they ate, and that when they died, for now they must die, they would return to dust again.

But something worse than this happened on account of their sin. Before they disobeyed God, their hearts were good, but now they were sinful.

Our heart is that part of us from which springs the desire to do

right or wrong. When we have a good heart that loves God, we want to do right; but when we have a bad heart that does not love God, we want to do wrong.

God had made Adam and Eve with good hearts, but they made their own hearts bad by sinning. Oh, how unhappy they felt!

After a while when little children were born, these children were like their father and mother—they, too, had sinful hearts; that is, they had something in their hearts that led them to disobey God.

Yet if these little children had died before they were old enough to know the difference between right and wrong, God would have taken them up to heaven; but just as soon as they knew that they were sinning when they did things which they should not do, they could never get to heaven without becoming sorry for their sins and asking God to forgive them.

With this sinful nature in their hearts, the people hardly knew the difference between right and wrong; so God gave them a law of ten commandments, besides some other laws telling them how to do right.

These laws were to teach them how to live to please God and go to heaven when they died, and to hold in check wickedness. And they had to offer sacrifices every day for their sins.

A good many tried to live right and obey God's commandments, but they found it hard to do with their sinful nature. They wanted to do right, but the sin in their hearts sometimes caused them to do wrong.

This, then, was why the people needed a Savior, or some one who could take this sin right out of their hearts, and make them like Adam and Eve were when God created them and placed them in the Garden of Eden. And this was why God sent his Son as a Savior, to take away our sinful natures and make our hearts as pure as Adam's was in the beginning.

God promised, when Adam and Eve first sinned, that a Savior should come. Many prophets, who lived afterward, told the people that he was coming.

But before he came, they said, Elias, who was John the Baptist, would be sent to tell the people to make ready for him by repenting of their sins.

Many believed what these prophets said would come to pass, and they waited and watched earnestly for the Savior's coming.

Joyful News to Zacharias.

—:—

AFTER many years the people were living in the land of Canaan, and were called Jews. They were still looking for the Savior. But they were expecting him to be some great king who would come to them in a very strange manner. He was called the Messiah, which means "anointed."

The Jews at this time were ruled by the Romans, a people of another nation; and they longed to have a king of their own to rule over them and to deliver them from the Romans. Many of them thought, "It will be all right when the Messiah comes; for he will be our king, and will free us from the Romans."

In the southern part of the land of Canaan there are a great many hills. In a town among these hills, just at the time the people were greatly expecting the Messiah to come quickly, lived a man whose name was Zacharias.

This man was a priest, and he and his wife Elizabeth were both old. They had never had any children to cheer their home; and now that so many years had passed by, they supposed that they never should have any. This must have been a great sorrow to them, for children are the greatest blessing a home can have.

The work of the priest in those days was to offer sacrifices to God for the sins the people committed.

This was a very particular work, and it had to be done just as God had commanded it should be, or the life of the priest was in great danger.

The Bible tells us of priests who died instantly because they were

not careful to obey all God's commandments concerning their work.

Zacharias and his wife were both good people, and were very careful to obey all God's commandments.

Years before, King David had divided the priests into what were called courses or companies. There were twenty-four of these courses. Each one took its turn in staying for a time at the temple to attend to God's worship there.

The course of priests to which Zacharias belonged was called the course of Abia.

Within the temple the priests began their work very early in the morning. Some of them cleaned the altar by taking away the ashes that had been left there from the day before, and put fresh wood on the fire, which was never allowed to go out. Other priests trimmed the lamps, and cleaned the golden altar of incense.

After this, one of the priests offered a lamb upon the altar of burnt offering, and another burned incense on the golden altar.

The time when the priests were offering sacrifices and burning incense was called the hour of prayer, and at these times the people came up to the temple to worship God, and stood in the court praying.

Every day lots were cast to know which part of the work each priest was to do.

On the day of which I am going to tell you, Zacharias was to burn incense upon the golden altar, and for this reason he went into the holy place at the hour of prayer.

Just at this time, while Zacharias was offering incense in the temple, some one appeared, or stood beside him.

How frightened Zacharias must have been! for he did not know that this was an angel from heaven bringing joyful news to him and his dear wife.

But the angel did not keep him waiting long. He said, "I am Gabriel, that stand in the presence of God, and am sent to thee with glad tidings." The angel told him that God was going to give him and his wife Elizabeth a son, and that they should call his name John.

And the angel told Zacharias that the child would become a prophet, and that many would rejoice at his birth; for he was to tell the people that their Savior was coming soon, and he would prepare the way for him.

Zacharias could not believe that this was true, and he asked the angel how it could be. But the angel told Zacharias that it was true, and that because he had not believed it God would punish him. He would be dumb, unable to speak, until the child was born.

The people wondered why Zacharias remained in the temple so long; and when he came out, they were waiting for him. But Zacharias could not speak a word to them, and they could see that the Lord had spoken to him.

When Zacharias' work in the temple was ended, he returned to his home.

The Angel's Visit to Mary.

—:—

IN the small town of Nazareth lived a young woman whose name was Mary. She had promised to marry a man by the name of Joseph.

Mary and Joseph were both descended from King David, but they were not rich. They really were quite poor, but they both loved God.

Now, Mary was a cousin of Elizabeth's, the wife of Zacharias.

About six months had passed since the angel Gabriel had visited Zacharias in the temple, telling him such glad news.

Again the angel came down from heaven. This time he came to the home of Mary. Mary was afraid when she saw the angel; but he told her not to be afraid, for the Lord was pleased with her, and was going to give her a son whose name should be Jesus.

And Jesus should be a king, the angel said—greater than any other king in the world, because he would be the Son of God.

After the angel had told Mary this, he left her, and went up into heaven again.

Mary was surprised, and she wondered why God had chosen her

to be the mother of his Son. But she was very happy; for she said, "My soul doth magnify the Lord."

The angel had also told Mary the good news about her cousin Elizabeth, and she hastened and went to visit her.

It was a long distance to the place where Elizabeth lived, but Mary went and paid her a visit. What a happy time they must have had, thinking of the little ones God had promised, and planning for them!

After a very pleasant visit Mary returned home; and the angel spoke to Joseph in a dream, and told him Mary's beautiful secret about the Son of God coming to earth as her little child, and told Joseph to call his name Jesus, for he should save the people from their sins.

Then Joseph at once took Mary to his own home as his wife. He was a carpenter, and he made his living in that way.

The Birth of John the Baptist.

—:—

God gave Zacharias and Elizabeth the son he had promised them. Zacharias had not been able to speak for a long time; for, you remember, the angel in the temple said that Zacharias would be dumb until the child was born.

When a child was eight days old, it was their custom to give it a name. When this little baby was eight days old, the neighbors and friends came in and wanted to call him Zacharias after his father; but Elizabeth said, "No; call him John."

They were very much surprised when Elizabeth said this, and turning to Zacharias, they made signs to know what name he wished him called.

Zacharias asked for a writing table, and wrote, saying, "His name is John," and at once he began to speak and praise God.

And he thanked God for keeping his promise about sending a Messiah. And then, turning to his little new-born son, he said, "And

THE BIRTH OF JOHN.

thou, child, shalt be called the prophet of the Highest: for thou shalt go before the face of the Lord to prepare his ways.''

That was just what the angel had told Zacharias in the temple. At that time Zacharias had not believed that what the angel said would ever come true; but now he believed it with all his heart.

When the friends left the happy parents, they told all they met what they had seen and heard, and many wondered what manner of man John would be.

We do not know much about John when a boy, but he grew to be a strong and good man, and the grace of God was upon him.

Jesus is Born.

—:—

You will remember I told you that Mary lived in the little town of Nazareth, and that she and Joseph, her husband, were both descended from King David. Now, the name of the king who was ruling over the Jews was Herod.

Herod had been made king by the Roman emperor, Augustus Cæsar; for the Jews were servants to the Romans at this time.

The Jews did not like Herod at all, for he was so cruel and wicked; but they could not help themselves, and they longed for the Messiah to come and deliver them from the Romans and rule the people himself.

The Roman emperor made the people pay him a certain amount of money as a tax; and in order to pay this tax, each person had to go to the city of his or her ancestors or fathers and be enrolled.

And so it happened that Joseph and Mary went from Nazareth to Bethlehem, where David used to live, to pay this money or tax.

It was a long journey—nearly seventy miles. They could not go on the cars or in easy carriages. They must either walk, or ride on donkeys.

No doubt, Mary was very tired when they arrived at Bethlehem; so they went to the inn, or place where travelers stopped, to sleep.

But the inn was full of people, and there was no room for them; so they went to the stable and stayed there.

While they were in the stable that night, God gave Mary the little son that the angel had promised her; and she called his name Jesus.

Mary had prepared clothes for the babe, such as they used in those days; and when she had dressed him, she laid him in a manger.

So you see, children, it was not in a beautiful house, such as rich people live in, that Jesus was born. He was born in a stable in Bethlehem. This was where Jesus, God's dear Son, was born.

Perhaps there were others in the stable, but they did not know what a glorious babe had been born. Mary must have been very happy.

Angels Visit the Shepherds.

—:—

At the time when this little babe was born in the stable at Bethlehem, other things happened that were of great interest.

Out in the country there were shepherds who stayed in the field at night to watch over their flocks.

There the fields had no fences around them, and there was great danger of the wild beasts' coming and killing the sheep. For this reason some one had to stay with the sheep all the time to keep them from getting lost or killed. These men were called shepherds.

David, who had been a great king many years before, was at first only a poor shepherd boy taking care of his father's sheep.

One day when he was caring for his flock, a lion came rushing out of the forest near by, and it would have killed one of the lambs; but David ran after him. God gave him strength, and David killed that lion. And another day a bear came in the same manner, and David killed it.

That had happened more than a thousand years before; but still

THE BIRTH OF JESUS.

29

the shepherds of Bethlehem were forced to watch their flocks by day and by night, lest some wild beast take them.

On the night that Jesus was born, some shepherds were out in the field keeping watch over their sheep.

All at once a bright light shone around them, and the angel of the Lord appeared.

The shepherds were frightened, and they could not understand what it all meant; but the angel said, "Fear not; for, behold, I bring you good tidings of great joy, which shall be to all people." And the angel told them that in Bethlehem was born a little child who was the Savior.

He meant Jesus; for, you remember, he was to change our sinful hearts into good hearts, and to save us from being punished in the judgment-day.

And the angel said that if these shepherds would go at once, they could see this little child. And the angel told them just how the babe would be dressed, and that they would find him lying in a manger.

As soon as the angel had finished telling the shepherds this, a multitude of angels appeared, singing and praising God for his goodness to the people who live upon this earth. And then the angels went up into heaven again, and the shepherds were left alone.

When the angels had left them, the shepherds said, "Let us now go even unto Bethlehem, and see this thing which is come to pass, which the Lord hath made known unto us."

So they left their sheep, and made haste to Bethlehem, and came into the stable. There they found Mary, and Joseph her husband, and the little child lying in a manger. And they were glad when they saw Jesus.

And after they had seen the child, they went out and told what the angel had said to them. And those who heard it were filled with wonder, for it was the first time they had ever heard of such a thing being done in the world. And the strange news spread fast.

Then the shepherds went back to their sheep in the field; and as they went, they thanked and praised God because he had sent his

Unto us
a Child is born,
unto us a Son
is given

ISAIAH.IX.6.

BETHLEHEM

31

32   BRINGING GLAD NEWS TO THE SHEPHERDS.

angel to tell them about Jesus, and had let them go to see him in the stable in Bethlehem.

Jesus Brought to the Temple, and Simeon's Joy.

—:—

Not many miles away was another and much larger city than either Nazareth or Bethlehem. Its name was Jerusalem, and it was the city where the beautiful temple had been built so many years before by Solomon, King David's son. And it was in this city that King Herod now lived.

Solomon's temple had been destroyed long before, but Herod had tried to rebuild it as nearly as possible like the first temple had been.

To this beautiful temple, Joseph and Mary brought the child Jesus to present him to the Lord.

Their law said that at such times they must bring a lamb to be sacrificed on the altar, but that those who could not afford to bring a lamb must bring instead a pair of turtle doves or two young pigeons.

As Joseph and Mary were poor, they brought, as their offering, two young pigeons.

I will tell you later on how Jesus became a sacrifice for the world, and yielded up his life.

Now, there lived in Jerusalem at this time a very old man named Simeon. He was a good man, and he had obeyed the commandments of God as well as he knew how. And he felt sure that he was not going to die until he saw the Savior. Day by day Simeon was looking for the Messiah to come.

On the day when Jesus was presented in the temple, the Spirit of the Lord directed Simeon, also, to go to the temple; and there he saw Jesus.

As soon as Simeon saw the child, he knew that this was the One for whose coming he had been waiting so long.

He took the child in his arms, and praised God for his goodness, and asked that he might die, for now he had seen the Savior.

SIMEON'S JOY.

And there was a woman named Anna, a prophetess, who lived near the temple. She was a widow and very old; but she worshiped God, with prayer and fasting day and night.

While Simeon was speaking she, too, came into the temple where Jesus was, and thanked God because he had let her see the Savior. And when she went out, she told many people the glad news.

Mary remembered all these things, and thought of them many times.

The Star and the Wise Men.

—:—

AMONG the many strange and wonderful things that happened about the time Jesus was born, was the appearance of a very bright star.

There were certain men living in an Eastern country who were very wise, and who, no doubt, had studied much about the stars in the sky as well as about many other things.

THE BETHLEHEM STAR.

These men knew by what they had read and heard that the time had come when God was going to send the Messiah for whom the Jews were looking; and when they saw this bright star, so different from the rest, they knew that it meant something. Some of them started at once, for they were very anxious to see the king God had sent.

It was a long, tiresome journey, but these men did not mind that; they were longing to see the Savior, who they felt sure had come down from heaven.

No doubt, they talked about Jesus all the way, and expected to see some great person in a beautiful mansion and longed to fall down and worship him.

They came to Jerusalem; but after they arrived there, they could not find Jesus. They spoke to the people, saying, ''Where is he that is born king of the Jews? for we have seen his star in the east, and are come to worship him.'' But the people did not seem to know.

When Herod heard what the wise men had said, that a child was born who would be king of the Jews, he thought of himself, and he was not pleased. He wanted to be king, and feared that Jesus was going to take the throne from him.

Then Herod hated the child from that moment, and made up his mind to kill Jesus if possible. But Jesus was God's Son, and no one could kill him unless God said so.

Herod called all the chief priests and scribes; for they were men who had studied the Bible a great deal, and who could explain what the prophets had said about Jesus. And Herod asked them where the Messiah or Christ should be born. Their answer was that he should be born in Bethlehem of Judea.

When Herod heard this, he called the wise men to him, and asked them all about the star they had seen in their own country. And he sent them to Bethlehem, and said, ''Go and search for the young child; and when you have found him, bring me word again, that I may come and worship him also.''

Now, Herod did not say this because he wanted to worship Jesus; it was because he hated him, and wanted to put him to death.

So the wise men left Jerusalem, and started to go to Bethlehem. As they were going, they saw the same star that they had seen in their own country.

THE WISE MEN FOLLOWING THE STAR.

This made them glad; for it moved on ahead of them, and guided them to Bethlehem. Then it stood still right over the house where the young child was. And when they went into the house, there they saw the young child with Mary his mother, and they fell down and worshiped the infant Jesus.

And they presented to him rich and costly gifts, which they had brought with them; for it was the custom in those days to take rich presents when going to visit a king.

Great Sorrow in the Land.

—:—

WE might imagine wonderful things about the visit of the wise men, but the Bible only tells us that they were very happy because they had found the Savior. And they fell down and worshiped him.

And when they had given him the treasures they had brought, they returned to their homes in the Eastern country.

God warned them before they left not to return to Herod nor let him know anything about Jesus. Herod wanted to know where Jesus was only that he might send soldiers to destroy him.

So the wise men did not go near Herod, but returned home another way; and Herod could not find out anything more about the young child.

Now, after Herod had waited a long time, and at last found that the wise men were not going to come back and tell him what he desired to know, he became very angry, and thoughts more wicked than ever came into his mind.

The death of Jesus was what he craved; for the wise men had asked, "Where is he that is born king of the Jews?" Herod, no doubt, thought of this saying very often; and fearing that when Jesus grew to be a man he would become king, he thought of this wicked plan to destroy Jesus: Herod sent soldiers, and told them to kill every little boy of two years old and under, in the town of Bethlehem and in all the country round about.

ON THE WAY TO EGYPT.

Oh, how terrible it must have been! Mothers could not save their babies. They were snatched from their arms by the cruel soldiers, and killed before their eyes.

But Joseph and Mary were not among these sorrowing parents. Jesus was not one of the children who were slain. With all Herod's trouble, he had failed to destroy the one whom he desired. The one child of whom he was afraid was now far away from Bethlehem.

The angel of the Lord had warned Joseph in a dream, and told him that Herod would seek to destroy Jesus. And the angel told him to take the young child and his mother, and flee into Egypt, and stay there until told to return.

Joseph did not wait. He rose at once, and did as the angel said.

At the death of Herod, the angel again appeared to Joseph, and told him it would be safe to return to his old home. Joseph obeyed, and he would have gone to Bethlehem; but he heard that Herod's son Archelaus was king, and so went to his old home in Nazareth.

The King's Plan Defeated.

—:—

In Bethlehem was weeping,
   Yes, weeping all the day;
Sad mothers there were mourning,
   Their grief no one could stay.
What meant such great lamenting?
   Ah! soldiers came, you see,
And slew each mother's darling—
   Her baby from her knee.

I'll tell a little story
   Of how it came about.
You see, the king had slyly
   Sent all these soldiers out;
For he had heard just lately
   A little child was born
Who some day might be taking
   The crown that he had worn.

This caused the king much worry,
  And brought a jealous thought;
Perhaps if he would hurry,
  The young child might be caught.
So that was why the army
  Had gone in haste that day
With orders that each baby
  'Neath two years old they slay.

But while the king was planning,
  An angel came one night,
And left this little warning:
  "The child must take its flight."
No time was lost by waiting
  To prove this warning true,
But Joseph soon was hast'ning
  With child and mother, too.

They left the place of danger,
  Nor shared the sorrow there;
They took the little stranger
  To Egypt with great care.
The trouble was all over
  When they from Egypt came.
This baby was our Savior,
  Christ Jesus was his name.

The Boyhood of Jesus.

—:—

THE Bible says very little about the boyhood days of Jesus; but we know that he lived in Nazareth, and that Joseph was a carpenter, and Jesus must have spent many hours helping Joseph with his work.

And as he grew, he was filled with wisdom and with the grace of God. Mary thought many times of the strange and wonderful things connected with his birth, and wondered what they all meant.

The Jews had certain feasts that they kept in remembrance of things that had happened years before. One of these feasts was more important than all the rest. It was called the Passover.

A great many years before this the Jews, who were then called the children of Israel, were slaves to the king of Egypt. This king was very cruel to them, and they were forced to work so hard that their lives were very miserable.

God was very much displeased with this king, and he told him

JESUS IN THE MIDST OF THE DOCTORS OF THE LAW.

to let the people return to their own country; but Pharaoh, for that was the king's name, would not let them go.

At last, God punished Pharaoh and all the people of Egypt as He would passed through Egypt
that He would cause every first born to die of the Egyptian's
But the children of Israel none of them were slain.
This thing made Pharaoh afraid, and he let the children of Israel

return to their own land in Canaan. But before they went God told them to prepare a feast.

They were to roast a lamb with fire, and eat it quickly just before leaving Egypt. And God said that they must remember the night He passed over their homes, and that they must always have a feast at that time each year. And they were to tell their children all about God's kindness in delivering them from Egypt.

They always remembered this time, and the feast was called the Passover. They ate it in Jerusalem once every year.

You remember that Joseph and Mary were living in Nazareth their old home, nearly seventy miles from Jerusalem. It was a long distance, but every year they went to Jerusalem to keep the feast of the Passover. When Jesus was about twelve years old, they took him with them.

When the feast was over, they started to return home, and they had gone quite a distance when they discovered that Jesus was not with them.

That is somewhat the way it is with some people to-day who start on their journey to heaven. They have seen Jesus in their midst, and they become careless and suppose that he is somewhere close.

All at once they wake up to the fact that Jesus is not with them, but is with those who are anxious to hear the wonderful story of his Father's love; and they can not find him without searching diligently.

We will not talk of that now, but that was just what Joseph and Mary had to do. They returned to Jerusalem, and after searching diligently for Jesus three days, found him in the temple.

There he was surrounded by the doctors of the law, and those who understood the Bible, both hearing them and asking them questions. And all that heard him were astonished at his understanding and answers.

Mary and Joseph were very much surprised and pleased to find how well he understood the Bible. But Mary reproved him for causing them so much trouble and worry, and told him that they had thought he was lost.

44   "SON, WHY HAST THOU THUS DEALT WITH US?"

Jesus asked them whether they did not know that he must be about his Father's business. Mary thought of this answer many times. But Jesus obeyed and went home with her to Nazareth, and remained there helping Joseph until he was thirty years old.

Many people loved Jesus, and they were surprised at his great wisdom; but only a few knew that he was the Son of God. The time had not come for them to know this publicly.

The Story of John the Baptist.

—:—

WE now come to the time when the Jews heard that a prophet was living in their land. In the days gone by there had been many prophets. These were men who listened for God to speak to them. After God had spoken, they would tell the people his words.

But many years had passed since there had been a prophet in the land; and when the people heard the joyful news, they went and listened to his words, that they might know what message God was sending them.

This new prophet was none other than John, son of Zacharias and Elizabeth. You remember that I told you what the angel told Zacharias in the temple—that John would prepare the way for the Savior.

And after he was born, his father said, "And thou, child, shall be called the prophet of the Highest: for thou shalt go before the face of the Lord to prepare his ways."

John lived in the wilderness, where he was alone with God and listened to God's voice. He did not look nor dress like other men. His clothes were made of rough cloth, woven from camel's hair; around his waist was a girdle of skin; and he ate locusts and wild honey.

And this was what John said: "Prepare ye the way of the Lord, make his paths straight." This meant that the Savior was coming, and that the people must get ready to receive him, by confessing their sins. Then they must be sorry because they had disobeyed God, and they must promise God that they would not sin any more.

And John said he would baptize them, which meant that he would lay them down quickly under the water, and lift them right out again. This was to signify that they were washed from their old sins, and to show that they never intended to sin any more.

You know when any one dies, he is buried in the ground. And to be baptized, means that you are dead to sin, and that you do not mean to sin any more. And when you are baptized, it represents the new life you mean to live.

John baptized many people who were sorry for their sins, and who had asked God to forgive them; and the people called him John the Baptist. He did not know who the Savior was, for he lived many miles from Nazareth, Jesus' home; but John knew that he was coming.

Some of the people wondered whether John were not the Savior they were looking for; but when they asked, he told them no. He said, "I baptize you with water; but there is one coming who will baptize you with the Holy Spirit, whose shoes I am not worthy to bear."

One day as John was preaching, and baptizing the people in the river Jordan, Jesus came from his home in Nazareth to be baptized.

Now, John did not know that this was God's dear Son; but something seemed to tell him that Jesus had never committed any sins to be sorry for. And John asked him why he came to be baptized. Jesus answered and said that it was God's plan, and right that he, as the Son of God, should submit to obey the ordinances of God; and then John baptized him.

As soon as this was done, and Jesus went up out of the water, a wonderful thing happened. The heavens were opened unto him, and he saw the Spirit of God descending like a dove and lighting upon him. And a voice from heaven said, "This is my beloved Son, in whom I am well pleased."

John then knew that Jesus was the Son of God, the Savior sent

JOHN THE BAP-TIST PREACH-ING IN THE WIL-DER-NESS.

47

from heaven; for he had been told that this would be the sign by which he would know the Savior.

Jesus was now about thirty years of age. And he went out into the wilderness, and stayed there alone for forty days and nights. All this time he ate nothing, but spent the time in prayer to God. Afterward he was hungry.

Satan Tempts Jesus.
—:—

You remember how Satan tempted Eve to disobey God, and in this way caused every one to be born with sin in his heart. And when Satan saw Jesus coming to take this sinful nature from the people, and make their hearts pure, like Adam's and Eve's were before they yielded to the voice of the tempter, he thought he would try to prevent him.

For forty days he tempted Jesus in every way that we are tempted. All this time Jesus was in the wilderness, and he had eaten nothing. The last temptation was that he would exercise his divine power to prove that he was really the Son of God.

Knowing that Jesus was hungry, Satan thought to tempt him with something to eat, the same as he did Eve. He said, "If thou be the Son of God, command that these stones be made bread." But Jesus answered him by quoting passages from the Bible. He said, "It is written, Man shall not live by bread alone, but by every word that proceedeth out of the mouth of God."

How different was this temptation from that of Adam and Eve's! There they were in the beautiful garden, with all they could desire to make them happy; but with the first temptation they yielded to sin. While Jesus was in the lonely wilderness wanting food, Satan came and tempted him to eat to satisfy his hunger. But Jesus believed that God would supply his needs, and he would not distrust nor disobey him.

Then Satan tried another plan to make Jesus sin. He brought

him to Jerusalem, and set him on a pinnacle of the temple, and said to him, "If thou be the Son of God, cast thyself down: for it is written, He shall give his angels charge concerning thee: and in their

JESUS COMMANDS SATAN TO FLEE.

hands shall they bear thee up, lest at any time thou dash thy foot against a stone''; but Jesus answered, "Thou shalt not tempt the Lord thy God."

And then Satan took him into a very high mountain, from which he could see many kingdoms and their glory. And he told Jesus that he might have all these things if he would only fall down and worship him.

Jesus then told him to go, for God was the only one who ought to be worshiped. Then Satan left and angels came and gave Jesus the things he needed.

Thus Jesus overcame all of Satan's temptations, and went about teaching the people. He knew now just what temptations the people would have; for Satan had tempted him on every line upon which they would be tempted—first, the appetite; secondly, pride; and thirdly, the love of gain.

In none of these things had Jesus disobeyed God, and now he was ready to tell the people that he was the Savior for whom they had been looking.

○✦○✦○✦○

The Lamb of God.

—:—

When Jesus had been tempted on all points on which we are liable to be tempted, he returned from the wilderness to the place where he had been baptized.

The next day John the Baptist saw him, and said: "Behold the Lamb of God, which taketh away the sin of the world! This is he of whom I said, After me cometh a man which is preferred before me; for he was before me. This is the Son of God."

John called Jesus the Lamb of God, because he was to be offered up as a sacrifice on the cross, as the lambs were offered upon the altar.

Two men that heard John the Baptist's words, followed Jesus. One was Andrew, and the other, though not named, is supposed to have been John.

When Jesus saw them following him, he asked whom they were seeking? They answered by calling him "Master," and by asking where he was staying. Jesus said, "Come and see." And one of them, named Andrew, brought his brother Simon Peter, also.

Andrew told his brother that he had found the Messiah, the one for whom they had been looking so long. The next day Jesus found Philip, and said, "Follow me."

Philip was very glad when he found Jesus, and he went and

told his friend Nathanael that he had found him of whom Moses and the prophets had written, Jesus of Nazareth.

Nathanael could scarcely believe that Philip's words were true; for he said, "Can there any good thing come out of Nazareth?" (But, you remember, Jesus was born in Bethlehem of Judea, where the prophets said he would be born.) Philip's answer was, "Come and see."

When Jesus saw Nathanael coming, he said, "Behold an Israelite indeed, in whom is no guile!"

These words surprised Nathanael, and he could not understand how Jesus knew him so well. But when Jesus said, "Before that Philip called thee, when thou wast under the fig-tree, I saw thee," he believed, and said, "Thou art the Son of God; thou art the King of Israel." Perhaps the place under the fig-tree was a place of secret prayer that Nathanael supposed no one but himself knew anything about. If this were true, it is no wonder that he was convinced.

Jesus asked Nathanael if his reason for believing was because he had said, "I saw thee under the fig-tree," and then he said, "Thou shalt see greater things than these."

Thus these five became disciples or followers of Jesus.

Jesus Visits His Old Home.

—:—

JESUS, we have seen, left his home in Nazareth to be baptized by John in the river Jordan. Some time afterward he returned to Nazareth, where his mother still lived.

Mary's heart must have been glad when she learned that there were other people who were beginning to see and believe that Jesus was the Son of God.

On the Sabbath-day when the people met in the synagogue to worship God, Jesus stood up to read, and he read from the book of Isaiah these words: "The Spirit of the Lord is upon me, because he hath anointed me to preach the gospel to the poor; he hath sent me to heal the broken-hearted, to preach deliverance to the captives, and recovering of sight to the blind, to set at liberty them that are bruised, to preach the acceptable year of the Lord.''   See Luke 4: 18, 19 and Isa. 61: 1.

And he closed the book, and gave it again to the minister, and sat down.   And the eyes of all were fastened upon him.

After this, Jesus told them that this scripture was now fulfilled.

The people were all surprised at the words of Jesus, and they wondered much at what they heard; for had not Jesus lived among them all his life?   Some said, "Is not this Joseph's son?" and they could not believe that he was God's Son.

But Jesus was not surprised; he knew just how it would be. Every one could be saved, who would obey God's call to repentance, and would desire salvation.   Jesus could not save any against their will.

The people of Nazareth were so angry that they wanted to kill Jesus because he told them the truth, and they took him to "the brow of the hill whereon their city was built, that they might cast him down headfirst."

But God's time had not come for Jesus to die, and he passed through their midst, and went away to the city of Capernaum.   Here the people heard him, and wondered at his words and wisdom.

The Wedding of Cana.

—:—

And now I am going to tell you of the first miracle Jesus did. A miracle is any wonderful thing that is done, that no man could do of himself.

Jesus was invited to a wedding or marriage in Cana, which was a small place not far from Nazareth, his old home.   And we find that Jesus went.   His disciples and mother went also.

It was the custom to prepare a great feast whenever a marriage

took place, and often this feast would last a long time; and wine was served at such times.

Now, these people must have been poor, and not able to provide as much wine as was needed for the feast; for we read that when they wanted more wine, there was none.

THE FIRST MIRACLE.

When Mary, the mother of Jesus, saw that the wine was gone, she went and told Jesus. Mary believed that Jesus could help them, and bade the servants do whatever he told them. Then a very wonderful thing happened.

There were usually large stone jars kept in each home for the

purpose of holding water; for the Jews liked to wash their hands and their feet often. Jesus told them to fill these jars with water, and they filled them to the brim.

When the jars were all full, Jesus said, "Draw out now and bear unto the governor of the feast. And they bare it." When the governor had tasted of the water that was made into wine, he called the bridegroom to him, and said, "Every man at the beginning doth set forth good wine, but thou hast kept the good wine until now." He did not know of the miracle that Jesus had done, but the servants knew.

This was the first time that Jesus used the power God had given him, to do what no other man could do.

When his disciples saw this miracle, they believed on Jesus more fully than they did before.

After this, Jesus went with his mother, his brethren, and his disciples to a place called Capernaum, on the shore of Galilee. But they did not stay there long; for the feast of the Passover was near, and you remember that Jesus went up every year to attend it.

The Feast of the Passover.

—:—

As Jesus went up to Jerusalem and passed on his way up to the temple, how sorrowful his heart must have been to see the great crowd of people with hearts so full of sin, and to know that the greater part of them would never be saved. The Passover feast was kept by many of them only as a sort of holiday.

When Jesus reached the temple, he beheld a sight that was still more sad. There in the beautiful temple that had been built as a house where they could worship God, were men who had brought many things to sell, such as oxen, sheep, and doves. These, they knew, would be needed as sacrifices, and their hearts were so hardened by sin that they dared to make their money in this way.

What did Jesus do when he saw them? He made a whip of many

small cords, and he drove them all out of the temple, and also the sheep and the oxen; "and he poured out the changers' money, and overthrew the tables."

THE MONEY CHANGERS DRIVEN OUT.

He said to those who sold doves, "Take these things away; make not my Father's house a place to buy and sell in." Then his disciples remembered something they had read in the Bible: "The zeal of thine house hath eaten me up," and they thought that this was what these words meant.

Although the men whom Jesus had driven out of the temple hated him, yet they knew that they had done wickedly to allow such deeds to be done in the temple, and they did not dare to resist or complain.

After their surprise was over, some of the Jews came to him to ask by what authority he did these things.

There had been many wonderful things done by the old prophets: the waters of the Red Sea had rolled back before Moses (Ex. 14: 21); Samuel had brought down a storm of thunder and rain (1 Sam. 12: 18); and Elijah had called down fire from heaven to burn up his sacrifice. 1 Kings 18: 37, 38. Now what sign was Jesus going to show them.

But Jesus would not do as they wished—give them a sign. He wanted them to look at his life and actions. These would be enough to convince them that he was the promised Savior.

However, he gave them a very strange answer. He said, "Destroy this temple, and in three days I will raise it up."

The Jews did not know what to think when Jesus said this. They said that it had taken forty-six years to build that temple, and asked if he thought that he could rebuild it in three days. But Jesus was speaking of what they would soon do to him, for he knew that they would crucify him.

He meant that although they would destroy his body, he would rise from the grave the third day.

His disciples remembered these words, although they did not then understand them. But after Jesus had risen again from the dead, they wrote them down, so that we, too, might know them.

But there were many at the feast who did believe that Jesus was the Son of God.

Nicodemus the Pharisee.

—:—

THE Pharisees were a people who believed that a Messiah was coming to be their king; but they were very proud, and thought themselves better than any one who was not a Pharisee. They tried to show, by their strict and careful way of living, how good they were; but in their hearts were many unkind thoughts of others.

JESUS TALKING TO NICODEMUS.   57

They thought that when the Messiah did come, he would be just like other kings on the earth, and that when he saw what good lives they were living, he would give them the chief places in his kingdom, and make much of them.

Now, the Messiah had come. He was Jesus of Nazareth. But these proud Pharisees could not believe that he was the One for whom they were looking.

They talked about it much, and the miracles that Jesus was doing filled them with wonder. If only he were rich, they might believe that he was the One for whom they were looking.

Now, there was one of these Pharisees named Nicodemus, who thought over the things he had heard about Jesus. He felt that he should like to know more, and so decided to go to Jesus and learn for himself. The Bible says he went by night. Perhaps he was ashamed to go in the day time, for fear of being seen.

And he said to Jesus, "We know that you are a teacher come from God: for no man can do these miracles that thou doest, except God be with him."

Jesus knew that Nicodemus' heart was not right, and so he told him that if he were not born again he could never see the kingdom of God, nor understand the things which he heard and saw.

How surprised Nicodemus was at this answer! He said, "How can a man be born when he is old?" But Jesus meant that unless a man's heart was cleansed from sin, and he became as a little child before it knew what sin was, he could not enter heaven.

You remember I told you that all little children are born with sin in their hearts; but when they die, they go to heaven. Perhaps this was what Jesus was telling Nicodemus; but the proud Pharisee could not understand, and he said, "How can these things be?"

Jesus said, "Are thou a teacher in Israel, and yet dost not know these things?" And he said that it would be useless to tell him of heavenly things if he could not understand earthly things.

Many years before, Moses lifted up a serpent made of brass, for the children of Israel to look at when they were in the wilderness.

Many of the people had been bitten by fiery serpents, and Moses said that if they would look at the serpent he was holding up before them, they would live, and not die. Many did look and were saved.

And Jesus said that as Moses had lifted up the serpent in the wilderness, even so must the Son of God be lifted up, and that who- ever believed on him should not die, but should have everlasting life.

Jesus thus spoke of his death, of his being nailed to a cross and lifted up; and he said it was because God loved the world so much that he sent his own Son to save them. But the people had become so sinful that they loved to do wrong rather than right.

Nicodemus the Pharisee.

There was a man in Israel,
    A ruler 'mong the Jews,
Who came to Jesus late one night
    To hear the gospel news.
He'd heard the preaching of the day,
    And felt it was God's Word;
But, then he knew how hatred filled
    The hearts of some who heard.

These enemies of Christ were men
    Who stood in great repute:
But many words that Jesus said
    Had often caused dispute;
And as these men were rulers, too,
    And all proud Pharisees,
Perhaps this man went in the night,
    Lest he might them displease.

Perhaps he wished they might not know
    Of Christ more truth he'd hear;
But this we know: his trip at night
    Would make it so appear.

He said, "Rabbi, a teacher true,
  Thou'rt surely from above;
The miracles that thou hast done
  This fact to all should prove."

Then Jesus answered him in words
  That did not seem quite plain;
He said that those who'd live above
  Must all be born again.
So Nicodemus said at once,
  "How can this ever be?"
The mystery was very great,
  Its truth he could not see.

Now, Jesus meant all must be born
  In God's great family,
And Nicodemus might have seen
  The truth most easily.
He thought Christ meant the fleshly birth
  Which made the truth seem dim;
So Jesus with great care explained
  The myst'ry unto him.

Then Jesus said it seemed so strange
  This man should be so slow
To understand the mysteries
  He surely ought to know;
For he had been a ruler long,
  And Israel oft had taught:
It was so queer he could not see
  The truth which now he sought.

And then Christ told how God had sent
  His dear and only Son,
That sin might be condemned through him,
  Man's future home be won.
And last he said that ev'ry one
  Who would God's truth reject
Must live forever with the lost,
  And punishment expect.

Just how Christ's words affected him
  The Bible does not tell,
But we are sure a purer light
  Upon this man now fell.
He must have been convinced that night
  That Jesus was God's Son;
This we infer from an event
  That happened later on.

The Pharisees were trying hard
  To find some lawful way
By which they might destroy the one
  They so much wished to slay;
But ev'ry way which they had found
  No satisfaction brought,
For none agreed, and all their plans
  Had thus far come to naught.

At last a band of men were sent
  With this command: "Go bring
The one who dares to call himself
  The Jews' long-promised king."
These men obeyed; but what took place,
  And all they heard that day,
Made them afraid to touch the one
  Whom they'd been sent to slay.

The people said, "This man must be
  The One for whom we seek,
For no one else could utter words
  Like those we hear him speak."
Some said, "He is a prophet true;"
  And some, "'T is Christ indeed;"
While others said: "Nay, 't is not so!
  How doth the scripture read?"

While still the people argued there,
  The officers returned,
And told the priests and Pharisees
  The things which they had learned;

They said that never man thus spoke,
   And this reply received:
"How is it that ye think this way?
   Are ye, too, all deceived?

"Do any of us learned men,
   Or any Pharisee,
Believe this man the promised Christ,
   Who comes to set us free?
The people that are thinking thus
   Know not the law we read.
Doth Christ come out of Galilee?
   Nay, he's of David's seed,

"And from the town of Bethlehem."
   Yes, this was surely true;
But Jesus was from this same town,
   Of David's lineage, too.
A voice that had been silent spoke,
   And said in accents clear,
"How is it that ye judge a man
   Before his case you hear?"

Now, Nicodemus was the one
   Who asked this question there.
(You know he was the Pharisee
   Whom Jesus taught with care.)
His words brought quickly this retort:
   "Art thou from Galilee?
Go search and look, for from that place
   There can no prophet be."

No more was done that night, we read;
   But later on we find
The Pharisees succeeded quite
   The one they sought, to bind.
Though falsely tried, they found a way
   Their hate to satisfy;
For God had planned long, long before
   That his dear Son should die.

Now, Nicodemus saw that time
  With sad and aching heart.
Although a ruler in the land,
  In this he took no part;
But when the cruel deed was o'er,
  He came with spices sweet,
Which round the form of one were bound
  Whose work was now complete.

John's Last Testimony of Jesus.

—:—

When the feast of the Passover had ended, Jesus and his disciples went into the cities of Judea, preaching, and baptizing the people. And at the same time John the Baptist and his disciples were preaching and baptizing in the cities farther north.

Then the Pharisees spoke to John's disciples of Jesus, and said that he was baptizing more disciples than John, and asked him whether it were right. Now, Jesus did not baptize any one, but his disciples baptized people in the name of Jesus.

John answered: "Did I not tell you, I am not the Christ, but am sent before him? He must increase, but I must decrease. The Father loveth the Son, and hath given all things into his hand."

And John said that whoever (that means you and me) would believe that Jesus was God's Son should be saved and have everlasting life; but that God's wrath, or anger, would be upon all who would not believe on his Son.

Afterward John continued to preach, but his work was nearly ended. God had sent him into the world to tell the people that his Son, Jesus, was coming, and to get them ready to receive him. And Jesus had come, and the people were gathering to hear him and know what he would say to them of heaven.

John the Baptist at one time made King Herod angry with him by telling him that he had done wrong in marrying his brother Philip's wife. This king was called Herod; but he was not the Herod who was ruling when Jesus was born, for you remember that that Herod died.

Now, this king had taken his own brother's wife while his brother was still living.

This woman's name was Herodias. When she knew what John had said concerning her late marriage, she hated him, and decided she would have him killed if possible.

Herod would have put John the Baptist to death; but he knew that the Jews all thought John was a prophet, and he was afraid to kill him. So Herod had him bound and put into prison.

When Jesus heard that John was cast into prison, he went from one town to another preaching, and saying, "The time is fulfilled, and the kingdom of God is at hand: repent ye, and believe the gospel."

After John had been in prison a long time, Herod, on his birthday, made a grand feast for all the great men of Galilee. And the daughter of Herodias came in and danced before them. Herod was greatly pleased with her for this, and he said, "Ask of me whatsoever you wish and I will give it thee, even to the half of my kingdom."

What a rash thing for a king to say! The girl went at once to her mother and said, "What shall I ask?" And her mother said, "The head of John the Baptist." She meant that she wanted John's head cut off; and her daughter hastened back to the king, and told him to give her John's head in a large dish.

The king was very sorry when he heard this, yet he had promised; and so he sent soldiers to the prison, who cut off John's head and brought it in a dish and gave it to the girl, and she gave it to her mother.

When John's disciples heard of this, they went and took up his body. And they carried it lovingly, and laid it in a tomb. Then they went and told Jesus what had happened, and Jesus comforted them.

Jesus at Jacob's Well in Sychar.

—:—

ONE day Jesus went to Sychar, a city of Samaria. This was near the piece of ground that Jacob had bought at one time and had

THE WOMAN AT JACOB'S WELL.

65

given to his son Joseph; and when the children of Israel returned from Egypt, they brought Joseph's bones and buried them there. Josh. 24: 32.   And Jacob's well was also there.

Now, the people of Samaria were not altogether of the same race as the Jews.   A great many years before, the king of Assyria had taken most of the children of Israel captive; that is, made them his slaves.   Then he sent some strange people back to that part of the country; and they made their homes in Samaria, and mixed with the children of Israel that were left there.

After a while the children of Israel that had been taken captive returned to their old homes, but they did not like the people that were living in Samaria.   They had many quarrels, and they would not have any more to do with one another than was necessary.

They had felt thus for many years; and the Samaritans had their place of worship in Mt. Gerizim instead of in Jerusalem.

Now, it happened that Jesus must pass through Samaria.   Jesus would not help **nor** encourage them in their quarrel.   He loved all men, and he wanted to see the Samaritans saved as well as the Jews or any one else.

It happened that when he reached Jacob's well, he was very tired, and he sat down to rest.   It was nearly noon, and his disciples had gone to buy something for their dinner.

While he was resting, he wished for some of the nice, cool water from the well; but it was deep, and he had nothing with which to draw the water.   Then one of the women of Samaria came to the well to draw some water, and Jesus asked her to give him a drink.

How surprised she was to hear Jesus ask her to give him a drink! And she said, "How is it that thou, being a Jew, askest drink of me, who am a woman of Samaria? for the Jews have no dealings with the Samaritans."   Jesus answered that if she knew who was asking her for a drink, she would have asked of him, that he might have given her living water.

She did not understand what Jesus meant by 'living water''; but she soon saw that he was a great prophet, and she asked him a

question which had long puzzled her and her people. She said, "Our fathers worshiped in this mountain; and ye say that Jerusalem is the place where men ought to worship."

Jesus answered her, "Ye worship ye know not what: we know what we worship; for salvation is of the Jews." But he also said the time was coming when they would not go up to Jerusalem, neither on that mountain, to worship the Father. God is a Spirit, he said, and those who worship him must worship him in spirit and in truth.

The woman said, "I know that Messiah cometh, which is called Christ: when he has come, he will tell us all things." Jesus said, "I that speak unto thee am he." Then the woman hastened back to tell her friends that she had found the Savior, and they came at once to see him.

The disciples were very much surprised that Jesus would talk so earnestly with a Samaritan woman, but they did not ask him any questions.

While the woman was gone to tell her friends, his disciples brought the food they had bought, and asked him to eat. But Jesus answered that he had food to eat that they knew not of.

They did not understand what he meant, and asked if any one had brought him food; but Jesus said, "My food is to do the will of him that sent me, and to finish his work." This explained what he meant. He loved to do his Father's will more than to eat or to rest, or even his life.

Then many of the Samaritans came to see Jesus, and they believed on him because they heard what the woman said of him. For she had said, "Come, see a man, which told me all things that ever I did: is not this the Christ?"

As they listened to Jesus, they forgot that he was a Jew, and they longed to have him stay with them. So Jesus remained two days in the city. And many more believed because of his own word; and they said to the woman, "Now we believe, not because of thy saying: for we have heard him ourselves, and know that this is indeed the Christ, the Savior of the world."

Jesus Telling How the Gentiles will Receive Him.

—:—

THE people of Nazareth were too ignorant and too selfish to receive the good news Jesus had to bring them.   They had driven him from their midst.

Jesus had told them two stories from the Old Testament, which showed that in the time past the Gentiles had sometimes been more ready to accept the gifts of God than had the Jews themselves.

The first story was about the great prophet Elijah.   He lived in the reign of Ahab, a wicked king, whose sins were so great that God punished him by not sending any rain upon the earth for three years and six months. Jas. 5: 17.   This caused a terrible famine in the land.

And God sent Elijah into Zarephath, a city of the Gentiles, to dwell, and said, "I have commanded a widow woman there to sustain thee."   As Elijah drew near to the gate of the city, he saw the widow gathering sticks, and asked her to give him something to eat.

But the famine had reached even to this place, and she answered; "I have only a handful of meal in a barrel, and a little oil in a cruse; and now I am gathering two sticks, that I may go in and dress it for me and my son, that we may eat and die."

But Elijah said unto her: "Fear not; go and do as thou hast said; but first make me a little cake, and bring it unto me.   After this make for thee and thy son."   And Elijah said, "The barrel of meal shall not waste, neither shall the cruse of oil fail, until the Lord send rain upon the earth."

When the poor woman heard these words, she received him gladly, and shared with him the food of which she had expected to make her last meal.   And it was as Elijah said—they had plenty until the rain came.

The other story was about Elisha and Naaman the leper.   Now, Naaman was of the country of Syria.   The Syrians had in war taken a little girl from the people of Israel.   This little girl became a slave in the house of Naaman.

Naaman was a brave man, and a great general; but he had the dreadful disease leprosy, which no one could cure. But when the little servant girl heard of it, she said, "If my master would go to the prophet in Israel, he would recover him of his disease."

Naaman wished very much to get well, and went to Samaria to the prophet of Israel. Elisha told him to go and bathe himself seven times in the river Jordan, and he would be made well. This he did, and God healed him.

When Jesus had told the people of Nazareth these two stories, he said, "Many widows were in Israel, but Elijah was sent to a widow in a Gentile city; and many lepers were in Israel in the time of Elisha, but none of them were cleansed, saving Naaman the Syrian."

Jesus told the people this to show them that the Gentiles would then more gladly hear and receive his teaching than would they who were known as the people of God.

By the story of the woman at the well, you can see how gladly the people of Samaria received Jesus.

The Nobleman's Faith.

—:—

Two days had passed since Jesus had preached to the people in Samaria, and he now went into Galilee to visit the towns and cities.

Nazareth was in Galilee, where the people were made so angry when Jesus told them that the Gentiles were as near to the kingdom of heaven as themselves. Jesus knew how they felt toward him, for he had told them that a prophet had no honor in his own country.

But when he came to the other towns of Galilee, the people gladly listened to his words; for they remembered all the things he did at Jerusalem during the feast. And Jesus again went into Cana, where he had made the water wine.

Now, in Capernaum, a city about thirteen miles from Cana, lived a certain nobleman, whose son was very sick, and ready to die. His parents had done all they knew to do for him, but still he grew worse.

When the nobleman heard that Jesus was in Cana, he was glad; for he had heard of the miracle concerning the wine, and he felt sure that Jesus could heal his son. So he went at once to Cana.

The nobleman soon found Jesus; for every one was now filled with wonder, and much was said of the man who claimed to be the Son of God.

How glad Jesus must have been to see the man come to him in his trouble! for Jesus is always glad when any bring their troubles to him.

The nobleman had great faith. He believed that if Jesus but saw his son, he would be healed. Jesus told the nobleman to return home, for the child was well. The nobleman believed that what Jesus said was true; and on his way home he met his servants, who were bringing him the good news that his son was better.

He asked his servants at what hour the child began to get better; and when told, he knew that it was the same hour that Jesus spoke the words, "Thy son liveth." Then he told his household how the word of Jesus had been able to cure his son, and they all believed that he must be the Son of God.

This was the second miracle that Jesus did in Galilee.

The Pool of Bethesda.

—:—

THE Jews had many feasts in Jerusalem, and now they were to have another, and Jesus went up to it.

Now in Jerusalem where the sheep were brought to be sold, was a pool of water. The pool was called Bethesda, and around it were five porches, in which were laid a great many persons that were sick, or lame, or blind. These people believed that at certain times an angel came down into the pool and caused the water to move or be troubled, and that whoever stepped into the troubled water first would be healed of whatever disease he had.

When Jesus came to the pool, he saw a certain man there who had been sick for thirty-eight years. This was a long time, and Jesus felt very sorry for the poor man. How loving and thoughtful the dear Savior was of all who were needing help in any way. His heart was touched, for he asked if the man would like to be made well.

THE POOL OF BE-THES-DA.

The man answered him, "Sir, I have no man, when the water is troubled, to put me into the pool: but while I am coming, another steppeth down before me." Jesus said to him, "Rise, take up thy bed, and walk." And immediately the man was made well, and he took up his bed and walked. This happened on the Sabbath-day.

Now, the Jews kept Saturday as the Sabbath, because in their law or Bible it said that they must keep the seventh day holy. God had been six days in creating the earth and all upon it, and he rested on the seventh day, and hallowed it. And the Jews were taught that it was wrong for them to do any kind of labor on that day.

But Jesus wanted them to get where they would want to keep every day for the Lord; that is, not on any day do bad things, nor feel bad things in their hearts. For although the Jews kept the Sabbath-day by not doing any work, they thought many bad and wicked thoughts, and were far from being holy.

So now the Jews, wishing to find fault with Jesus, said to the man, "It is the Sabbath-day, and it is not lawful for thee to carry thy bed." The man answered, "He that made me well, said, Take up thy bed and walk." Then they asked who had made him well. But the man did not know who it was, for many people were there at the time when he was healed.

After this, Jesus saw in the temple the man whom he had made well. And Jesus said, "Behold, thou art well: sin no more, lest a worse thing come unto thee." Then the man knew that it was Jesus who had healed him, and he went and told the Jews. And the Jews persecuted Jesus and tried to kill him because he had done these things on the Sabbath-day.

But Jesus answered them, "My Father worketh hitherto, and I work." Then the Jews sought all the more to kill him; for he had not only broken the Sabbath, but had made himself equal with God. But Jesus said: "If I bear witness of myself, my witness is not true. There is another that beareth witness of me." Here Jesus spoke of John the Baptist.

But Jesus said, "I have a greater witness than that of John: for the works that I do, bear witness of me, that the Father hath sent me." And he told them to search the Scriptures, and see what the prophets had spoken of him.

JESUS PREACHING TO THE PEOPLE FROM A BOAT.

Fishing in the Sea of Galilee.

—:—

JESUS went about all the country of Galilee preaching to the people, and telling them how they must live to get to heaven. One day as he was walking near the Sea of Galilee, he saw Peter, Andrew, James, and John out in boats fishing.

When Jesus saw them there, he entered into Peter's boat while they were washing their nets; for they had been fishing all night, and had caught nothing. And Jesus preached to the people from the boat; for many people were standing on the shore, waiting to hear what he would say to them.

When Jesus had finished speaking to the people, he told Peter to let down his net into deeper water; but Peter answered, "Master, we have toiled all the night, and have taken nothing; still, at thy word I will let down the net." And when they had done this, they enclosed a great multitude of fishes; and their net broke, and it would not hold them all. They then called to their partners, James and John, to help them; and they filled the ships so full of fish that they began to sink. Then they realized that this was another miracle.

Peter fell down at Jesus' feet, and confessed that he was a sinful man. But Jesus said, "Fear not; for I will make you fishers of men. And when they had brought their ships to land, they left all, and followed Jesus."

❀❀❀❀❀

A Man Possessed with Evil Spirits.

—:—

WHEN Jesus and the fishermen had left the seashore, they went up into Capernaum. There they found the people anxious to hear what they had to say, and they went into the synagogue to teach them.

All at once some one cried out: "Let us alone; what have we to do with thee, thou Jesus of Nazareth? art thou come to destroy us? I know who thou art, the Holy One of God."

The man who spoke these words was possessed with evil spirits. He had no control of himself. Sometimes he was thrown into the

A GREAT MULTITUDE OF FISHES.

75

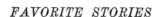

water and sometimes into the fire, and now the evil spirits made him speak these words.

Jesus stopped preaching when he heard this, and rebuked the spirits, saying, "Be quiet, and come out of him." Then the spirit cried with a loud voice, but it came out of the man.

How it surprised the people to see this! They said, "What thing is this? for he commandeth even the unclean spirits, and they do obey him."

When the service in the synagogue had ended, Jesus went home with Peter, who was a married man. When they reached the house, they found that Peter's wife's mother was very sick with a fever, and could not rise from her bed.

Jesus went to her, took her by the hand, and lifted her up. The fever left her at once, and she was well, and able to wait upon them.

The news of this wonderful cure and of the healing of the poor man possessed with evil spirits was soon known all over Capernaum, and all who had friends that were sick or afflicted brought them to Jesus, and he healed them.

It seemed that all the people in the city were gathered at the door. And devils, also, came out of many, crying out, and saying, "Thou art Christ, the Son of God."

Very early the next morning Jesus arose and went away to a quiet place where he could be alone with God. He wanted to pray to his Father, who would give him comfort and strength.

The Mission of Jesus.

—:—

ALTHOUGH Jesus brought healing for the many poor afflicted people, his mission was also to heal their souls, and to teach them how they could live pure, sinless lives in this wicked world.

Jesus could not spend all his time in Capernaum with the people there, so we find him preaching in the different towns of Galilee. The Bible says, "He went about all Galilee, teaching in their syna-

PETER'S WIFE'S MOTHER.

77

gogues, and preaching the gospel of the kingdom, and healing all manner of sickness and all manner of disease among the people.''

And great multitudes of people followed him from Galilee, from Decapolis, from Jerusalem, from Judea, and from beyond Jordan.

When he saw the great crowds of people following him, he felt that the time had come when he must teach them what was meant by the kingdom of heaven, of which he had been speaking so much. It was something so grand and noble that many of them would be unable to understand him, and would be angry and leave him; but they must all hear, and some would believe.

It was a very solemn hour in the life of Jesus, for the words that he was going to speak were not only for them, but for all men who would live after them, even to the end of the world.

And when Jesus had called his disciples to him, he chose twelve of them to be with him. These twelve were called apostles, which means messengers, or ''sent ones.'' They were: Peter and Andrew, his brother; James and John, his brother; Philip and Bartholomew (supposed to have been Nathanael); Thomas and Matthew the publican; James, the son of Alphæus; Thaddæus, Simon, and Judas Iscariot.

To these twelve Jesus gave power to heal the sick, to cleanse the lepers, to raise the dead, and to cast out devils. And Jesus sent them out to preach to ''the lost sheep of the house of Israel.''

Jesus spoke of the Jews as ''lost sheep.'' They were the chosen people of God; but they had committed so many sins, and had worshiped idols so many times instead of the true and living God, that Jesus counted them as ''lost sheep.'' But he had come as a Shepherd, and he wanted to gather them together again into one fold, and care for them for his Father in heaven.

Many of the words and teachings of Jesus were so deep that even his disciples did not understand them; but they knew that Jesus was the Son of God, and they went out among the people and preached as Jesus had told them—that the kingdom of heaven was at hand.

CHRIST HEALING ALL MANNER OF DISEASES.

79

Jesus and His Kingdom.

—:—

JESUS, you remember, was born a king. He was the king whom God had sent from heaven to rule over the Jews. But Jesus was not going to rule over them as any other king had ever done before.

His kingdom was made up of people who loved him with all their hearts, and who were willing to suffer and die, if need be, for him. And they must be willing to give up all they had in this life, too, for his sake.

It made the Pharisees angry to hear Jesus called their king. They could not understand how this could be; and they said and did so many cruel things to Jesus that he told them plainly that unless they would have their hearts cleansed they could never enter his kingdom. To simply keep the law was not enough.

Now, their hearts were full of hatred and murder, which they believed in keeping covered up; but even though they tried to keep the sin in their hearts covered, it would show itself.

One time when Jesus was talking to the Pharisees, he said that they made the outside of the cup and platter clean, but that the inside was full of unclean things; and he said that they must first cleanse the inside of the cup and platter, and that then the outside also would be clean. And he called them hypocrites, which meant that they were trying to appear to be what they were not.

But the time had come when Jesus wanted his disciples to know just what the kingdom of heaven was; so he took them with him, and went up into a mountain. And there he taught them that although they were poor men, yet they were rich in heavenly things, and were heirs of his kingdom.

Sermon on the Mount.

—:—

WHEN Jesus had called his disciples near him in the mountain, he told them many things.

THE SER-MON ON THE MOUNT.

They were astonished at his words, and a silence fell upon the great crowds of people that gathered around.

He told them that those who were poor in spirit, that is, sorry for their sins, theirs was the kingdom of heaven, and that all who were sorry for their sins should be comforted. And he said that the meek or humble should inherit the earth, and that those who wanted to be saved should have the desire of their hearts.

And he said that if they would show mercy, they should obtain mercy, and that the pure in heart should see God.

And Jesus said that the peacemakers, that is, those who will not quarrel themselves, and who try to keep others from it, should be called the children of God. And he said that if they were treated cruelly and persecuted, they should be glad; for their reward in heaven would be great. For even the prophets in olden times were treated in the same way.

And then Jesus told his disciples that they must let their light shine; that is, let others know that they were saved and had pure hearts, and then live so that those around them would see that what they said was true. In this way others might be led by their example to love and obey God, and would become great in the kingdom of heaven.

But if they, like the Pharisees, only taught the things they had heard, and did not live them, their life would be no better in God's sight than the life of the Pharisees.

And Jesus said, "Think not that I am come to destroy the law, or the prophets: I am not come to destroy, but to fulfil them." Jesus meant that he had come to teach men how to understand the will of God and obey his commandments in a higher and truer sense than had been possible before. Not only were they to keep from doing all wicked actions, but even the very thoughts of their hearts must be pure and free from sin.

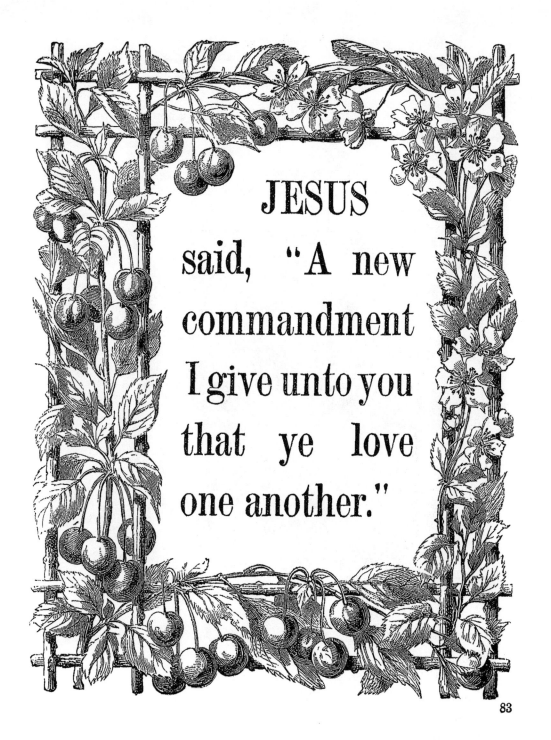

JESUS said, "A new commandment I give unto you that ye love one another."

Jesus Teaching His Disciples.

—:—

JESUS said that in the law they had read, ''Thou shalt not kill''; and if any one did kill, the murderer was to be punished for it. But now it was different; for if any one became angry with his brother and hated him, he would be a murderer in God's sight, and could not enter heaven until he repented; that is, became sorry, and asked his brother's forgiveness.

JESUS TALKING TO HIS DISCIPLES.

By ''brother,'' Jesus did not simply mean brothers in the same families. You remember that Jesus was in a hill near the Sea of Galilee, and that he was teaching his disciples how to live, and how to preach to the people.

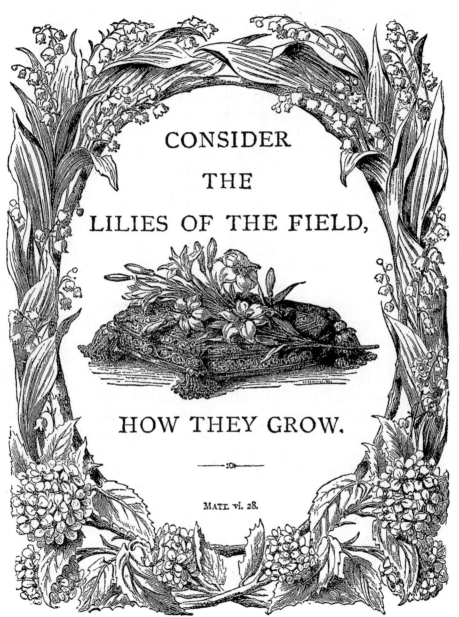

CONSIDER
THE
LILIES OF THE FIELD,

HOW THEY GROW.

MATT. vi. 28.

And Jesus wanted them to know that God was now their Father and the Father of all; then, all men must be brethren.

And Jesus wanted them to have true love for all people in the world; for he said, "Thou shalt love thy neighbor as thyself."

By the law they had been taught to love their friends, and to hate their enemies; but Jesus said, "Love your enemies, bless them that curse you, do good to them that hate you, and pray for those who treat you cruelly." And he told them to remember that they were all God's children, and that God made the sun to shine and the rain to fall upon the good and bad alike.

Jesus said that if they simply loved those who loved them, they were no better than the publican or sinners, for they did that; but that they must be perfect, as their Father in heaven is perfect; that is, they must love and do good to all.

Then, too, they must be careful not to be like the Pharisees, who when they did any good deed, told every one they could about it, that it might seem as if they were doing much for the Lord. If they did this, their heavenly Father would take no notice of their good deeds. They must do good, expecting God, not men, to see them.

And Jesus taught them to pray much, but not to pray as the Pharisees prayed; for they loved to stand on the street corners and in other public places, where men could see them praying. God loved the prayer that came from a sincere heart in some secret place where no one could see the person praying.

And then Jesus taught them a prayer, which is known as the Lord's Prayer.

A Lesson from the Birds and the Lilies.

—:—

THEN Jesus went on to teach them that they must not be anxious or worry about the future, for fear they would not have enough to eat or drink or wear; for their heavenly Father knew just what they were needing.

BEHOLD THE FOWLS OF THE AIR.

"Behold," he said, "the fowls of the air: for they sow not, neither do they reap, nor gather into barns; yet your heavenly Father feedeth them.   Are ye not much better than they?

"Which of you by taking thought can add one cubit unto his stature?"

"Consider the lilies of the field, how they grow; they toil not, neither do they spin: and yet I say unto you, That even Solomon in all his glory was not arrayed like one of these."

Therefore do not say, "What shall we eat?" or, "What shall we drink?" or, "Wherewithal shall we be clothed?"   But seek ye first the kingdom of God, and his righteousness, and all these things shall be added unto you.

Lay not up for yourselves treasures upon earth, where thieves break through and steal, and things spoil and decay; but lay your treasures up in heaven, for there they will be safe.

Where your treasures are, there also will be your heart; for you will be thinking about them.   So if your treasures are in heaven, your heart will be in heaven also.

And he told them never to judge their brother hastily, but to remember that they, too, must be judged by their heavenly Father, and to be careful that they did not see something in their brother that was really in themselves.   But when they were sure that there was nothing wrong in their own lives, then they could go to their brother and tell him about his fault.

And he said, "Give not that which is holy unto the dogs, neither cast ye your pearls before swine, lest they trample them under their feet, and turn again and rend you."   This was to show the disciples that there were people to whom it would do no good to talk.   These he compared to dogs and swine.

Lastly he told them that whatsoever things they desired men should do unto them these same things they must do to others.   This was the true way to keep the spirit of the law, and the only path that would lead them to heaven.   But they must beware, for false prophets would come and try to lead them into a road that was broad and easy to travel.

Let thy Garments be Always White.

Eccles. ix 8

J.H.Hipsley

89

Enter in at the strait gate, where the way is narrow; for this way will lead unto life, and very few find it. For wide is the gate, and broad is the way, that leadeth to destruction and despair, and many there be which go in thereat. Not every one who saith, "Lord, Lord," shall enter into the kingdom of heaven; but he that doeth the will of my Father which is in heaven. Many will wish to enter, but it will be too late.

○✤○✤○✤○

Consider the Lilies.

—:—

If in your heart you seem to grieve
Because you do not much receive
Or to some height you don't achieve,
    Consider then the lilies.

When trials come to press you sore
And you begin to count them o'er
And think there's many on before,
    Consider then the lilies.

Perchance a friend you thought was true,
Because of Christ deserted you,
And said harsh things about you, too:
    Consider then the lilies.

They do not spin, they do not toil,
They know not of earth's great turmoil,
Nor care for articles that spoil;
    Consider, then, the lilies.

They're dressed in garments snowy white,
No care for fear they're not dressed right;
They're pure as heaven in God's sight:
    Consider, then, the lilies.

THE HOUSE BUILT UPON THE SAND.

The Rocky and Sandy Foundations.

—:—

In order that he might impress his words upon the minds of his disciples, Jesus told them a story of two men, who each wished to build a house.

Now, one of these men was wise, and his first thought was to find a good firm place upon which to build his house. He knew that although the sun might shine ever so bright, there would be fierce storms, and he wanted his house to stand, no matter how hard the wind might blow or the rain fall.

So when he had digged deep, he found a large rock, and upon this he built his house. And he laid the foundation carefully, in order that no storm, however fierce it might be, could overthrow his house.

But it was not so with the other man. He thought only of the pleasant part, and chose the easiest way.

Upon the nice soft sandy ground by the seashore, he found a place where he had no trouble about making a foundation. Everything seemed to work in his favor, and in a very short time he had a house all complete and ready to live in.

But ah! one day it began to rain, and the wind blew very hard. Slowly the water began to rise, and soon reached the spot where his house was standing. Then it did not take long for the cruel waves to wash away the sand from beneath the house, and—what was the result? It fell, and great was the fall of it.

Looking up in the midst of his trouble, he saw the beautiful house his friend had built. Did he expect to see it fall, as his own had done? Ah, no!

His friend had taken great care to prepare for storms; for he knew that they would come, and there stood his house safe and secure. All the storms that could beat about it did not shake it in the least.

This story had two meanings, and it was called a "parable." Jesus often spoke in parables, and in this way taught his disciples many things that they could not have understood in any other way.

This time Jesus wanted them to see how careful all must be when they started out to serve God. If they would listen to his teachings and do the things he taught them, then they would be like the wise man who built his house upon a rock.

But those who listened to his teaching and would not do as he taught, were like the foolish man who built his house upon the sand.

These two men represented the righteous and the wicked. The righteous would be saved through trial and temptation, but the wicked would be destroyed and lost.

When Jesus had finished his sermon on the mount, the people wondered at what they had heard.

As they talked among themselves about the word he had spoken, they asked each other what it could mean; for he did not preach like any one else whom they had ever listened to, and his doctrine was so new, and something they had never heard before. It seemed to raise and point them to a purer and higher knowledge of God than they had ever known or realized before.

The Centurion's Faith.

—:—

GREAT multitudes of people followed Jesus as he came down out of the mount, some curious to know what he would say or do next, and some because they believed his words—that God had sent him to save them from their sins.

Capernaum being close, Jesus went there; and as he was entering the city, some of the elders of the Jews came to him, saying, "There is a certain centurion [or Roman officer] among us whose servant is very sick. This man has heard of thee, and has sent us to ask that thou wilt come and heal his servant."

And the Jews told Jesus that the centurion was worthy; for he loved their nation, and had built them a synagogue to worship God in.

When Jesus heard this, he went with them. And when he came near the house, the centurion sent friends to him, saying, "Lord, trouble not thyself; for I am not worthy that thou shouldest enter under my roof: wherefore neither thought I myself worthy to come unto thee: but say in a word, and my servant shall be healed."

And the centurion said that he was an officer with many soldiers under him. When he said to one "Go," the soldier had to go; and when he said to another "Come," he came; and his servants knew that they must do just as they were bidden.

When Jesus heard all this, he wondered. Here was a rich man that could command so many people, who knew they must obey him, and yet he did not feel worthy to come near enough to Jesus to ask him to heal his servant, but believed a word from Jesus would be all that was necessary.

Jesus turned to the people, and said, "I have not found so great faith, no not in Israel." Here was a Gentile with great faith—even greater faith than Jesus had found among the Jews.

Jesus said that many would come from the east and from the west, and would sit down with Abraham, Isaac, and Jacob in his kingdom in heaven; but that the unbelieving Jews and all others that did not have faith would be cast out into darkness, where would be weeping and gnashing of teeth. This Jesus said to show them the necessity of their believing in him.

And then he sent word to the centurion, and told him to believe and according to his faith his servant would be healed. When the messengers returned to the house, they found the servant well that had been sick.

○✣○✣○✣○

The Dead Man Raised.

—:—

Jesus did not stay long in Capernaum, but went down to a city called Nain. This city was about twenty-three miles from Capernaum, yet his disciples and many of the people went with him.

As they drew near the city, Jesus saw that something very sad had happened. A company of people were carrying a dead man. He was the only son of his mother, who was a poor widow.

We know that Jesus pitied the poor mother, for his heart was

JESUS AND THE CENTURION'S FRIENDS.

always full of love and pity for all who were in trouble. When he saw her, he said tenderly, "Weep not." Then he stopped the procession, and spoke to the young man who had died, saying, "Arise," and the man sat up, and he was able to speak once more. What joy must have filled the poor mother's heart!

When the people saw this miracle, great fear fell upon them all, and they thought that Jesus must be a prophet. And his great works were spoken of far and near.

THE WIDOW'S SON RESTORED TO LIFE.

Some asked whether he were really the Christ or whether they must look for another. Jesus told them to look at the things which they had seen and heard—how the blind saw, the lame walked, the lepers were cleansed, the deaf made to hear, the dead were raised, and the gospel preached to the poor. Was not this enough to show that he was the Christ, the Messiah they were looking for? And he said that the law and all the prophets until John the Baptist had prophesied of his coming.

The people were looking for Elijah to appear on earth again before their Messiah came, for Malachi had prophesied that he would come; but Jesus said that Elias had come already, meaning John the Baptist. And he spoke of the shameful treatment of John, and said that he himself also must suffer many things at the hands of the Jews.

And Jesus spoke against the wickedness of the different cities and people that had seen his mighty works and that would not receive him. He said that even the people of Sodom and Gomorrah were not so guilty as they were, for they had never had the light of the gospel preached to them.

Jesus then said such sweet words—words that have come down even to us: "Come unto me, all ye that labor and are heavy laden, and I will give you rest. Take my yoke upon you, and learn of me; for I am meek and lowly in heart, and ye shall find rest unto your souls. For my yoke is easy, and my burden is light."

In the House of Simon the Pharisee.

—:—

THE Pharisees had taken very little notice of Jesus up to this time; but they could not help seeing the great and mighty works that he was doing among them. So one day a Pharisee named Simon invited Jesus to dine at his house.

Although Simon invited Jesus to eat at his house, he did not show him any real kindness of feeling, and he was ready to find all the fault with Jesus that he could.

Their customs were different from ours. When any one went into a house tired and dusty from walking, the host usually had water brought, so that the visitor might wash his hands and feet. But this Pharisee did not do this for Jesus.

Another odd custom to us was the manner in which they ate their

7

meals. Instead of sitting up to a table as we do, they reclined upon couches, with their feet away from the table.

While Jesus was eating his dinner, a woman who had led a very wicked life entered the room. She had listened to the words of Jesus before, and she was very sorry for all the sins that she had committed, and she longed to do something for Jesus that would show him how sorry she was, and how much she loved him.

So when she saw him sitting at the Pharisee's table, she took a box of very costly ointment, and stood at his feet.

She began to weep bitterly; and as she wept, her tears fell down upon the feet of Jesus. When she saw this, she stooped down and with her long hair wiped his feet, and then she kissed them, and poured upon his feet and upon his head the ointment that she had brought.

When the Pharisee saw what the woman had done, he was very much displeased with Jesus, and thought, "If this man were a prophet, he would have known what a wicked life this woman has led; for she is a sinner."

Now, the Pharisees thought that they were too good and holy to let sinners touch them. But Jesus saw only the heart. He looked in pity upon this poor woman, whose life he knew had been very sinful. He also looked at the heart of the proud Pharisee, and there he saw the same things that had prompted the woman to commit sin. The difference was, the world could see the one, and not the other.

The Two Debtors.

Jesus told Simon the Pharisee that he had something to say to him, and then he told him of a certain man who had two debtors. The debt of one was much larger than that of the other.

At last, when the time came to pay the debt, they had no money. So they went to the man and told him, and he frankly forgave them both.   Then Jesus said, "Tell me therefore, which of them will love him most?"

Simon answered and said, "I suppose that he, to whom he forgave most."

Then Jesus said, "Thou hast rightly judged"; and turning to the woman, he said, "Seest thou this woman?   I entered into thine house, thou gavest me no water for my feet: but she hath washed my feet with tears, and wiped them with the hairs of her head.

"Thou gavest me no kiss: but this woman, since the time I came in, hath not ceased to kiss my feet.   My head with oil thou didst not anoint: but this woman hath anointed my feet with ointment.

"Wherefore I say unto thee, Her sins, which are many, are forgiven; for she loved much: but to whom little is forgiven, the same loveth little."

What reproof this was for Simon!   This was a lesson of the great debt of gratitude that sinners owe to God.   He forgives and takes away their burden of sin.   And the one who has committed the most sin, generally feels the most thankful.

Then Jesus said to the woman, "Thy sins be forgiven thee: thy faith hath saved thee.   Go in peace."

And the people wondered how Jesus had power to forgive sins as well as to heal the bodies of the sick people.

✪✦✪✦✪

Jesus Reproves the People.

JESUS spent some time in visiting the different cities of Galilee. Many came to him who were possessed with evil spirits, and he healed them, "insomuch that the blind and dumb both spake and saw."   All the people were amazed and said, "Is not this the Son of David?" They could not understand the mighty works that they saw done in their midst.

The Pharisees said, "This fellow casts out devils by Beelzebub, the prince of devils."   But Jesus, knowing their thoughts, as well as words, told them that a kingdom which was divided against itself could not stand, and said, "If I by Beelzebub cast out devils, by whom do your children cast them out?" And he told them that Satan could not drive himself out of any person.

"But if I," he said, "with the finger of God cast out devils, no doubt the kingdom of God is come upon you."

Then Jesus said that every sin that man might commit would be forgiven him, except one. That was the sin against the Holy Ghost.

We can almost imagine we see and hear the people asking one another what Jesus meant. No doubt they thought that it was because they had said, "He hath an unclean spirit."

Jesus knew that they could not understand then, but that the day was coming when it would be made plain. They were going to crucify him; that is, nail him to a cross of wood, and let him hang there until he died. They would say many hard things about him; but if they were sorry, God would forgive them, and then they would know that he was truly God's Son.

But if when they knew this and that Jesus had cleansed their hearts from every sin they should again say that Jesus was only a common man and that he had never done anything for them, it would be as though they had crucified him again, and God would not forgive them.

A good many people fear they have committed this sin, because they have allowed trials, persecutions, or a failure to do their duty, to come between their souls and God, and in this way became backsliders. And Satan tries to bring against souls everything that he can to deceive them. No wonder, then, that he tries to make them think they have committed the unpardonable sin.

But it all depends upon the true state of the heart. As long as they have a desire to serve God, and can be sorry for their sins, God can forgive them, and will if they will turn to him.

It is dangerous to put off salvation one moment after the grace of God has leaked out of the soul through carelessness or in any other way, as it opens the way for Satan to deceive.

But people who find that they are under a deceiving spirit should at once seek help from the Lord through earnest prayer, and he will deliver and save them.

○✢○✢○✢○

The Sign of Jonah.

J ESUS was asked one day by the Pharisees to give them a sign from heaven, but he said, "There shall no sign be given but the sign of the prophet Jonah."

Many years before, God had sent a prophet named Jonah to the wicked city of Nineveh. Jonah did not want to go, and he tried to run away from the Lord. But the Lord knew all about Jonah and his plans, and he sent a great storm, which rocked the boat so hard that was taking him away from Nineveh that there was great danger of its going to pieces.

The sailors were greatly frightened, and they cried to their gods, or idols, to save them; and they cast their wares into the sea to lighten the ship. But Jonah was asleep through it all.

Then the shipmaster went to him, and said, "What meanest thou.

O sleeper? Arise, call upon thy God, if so be that God will think upon us, that we perish not.'' Then Jonah told them that he feared God, and that he was not going where God had told him to go. And he said to them, "Take me up, and cast me forth into the sea; so shall the sea be calm.'' It was very hard for the men to do this, but at last they threw Jonah into the sea, and it at once became calm.

Now, the Lord had prepared a great fish to swallow Jonah, and he was within this fish three days and three nights.

Then Jonah prayed to the Lord, and said he would do anything the Lord wanted him to do. "And the Lord spake unto the fish, and it vomited out Jonah upon the dry land.''

A second time God spoke to Jonah, and told him to go to Nineveh and preach to the people of that place, and this time he went. Jonah told them that in forty days their city would be overthrown.

Now, the people of Nineveh knew there was a true God, and they did not want to be destroyed; so they fasted and prayed, and God forgave them, and they were not destroyed.

When Jesus referred to this as a sign, he meant that as Jonah was three days and three nights within the fish, so the Son of God would lie in the grave, after they had crucified him, three days and three nights.

And Jesus said that the people of Nineveh would not be as guilty in God's sight as these Pharisees were. For the people of Nineveh were sorry for their sins and repented; but these had listened to the words of a far greater prophet than Jonah, even Jesus, God's Son.

Who Are Christ's Relatives?

—:—

WHILE Jesus was still talking to the people, some one came to him and said that his mother and brethren wished to speak with him.

Now, Jesus loved his mother and his brethren very dearly; but he wanted to show the people how much he loved those who would forsake their sinful lives and become servants of God. So he said,

"Who is my mother? and who are my brethren?" Then stretching out his hand toward his disciples and those who believed on him, he said, "My mother and my brethren are these which hear the word of God, and do it."

Strange as these words must have sounded, those who were saved knew they were true. The Christian loves everybody, but there is a tie binding those who are saved which is far greater than the love that binds earthly families together.

What a blessed thought it is to think that we may be counted as the brothers and sisters of Jesus! And, children, you do not have to wait until you become men and women before you can become related to Christ. No, indeed; Jesus wants you to give your hearts to him as soon as possible.

How sweet it is to see little children saved and able to testify that God is their Father and Jesus their brother, and that they are in the family of God!

At one time Jesus said that unless people became as little children they could not enter into the kingdom of heaven. So you see that even grown people must, before they can be saved, feel as though they were little children.

Jesus continued to preach to the people, and many believed on him; but the Pharisees saw by his preaching that their own hearts were not right, and instead of seeking to get right and accepting him as their Savior, they did all they could against him. They tried to get him to say something that they could use against him. But the time for this had not come.

Jesus warned his disciples, saying, "Beware ye of the leaven of the Pharisees, which is hypocrisy." He meant the sin that the Pharises were covering up in their hearts.

And he said: "There is nothing covered that shall not be revealed; neither hid that shall not be made known. Therefore, whatsoever ye have spoken in the darkness shall be heard in the light; and that which ye have spoken in the ear in closets shall be proclaimed upon the housetops."

Jesus told them not to be afraid of those who could kill the body, but to fear him who, after he had killed the body, had power to cast into hell. This was God.

And then he told them that God, their Father, would take good care of them. Even the little sparrows, he said, were all remembered by God. The care for his children was so great that even the hairs of their heads were numbered, and could they not trust him to care for them—his own dear children? They were of more value than many sparrows.

They might have to suffer many things, and have many hard questions asked them; but they must not wonder at this, nor try to think of some good answer. God would care for them and teach them what to say.

The Barren Fig-tree.

—:—

A man possessed a vineyard,
　Where grapes in plenty grew,
And he who was the dresser
　Picked grapes there not a few.

The owner came with pleasure
　To view his vineyard o'er,
And saw the crop increasing
　Each year more than before.

He saw, on one occasion,
　A spot which idle stood,
And planted there a fig-tree,
　Young, vigorous, and good.

In time he thought the fig-tree
　Was old enough to bear,
So came one day to see it,
　But no fruit found he there.

" Are not two sparrows sold for a farthing? and one of them shall not fall on the ground without your Father."

" Fear ye not, therefore, ye are more value than many sparrows."

" The foxes have holes, and the birds of the air have nests; but the Son of man hath not where to lay His head."

THE UNFRUITFUL TREE.

Then speaking to the dresser,
"Just cut it down," said he;
"Why let it longer cumber
  The ground, or hindrance be?"

The dresser was kind-hearted
  And said: "Lord, not this year;
I'll dig about and tend it,
  And possibly 'twill bear.

"But if it then bears nothing,
  No longer I'll object;
I'll cut it down, and quickly:
  Such trees we should reject."

A little lesson, children,
  From this same tree we learn:
Those in the Lord's great vineyard
  Their right to stay must earn.

For all who there are idle
  Will share the fig-tree's fate,
And they may not discover
  They're cut off till too late.

Parable of the Rich Man.

JESUS one day told the people a story about a rich man. He did this that he might impress upon their minds how uncertain life is, and how little riches are worth to any one when he comes to die.

This man had much good land. It had yielded so much substance year after year that he had become very rich. His barns were large and roomy; but everything increased so fast that at last he found his barns were not large enough to hold all that the ground brought forth.

Then this man should have thought, "What can I give to the poor people around me, who are not blessed as I am?" But he did not think of doing this at all.

Instead he thought, "What shall I do, because I have no room where to bestow my fruits?" Then he thought, "This will I do: I will pull down my barns, and build greater; and there will I bestow all my fruits and my goods. And I will say to my soul, Soul, thou hast much goods laid up for many years; take thine ease, eat, drink, and be merry."

When this man had finished speaking thus, the voice of God said, "Thou fool, this night thy soul shall be required of thee: then whose shall those things be, which thou hast provided?"

Jesus told the people it would be so with all who would try to lay up riches for themselves in this world, and did not care whether they pleased God or not. They would have to die some day, and would have to leave their riches to be enjoyed by others, while they went away to a world where they would have to suffer torment and misery.

They need never fear that they would not have enough food to eat or clothes to wear; for their life was more than their food, and their body more than what they would wear. God created both their life and their body, and he would not let them suffer for food and clothes.

He told them to think about the birds, and see how God cared for them. They never planted anything, and yet God fed them; and then the lilies, how beautifully they were dressed, and yet they did not work nor make their garments. Even Solomon, who was once the great wise king who ruled over the children of Israel, did not have such beautiful garments.

If God cared so much for the birds and the lilies, and clothed and fed them with such care, they need never fear but that he would care for them if they would only trust him.

They must not be anxious for these things, but they must be sure to lay their treasures up in heaven. They need never fear that there thieves or moths would destroy their treasures.

THE PARABLE OF THE RICH MAN WHO SET UP GREATER BARNS.

ST LUKE XII.

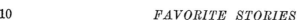

And Jesus told them that they must be ready and waiting, as servants who were waiting for their master to come home. When he came and knocked, they must open to him at once.

He wanted them to know that he would not always be with them. After his death he would go to heaven; but some day he would come back to this earth, gather all his people together, and take them back to heaven with him. And he told them that they must watch for his coming, or he might come when they were not expecting him.

Parable of the Sower.

—:—

While teaching the people
  About God one day,
Christ's foll'wers were startled
  By hearing him say,
"A sower went forth to
  Sow seed by the way;"
And then they all wondered
  How the truth he'd display.

With great care they listened;
  Now here's what they heard:
"Some fell by the wayside."
  (The seed meant God's word,
But some way it never
  To their minds occurred;
And though they all listened,
  In judgment they erred.)

The seed Jesus mentioned,
  By fowls were soon found;
They quickly devoured
  Each seed, good and sound.
Then, some fell on stony
  Or hard, rocky ground,
Where the soil was deficient,
  Great rocks lying round.

THE RICH FOOL.

The sun, shining brightly,
  Sent forth such great heat
That the tiny seeds, sprouting,
  Its rays could not meet;
They withered and perished
  Ere growth was complete
Or fruitage was gathered
  For others to eat.

Then some fell where thorns grew
  So rank and so tall
That small seeds were hindered,
  If grown there at all;
The harsh, cruel briars
  Seemed so to enthrall
That young plants were famished,
  And soon had to fall.

Now, some fell on good ground,
  Perhaps just a few;
But all of this sprouted,
  And rapidly grew.
The rain fell in plenty,
  No drought this seed knew;
'Twas indeed a fine harvest
  For the reapers to view.

When Jesus had finished
  This parable queer,
He saw his disciples
  Come gathering near.
The Savior knew what they
  Were longing to hear,
So he quickly endeavored
  To make all things clear.

He said that wherever
  God's word should be taught,
A foe would endeavor
  To bring it to naught.

PARABLE OF THE SOWER.

Perchance he succeeded
  And gained what he sought,
'Twould be like the wayside
  Seed—hastily caught.

The hard, rocky places
  Were where the truth came
Into hearts that with gladness
  Accepted the same,
But who were not willing
  To suffer the shame
All Christians must suffer
  For Jesus' dear name.

Life's cares were the harsh thorns
  That sprang in the heart.
These hindered the small growth
  Made there in the start;
Then the greed and desire
  For gain did their part:
'Twas no wonder this soul had
  No fruit to impart.

The good soil, which yielded
  Much fruitage, was found
In hearts of the people
  Whose judgment was sound.
They heard the whole gospel,
  Then tried to expound
The glad truths to others,
  Who gathered around.

These were not offended,
  Their hope was secure,
Were fully decided
  To always endure.
Great wealth and false pride
  Could never allure
Their hearts from the kingdom
  They meant to secure.

The disciples, rejoicing,
    Could then understand;
The story no longer
    Seemed strange, it was grand;
For Jesus had called them
    His own chosen band,
And this would encourage
    And help them to stand.

The parables were given
    By Jesus below,
To tell of his kingdom
    And God's love to show,
To direct to and guide in
    The path we should go
If heaven we'd enter
    And God's favor know.

Parable of the Candle Hid under a Bushel.

—:—

One time Jesus asked his disciples a strange question. He said, "Is a candle brought to be put under a bushel, or under a bed? and not to be set on a candlestick?" And then he said, "No man, when he hath lighted a candle, covereth it with a vessel, or putteth it under a bed; but setteth it on a candlestick, that they which enter in may see the light."

Jesus was comparing people who had salvation to a candlestick, and their experience to the light of the candle. And he wanted to show how foolish it would be for a saved person to try to hide what God had done for him. "For nothing is secret, that shall not be made manifest; neither anything hid, that shall not be known and come abroad."

And Jesus said, "Take heed therefore how ye hear; for whosoever hath, to him shall be given; and whosoever hath not, from him shall be taken even that which he seemeth to have."

It may be seen by this parable how very important it is that those who are saved do all they can to let their light shine, and not be as the candle under a bushel, where no one can see the light.

There are many ways in which they can let their light shine. One good way is to read the Bible much, and pray very often. Another is to look around you every day, and see if you can not help somebody. Oh, there are so many ways of helping people!

Perhaps you might see no one else than poor little brother, who was feeling sad because some of his toys were broken or would not work to suit him. You could go to him and say, "Come, let me see what is the matter," and then try to make him feel happy again. This would be letting your light shine.

I am sure you could see many such ways in which you could do good to those around you. And the one you were helping would not be the only happy one; for Jesus said, "With what measure ye mete, it shall be measured to you; and unto you that hear shall more be given." So you see that by helping others we let our light shine, and make others happy; but we are the happiest, for we know that we are doing what Jesus told us to do.

"Let your light so shine before men, that they may see your good works, and glorify your Father which is in heaven."

Parable of the Wheat and the Tares.

—:—

ANOTHER parable was spoken by Jesus about the sowing of seed. This time he said, "The kingdom of heaven is likened unto a man which sowed good seed in his field. But while men slept, his enemy came and sowed tares among the wheat, and went his way. But when the blade was sprung up, and brought forth fruit, then appeared the tares also.

"So the servants of the householder came and said unto him, Sir, didst not thou sow good seed in thy field? from whence then hath it tares?

THE
PARABLE OF THE TARES.
MATT. XIII.

"He said unto them, An enemy hath done this. The servants said unto him, Wilt thou then that we go and gather them up?

"But he said, Nay; lest while ye gather up the tares, ye root up also the wheat with them. Let both grow together until the harvest: and in the time of harvest I will say to the reapers, Gather ye together first the tares, and bind them in bundles to burn them: but gather the wheat into my barn."

We can imagine that we see the man when his day's work was ended, going to his home to rest, and his servants resting also.

But while they are resting and enjoying a nice quiet sleep, an enemy comes and scatters tares in the wheat-field, and then goes away again.

Tares are much like wheat in appearance, but are harmful if eaten.

After a while the seed which had been sown began to spring up. Then the master's servants saw that the field was full of tares, also. They were much surprised and grieved, for they saw that much damage had been done by some one.

So they came to their master and said, "Sir, didst not thou sow good seed in thy field? from whence then hath it tares?" He told them that some enemy must have done this.

Then the servants asked whether he should like to have them go and gather the tares from among the wheat. He said no; for in gathering out the tares, they might also destroy or root up some of the wheat. It would be better, he said, to let both grow together until the harvest, and then he would have the reapers separate the two. Then the tares could be bound into bundles and burned, but the wheat would be taken to his barn.

The disciples could not understand this parable; so when they were alone with Jesus, they asked what it meant. Then Jesus said to them: "He that soweth the good seed is the Son of man; the field is the world; the good seed are the children of the kingdom; but the tares are the children of the wicked one; the enemy that sowed them

THE ENEMY SOWING TARES.

is the devil; the harvest is the end of the world; and the reapers are the angels."

And he said that as the tares were gathered and burned with fire, so it would be at the end of the world.

We sometimes wonder why people are allowed to live and do such dreadful things, but we must remember that in this world the good and the evil live side by side; but there is a day coming when God will separate the good from the evil.

And in that day those who have done evil will not be happy, for God will punish them for all the wrong deeds they have done. God is a loving and merciful God, but he is also a God of justice. He would like to see every one saved, but those who refuse to repent of their sinful ways will be punished.

But in that great day of which Jesus spoke in this parable, God will reward the righteous, or good people, and they will shine forth in the kingdom of heaven as the sun.

Be sure that you are among those whom Jesus called "the good seed," and not among "the tares."

<blockquote>
In the same field this seed had been sown,
Side by side it was placed and had grown,
And the same sun and rain it had known;
    But at last a day came
    Which brought judgment and shame:
For into the fire the tares were thrown;
    But the good and the choice
    Had great cause to rejoice,
For the Master knew they were his own.
</blockquote>

Parables of the Mustard Seed and the Leaven.

JESUS spoke a parable about the mustard seed, which is among the smallest of seeds. He said: "The kingdom of heaven is like to a grain of mustard seed, which a man took and sowed in his field:

which indeed is the least of all seeds: but when it is grown, it is the greatest among herbs, and becometh a tree, so that the birds of the air come and lodge in the branches thereof.''

It might seem strange to some that Jesus should take such things to represent the kingdom of God. But this was God's way of showing the people the wonders of the kingdom. One of the prophets said that he (Jesus) would speak many things in parables, and would utter many things which had been kept secret from the foundation of the world.

Jesus knew that because of sin in their hearts not many of the people would believe what he said, but that some would believe and would understand. If they would come to him, he would explain all they desired to know.

That is the way it is to-day. When we do not understand his words, we can go to him, and ask him what he meant; and he will tell us.

But let us return to the mustard seed, which was so tiny, and yet when it was planted in good soil became so large, even the largest of herbs, and was as a tree, where the birds could come and lodge in its branches.

So it is with our faith and love for God. Both may seem very small at first; but if we truly love God and are his children, God will cause our faith to become so great and our love for him so strong that others will see us and come to learn of Jesus and his kingdom.

And Jesus compared the kingdom of God to a little leaven, or yeast, which a woman hid in some meal. The leaven worked through all the meal, and it was changed into good light bread. This parable seems strange, and quite hard to understand; but when we think about the love of God, and how it is hid in the heart, and then notice how it works in the life of that one in whose heart it is hidden, we can better understand why Jesus compared it to leaven in the meal.

Parables of the Hidden Treasure, the Pearl, and the Net.

—:—

JESUS told his disciples some parables when he was alone with them.　One was about a man who found a treasure that had been hidden in a field.　This man was so happy when he saw the treasure that he wanted to own it for himself.　So at once he hastened away and sold all his own land, and bought that field.

That is the way with those who find salvation.　When they see what a great treasure it is, they at once have a desire to possess it for themselves; and not only are they willing to give up the enjoyments of this world, but they hasten to do so.

The next parable was of a merchantman, or man who bought things to sell them again.　This man in the parable bought pearls. Pearls are beautiful white stones.　They are found in oysters, and many of them are very costly.

Many people who can afford to do so, wear them as ornaments in rings, bracelets, and necklaces.　This is not right; for the Bible says 'to adorn ourselves in modest apparel; not with gold, or pearls, or costly array.'

But Jesus was not speaking to those who wore them.　He was trying to show his disciples the great worth of salvation.

Now, this merchantman was looking for pearls to buy.　At last he saw one more beautiful than any he had ever seen before; but it belonged to some one who asked a great price for it.　He asked more for it than the merchantman was able to pay without selling everything that he had.　But he wanted the pearl so much that he went and sold all that he had, and bought that one precious pearl.

This is the way persons feel who want to have their sins forgiven.　They are not happy, but instead they feel, oh! so miserable. They long for salvation; and when they see that to possess it they must give up all their sinful ways and everything that displeases God, how glad they are to give them up!

And the next parable was about a net that fishermen use.　Several of Christ's disciples were fishermen, you remember; so this was very easy for them to understand.

THE MERCHANT SEEKING GOODLY PEARLS.

Jesus said that as a net was cast into the sea, and gathered of every kind of fish, and when it was full it was drawn to the shore, and there the good fish were gathered into vessels, but the bad were cast away; so it would be at the end of the world. The angels will come forth, and take the wicked from among the just. And the wicked will be cast into a furnace of fire, where there will be wailing and gnashing of teeth.

When Jesus had finished telling his disciples these parables, he asked, "Have ye understood all these things?" and they answered, "Yea, Lord."

Then Jesus said that those who were instructed and understood what the kingdom of God was, were like a householder who brought out of his treasure things new and old.

All who have salvation can do this, for God helps them to understand the Bible; and they are able to teach others many things that before they were saved they themselves could not understand.

The Savior's Home.

—:—

The birds of the air have nests, we read;
  How true! and then again,
The foxes holes in which to go,
  Where shelter they obtain;
But the Son of man hath not a place
To call his own in this vast space;
Although a crown his head might grace;
  He knows naught here but pain.

But though the Christ no home possessed,
  And here such suff'ring bore,
He knew a home most beautiful
  His Father held in store;

THE PARABLE OF THE NET,

125

He knew 'twas but a season brief,
Then he would find such sweet relief
No more he'd know of sorrow, grief;
    He'd reign forevermore.

He did not wish an earthly home;
    He came to teach mankind,
For man had wandered long in sin,
    And to the truth was blind.
Christ came that all mankind might see
That from this sin they might be free,
And share his home eternally—
    Oh, what a Savior kind!

No Resting-Place.

—:—

EVERY parable that Jesus spoke meant something. He did not tell these things to amuse the people, but that they might understand and remember better the things he wanted them to learn.

As he taught the people about his kingdom in heaven, he told them that if they wanted to be his disciples, they must take up their cross and follow him. He meant they must follow his example, and do what was right, no matter how hard and unpleasant it might be. Things that were wrong might often seem more easy and pleasant to do; but these were the times to do the things that were right, and in this way they could bear the cross.

One evening after Jesus had been preaching to the people all day, a man came to him and said, "Lord, I will follow thee whithersoever thou goest." But Jesus wanted him to know how much it meant to follow him, and so he said, "Foxes have holes, and birds of the air have nests; but the Son of man hath not where to lay his head."

Jesus meant to tell the man that he was poorer than even the foxes and the birds. For they had homes of their own, where they

ON THE WAY TO ITS NEST.

might stay; but Jesus had no home, nor any place where he might go to lie down and rest when he was tired. Those who wanted to be his disciples must be willing to live just as he did if it were necessary.

Then Jesus spoke to another, and said, ''Follow me,'' but he was not ready; and still another said, ''I will follow thee; but let me first go and bid them farewell, which are at home at my house.'' But Jesus said, ''No man, having put his hand to the plow , and looking back, is fit for the kingdom of God.''

By this Jesus did not mean that it was wrong to be courteous to their friends; but that they who would follow him must care more about getting others saved than about the many little acts which they had been used to doing to their friends.

A Great Storm.

—:—

ONE evening Jesus and his disciples went into a boat to sail over to the other side of the Sea of Galilee.

Soon after they had started, the wind began to blow very hard. The great waves dashed against the boat, and it was soon full of water, and they were in great danger of being drowned.

But Jesus was very tired, having preached all day to the people; and he had lain down in the end of the ship, with his head upon a pillow, and he was sleeping soundly.

As the storm kept increasing, the disciples went to Jesus and awoke him, saying, ''Lord, save us: we perish.'' Their fear was great; for they did not have the faith of the centurion, who believed that Jesus was Lord of all. And Jesus said to them, ''Why are ye fearful, O ye of little faith?'' Then he arose, and said to the sea, ''Peace, be still''; and the wind ceased, and there was a great calm.

His disciples were astonished when they saw this, and they said, ''What manner of man is this! for he commandeth even the winds and waters, and they obey him?''

THE TEMP-EST ON THE SEA.

Soon after this, Jesus and his disciples landed on the other side of the sea in the country inhabited by the Gadarenes.

Gadara was a city five miles southeast of the Sea of Galilee. At this place and around it in the rocky hillsides were many tombs cut. These were rooms from ten to twenty feet square, and some larger, with small recesses or places cut out of them for dead bodies. Great stone doors with stone hinges were in front of these recesses, and it was up among these tombs that Jesus and his disciples now came.

Two Dangerous Men.

—:—

As Jesus and his disciples were walking along among these tombs, two men possessed with evil spirits met them. These men were very dangerous, and most people were afraid to go that way, fearing they might be killed.

One of these men was so fierce that he had often been bound with chains and had his feet placed in fetters; but these he would break in pieces, and no man could bind him. And always, night and day, he was crying, and cutting himself with stones.

When this man saw Jesus, he said, "What have I to do with thee, Jesus, thou Son of the most high God? I beseech thee, torment me not." Jesus asked him, "What is thy name?" and the evil spirits answéred, "Legion: for we are many."

At a little distance from the place where they were standing was a herd of swine feeding; and when Jesus commanded the unclean spirits to come out of the man, they asked whether they might enter the swine; and he said they might.

Then the unclean spirits went out, and entered into the swine. The swine at once began to run about, and then they all rushed over a steep place, and were drowned in the sea. There were about two thousand in the herd.

When the men who cared for the swine saw what had happened, their hearts were filled with fear, and they ran away to the city,

Matth 8, 28. 33

and told all that had happened—how the man possessed with devils had been delivered, and what had become of the swine.

When the people in the city heard this, they came out to see Jesus, and to find out whether these things were true. They found the man who had been so fierce and wild, sitting at the feet of Jesus, clothed, and in his right mind; and they were afraid.

As Jesus was leaving the place, the man who had been delivered asked Jesus to take him away in the ship; but Jesus told him to go home to his friends, and tell them what great things the Lord had done for him. The man obeyed his words, and told all his friends what a great change had taken place in his mind and body; and they could all see that his words were true.

Levi's Feast.

—:—

Jesus, having reached the other side of Galilee, went into the city of Capernaum. He found the people waiting for his return, and they were glad to have him once more in their midst.

One day Jesus and his disciples were invited to the house of a man whose name was Levi. This man made a great feast, and many guests were invited that were known as publicans and sinners.

Now, the Pharisees would not eat with this class of people; and when they saw Jesus and his disciples at the table, the Pharisees asked, "Why do ye eat and drink with publicans and sinners?"

Jesus told them that he had come to this world to save sinners, not the righteous; but the Pharisees could not and would not understand him.

Jesus spoke as often as he could about his reason for coming to this earth and about his death.

One day the disciples of John the Baptist came to Jesus, and asked, "Why do we and the Pharisees fast oft, but thy disciples fast not?"

Jesus told them that it was because he was with them. But the time, he said, would come when he should be taken from them; then they would fast.

And he spoke another parable, saying, "No man soweth a piece of new cloth on an old garment; else the new piece that filled it up taketh away from the old, and the rent is made worse."

By this little saying Jesus showed how impossible it would be to patch up the Pharisees' religion. Their profession was as an old garment; and if Jesus would try to patch is up for them, the rents would only be made worse.

Jairus' Daughter and the Happy Woman.

—:—

A RULER of the synagogue whose name was Jairus came to Jesus. This man was in great trouble; and when he saw Jesus, he fell down before him. His little daughter, he said, was very sick, and at the point of death; even now she might be dead. But he said that if Jesus would only go to his house and lay his hands on her, he knew she would be healed and live.

When Jesus heard this, he and his disciples went with the man, and many of the people followed them. Among the people who followed them was a woman who had been sick twelve years. She, in trying to be made well, had spent all her money upon doctors; but she grew worse all the time.

As she came behind Jesus, she thought, "If I may touch but his clothes, I shall be well "; and reaching out, she touched the hem of his garment. When she did so, she felt herself suddenly become well and strong, and she knew that she was healed.

Then Jesus surprised his disciples very much by turning around in the crowd and asking who touched his clothes. Peter said, "Master, the multitude press thee, and sayest thou, Who touched me?" But Jesus said, "Some one hath touched me"; and then the woman saw that she could not hide the thing she had done, and she came trembling, and fell down at his feet, confessing all the truth. Jesus said,

"Daughter, be of good comfort: thy faith hath made thee whole."

He was still speaking to the woman when some messengers came from the house of Jairus, saying, "Thy daughter is dead; trouble not the Master"; but Jesus said to Jairus, "Be not afraid, only believe."

When they reached the house, they heard a great noise; for it was the custom then to hire people to come and mourn when any one died. These people would cry aloud, and try to show the grief of the friends by many tears and lamentations. Jesus asked why they made such an ado, and said, "The maid is not dead, but sleepeth."

When he said this, the people laughed him to scorn, and said that they knew she was dead. Then Jesus put them all out except the girl's father and mother and three of his disciples—Peter, James and John. Then he went to the place where the little maid was lying, and said, "Maid, arise"; and she rose at once, and walked; for she was twelve years old. Jesus commanded them to give her some food. Her parents were astonished when they saw their precious child restored to them alive.

<hr>

Instructing the Twelve Apostles.

—:—

Now the time had come when Jesus wanted to send his disciples out into the world, that they might tell the people about the great kingdom of God of which they had been hearing so much. And he wanted them to tell the people how they must live if they would like to live in that kingdom.

So he called the Twelve together and told them that the time had come when they must go out into the cities and preach to the people.

He told them that they must first preach to the children of Israel; for they were the truly-chosen people of God, the ones God had intended to have for himself.

He said, "Take nothing for your journey, neither staves, nor scrip, neither bread, neither money; neither have two coats apiece." For these things would be provided for them. And Jesus told them that they must do all the wonderful things they had seen him do—

TOUCHING THE HEM OF HIS GARMENT.

135

heal the sick, cleanse the lepers, raise the dead, cast out devils; and that they must not charge for any of their services.

And Jesus said, "Behold, I send you forth as sheep in the midst of wolves: be ye therefore wise as serpents, and harmless as doves." And he told them that they would have to suffer many things for his sake, but that he would be with them, and teach them what they were to say.

"Ye shall," he said, "be hated of all men for my name's sake: but he that endureth to the end shall be saved. When they persecute you in one city, flee ye into another. The disciple is not above his master, nor the servant above his lord. It is enough for the disciple to be as his master, and the servant as his lord. Fear not them which kill the body, but are not able to kill the soul: but rather fear him which is able to destroy both soul and body in hell."

And Jesus told them that God took care of each little sparrow, and even numbered the hairs upon the heads of people; and that there was no need for them to worry, as God would care for all who were willing to follow his Son, and tell the people what had been done for them.

And he said they must not love their parents nor homes more than they loved to go and tell the people how to get saved; for this was their cross, and if they would not take up their cross, they were not worthy of his love.

Then he said, "He that receiveth you receiveth me, and he that receiveth me receiveth him that sent me."

And he also said that all who were good and kind to his disciples would be richly rewarded. Even if they did no more than to give them a drink of cold water, they would receive a blessing.

What a solemn time this must have been for the Twelve! No doubt they all felt that a great responsibility was placed upon them. When Jesus had finished commanding them, they went out and preached that men should repent. And they cast out many devils, and anointed with oil many that were sick and healed them.

And the twelve disciples were also known as the twelve apostles, for "apostle" means any one sent forth to preach the gospel.

The Twelve Return.

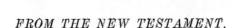

AFTER a time the apostles returned to the place where Jesus was preaching near the Sea of Galilee. They told him all the things they had done, and how they had taught the people.

Jesus was glad to see them again; and as there were so many people crowding around to hear and see all they could, Jesus took his disciples, and went across the Sea of Galilee in a boat, where they might be more to themselves.

But the people, when they found out where Jesus was, went as quickly as they could to the place. They must have been very anxious to hear Jesus, don't you think?

They were anxious to hear him, but many desired more to be made well than they did to hear about the kingdom of heaven. Jesus knew this, but he was so sorry for the poor sick people that he healed them. He saw that they were like sheep not having a shepherd, and so he began again to teach them many things.

When the evening drew near, the apostles came to him, and reminded him that it was nearly night, and that they were in a desert place away from all the stores. They asked Jesus to send the people away quickly, that they might go into the towns and villages near, and buy themselves food before it was too late.

But Jesus would not send the people away hungry at that late hour.

Now, Jesus knew what he was going to do; but to prove how much faith his disciples had, he said to one of them, "Whence shall we buy bread, that these may eat?" Philip was the one of whom the question was asked. He could not understand how they, away out there in the desert, could get enough bread to feed so many people.

Then Andrew said, "There is a lad here, which hath five barley loaves, and two small fishes: but what are they among so many?"

They must have felt somewhat as Moses did when he was in the wilderness and God told him he was going to give the children of Israel all the meat they could eat for a whole month.

Moses said: "The people among whom I am are six hundred thousand footmen; and thou hast said, I will give them flesh that they may eat a whole month. Shall the flocks and the herds be slain for them? or shall all the fish of the sea be gathered together for them, to suffice them?"

The Lord told him that he would soon see how it would come to pass. Then a great wind-storm was sent, which blew thousands of quails into the camp of Israel, and the people were two days and a night in gathering them.

Moses might have known from things that had taken place in the past that God meant to perform a miracle; but he soon saw the power of God manifested. And this was what the disciples saw.

Five Thousand People are Fed.

—:—

JESUS commanded his apostles to make all the people sit down in companies on the grass. There were about fifty in each company.

When the people were all seated, Jesus took the five loaves of barley bread and the two fishes that the lad brought, and looking up to heaven, thanked God for them. He then broke the loaves in pieces, and gave to the apostles; and he divided the fishes in the same way among them. Then the apostles gave them to the multitude. Jesus made those few loaves and fishes increase as they were given to the people until there was enough for them all.

Just try to think what a great crowd five thousand people would make, and then you can understand better what a great miracle Jesus performed. And there were even more than five thousand, for the women and the children were not counted.

When every one had eaten and was satisfied, Jesus said, "Gather up the fragments that remain, that nothing be lost"; and the disciples filled twelve baskets with the pieces that were left from the five loaves and the two fishes.

We might learn a little lesson from what Jesus said about the

FEEDING FIVE THOUSAND.

139

fragments. We should never waste anything, even though we seem to have more than we need. What is not needed for ourselves can be kept, and given to some poor person who may need it. God will bless all who remember the needs of others; but those who waste what they do not seem to need at the time will some day be sorry, for "wilful waste makes woeful want."

The people, when they saw this great miracle which Jesus did, felt that this must truly be the Messiah for whom their fathers and their fathers' fathers had been looking so many years. They had always pictured him up as a mighty king, and now they would have been glad to make Jesus their king.

But Jesus wanted them to understand that his kingdom was not of this earth, but of heaven; and that the enemies whom they ought to be fighting were not human beings, but evil thoughts and evil deeds.

At last, when all the people had been sent away, Jesus told his disciples to get into a ship and go to the other side of the sea without him. He would follow them later, he said; but now he wanted time to pray, and to be alone with his heavenly Father. He then went up into a mountain.

○✶○✶○✶○

They Thought He Was a Spirit.

—:—

It should not have taken more than two or three hours for the disciples to sail across the Sea of Galilee to Capernaum. But the night was very stormy, and at midnight the ship in which the disciples were, was still far from land.

Jesus was alone on the shore; but he knew they were having a hard time, and that the wind was against them. Although it was night, and dark all about him, yet Jesus could see them toiling in rowing their boat; and he went out to them, walking on the water.

When the disciples saw him walking toward them, they thought it must have been a spirit, and cried out with fear. But Jesus spoke to them, saying, "Be of good cheer; it is I; be not afraid."

How glad they must have been to know that Jesus was coming

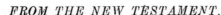

to help them out of their trouble! Jesus loves to help all who are in trouble, if they will only let him.

Now, Peter, when he heard Jesus speak, said, "Master, if it be thou, bid me come unto thee on the water." And Jesus said, "Come." Peter at once stepped out of the ship upon the waves to go to Jesus.

All went well at first until he thought of where he was. He could hear the fierce wind blowing about him, and hear the splash of the waves. This made him afraid, and he began to sink. Then he cried out, "Lord, save me!"

Jesus at once stretched out his hand and caught him, saying, "O thou of little faith, wherefore didst thou doubt?"

How strange it seems that Peter would doubt the power of Jesus to keep him from sinking! He was like the Christian of to-day when the storm of life is raging around him. Just as long as the Christian keeps his eyes upon Jesus, he is all right; but when he stops to listen to the fierce trials he has to meet, and thinks he is not able to bear them, he will sink, unless, like Peter, he cries out, "Lord, save me!" Then Jesus will answer, "O thou of little faith, wherefore didst thou doubt?"

When Jesus had saved Peter from sinking, they went to the ship, and the wind stopped blowing. Then those who were in the ship came and worshiped Jesus, saying, "Of a truth thou art the Son of God."

It was not long after this that they reached the other side of the sea. As soon as the people knew that Jesus had returned, they hastened to bring every one they could who was sick. Some were even carried in beds and laid in the street. They said that if they could only touch the hem of his garment they should be made well. And as many as touched him were made perfectly whole.

142   CHRIST WALKING ON THE SEA.

The Multitude Follow Jesus.

—:—

The next day after the multitude had been fed, the people searched for Jesus. They knew that he had not left in the ship with the disciples, but they could not find him in the desert where they were.

At last, when they saw that he was not in their midst, they, also, went in ships to Capernaum. When they found Jesus on the other side of the sea, they said, "Rabbi, when camest thou hither?" Jesus told them that they were not so glad to see him because of the miracles which he did the day before, but because they had eaten of the loaves, and were filled.

And he said, "Labor not for the meat which perisheth, but for that meat which endureth unto everlasting life, which the Son of man shall give unto you." The people did not understand, and they said, "What shall we do, that we might work the works of God?"

Jesus told them to believe that he was God's Son, and that he was sent to save the people from their sins. Then they asked him what sign they should see to prove that he was the Son of God, and said, "Our fathers did eat manna in the desert; as it is written, He gave them bread from heaven to eat."

Then Jesus answered: "Moses gave you not that bread from heaven; but my Father giveth you the true bread from heaven. For the bread of God is he which cometh down from heaven, and giveth life unto the world."

When the people heard this, they said, "Lord, evermore give us this bread." But still they could not understand that Jesus meant that he himself was the true bread of life.

Many were displeased with him, and they refused to believe that he was sent from heaven to be their Savior. He was not at all like the one for whom they were looking. A good many who had really believed on him before went back, and would not be his followers any more. Jesus then said to the Twelve, "Will ye also go away?" Peter answered: "Lord, to whom shall we go? thou hast the words of eternal life. And we believe and are sure that thou art that Christ, the Son of the living God.''

Then Jesus said that he had chosen them, but that one was his enemy. He meant Judas Iscariot, who, he knew, was going to betray and sell him to wicked men seeking his life.

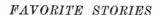

The Traditions of the Elders.

THE Pharisees tried in every way they knew to find something out about Jesus that they could use against him. They did not like to hear him tell them that they were not living right nor on the road to heaven. They wanted to get to heaven in their own way. That was by being very careful to do everything that Moses had commanded the children of Israel to do when they were in the wilderness. In fact, they wanted to get to heaven in their own way, and not in God's way.

Following the commands of Moses was all right for the children of Israel, for they had no better way; but now God had another way, and Jesus was trying to show the people what it was.

All their efforts to be good and to live right were not worth anything in God's sight so long as they would not love his dear Son, whom he had sent to save them.

At one time a few of the Pharisees came to Jesus. They brought with them some of the scribes, or men who claimed to understand and explain the Scriptures, or laws given to Moses. They believed that part of the laws had been given by God, but that some were given by Moses. They called those given by God the written, and those given by Moses under God's direction the oral law, and considered them as binding as the first. In this oral law were many commands such as not to eat without washing themselves very often. And every vessel used in cooking their food had to be washed in a certain way. There were many commands of this kind, which if they failed to keep, were as though they committed a great sin, and defiled themselves. These laws were called ''the traditions of the elders.''

Now, when these Pharisees and scribes saw some of the disciples of Jesus eat bread without first washing their hands, they found fault, and asked Jesus why his disciples did not keep these traditions. Jesus told them that they were deceiving themselves and others, too, by teaching the commandments of men instead of the commandments of God. And he told them how they had changed one of the commandments of Moses. In this way their tradition had done away with the word of God. And Jesus said they were hypocrites, which meant that they pretended to be what they were not.

Jesus then turned to the great crowd of people that was standing around, and said: "Hear and understand: not that which goeth into the mouth defileth a man; but that which cometh out of the mouth, this defileth a man. If any man have ears to hear, let him hear."

After Jesus had talked so plainly, his disciples came to him, and asked whether he knew that he had offended the Pharisees. But Jesus said: "Let them alone: they be blind leaders of the blind. And if the blind lead the blind, both shall fall into the ditch."

The disciples said they could not understand this parable, either; so Jesus told them that it was not what a man ate that defiled him, but that it was the evil thoughts which came from his heart. He named over several things, among which were pride, foolishness, deceit, covetousness, and murder, and said, "These are the things which defile a man: but to eat with unwashen hands defileth not a man."

The Syrophonician Woman.

Because of the way the Pharisees felt toward him, Jesus went away from Capernaum, where he had preached so many times, and had healed so many people. He went up into the land of Phonicia as far as the coast of the Mediterranean Sea, and visited the Gentile cities of Tyre and Sidon.

Jesus wished to rest and pray, for he often became very tired; and at this time he did not care to have the people know where he

10

was. But even here the people had heard of the many wonderful things he had been doing.

One day as he was passing along, a Gentile woman came begging him to have mercy on her daughter, who was possessed with a devil.

At first Jesus did not pay any attention to her, and his disciples supposed that he did not care to do anything for the woman because she was not a Jew. They said, "Send her away; for she crieth after us"; but this Jesus would not do.

Jesus will not turn any away when they come to him; but he wanted to try her a little, and see how much faith she had. So he said, "It is not meet to take the children's bread, and to cast it to dogs." But the poor woman was in earnest, and she did not care if her people were compared to dogs; for she quickly answered, "Truth, Lord: yet the dogs eat of the crumbs which fall from their master's table." How her words pleased Jesus! for he said, "O woman, great is thy faith: be it unto thee even as thou wilt."

When she returned to her home, she found her daughter perfectly cured, and lying upon the bed.

Once before Jesus had been surprised at the faith of a Gentile. You remember it was in the case of the Roman centurion. They had both shown more faith than the children of Israel, to whom Jesus had been sent.

○✷○✷○✷○

The Deaf and Dumb Man Healed.

—:—

JESUS did not remain in Tyre and Sidon long. He returned to the opposite side of the Sea of Galilee, and preached in the cities known as Decapolis. These were cities, about ten in all, which had been built by the Romans.

Great multitudes came and listened to his preaching. It was near the place where the man possessed with a legion of devils had been cured. At that time the people had been afraid of the great power of Jesus; but since then the man who had been healed had told so many about the wonderful work Jesus had done for him that now they were

THE WOMAN OF CANAAN.

anxious to see him and hear him talk.　They brought with them those who were lame, blind, dumb, maimed, and many others, and cast them down at Jesus' feet; and he healed them.

Among those who were brought to Jesus for healing, was a young man who was deaf and dumb; that is, he could neither hear nor talk. Jesus took him aside from the multitude.　Then he put his fingers

THE SICK ARE HEALED.

into his ears, and he spit and touched his tongue.　Jesus then looked up to heaven and sighed.　It made him feel sad to see so many suffering ones all about him.

Then he spoke a Hebrew word which meant ''Be opened,'' and the man could hear and speak plainly.

Jesus told them not to say anything about this and the other miracles that he did; but they did not heed his words, but told it only the more. The people were astonished, and they said, "He hath done all things well: he maketh both the deaf to hear, and the dumb to speak, the lame to walk and the blind to see. And they glorified the God of Israel."

Jesus Again Feeds the Multitude.

—:—

JESUS continued to preach to the people for three days, during which time they had nothing to eat. He was sorry for them; for he said to his disciples, "I have compassion on the multitude, because they have been with me three days, and have nothing to eat: and if I send them away fasting to their own houses, they will faint by the way: for divers of them came from far."

Perhaps his disciples thought of the time not long before this when Jesus fed a multitude even larger than this. But all they said was, "From whence can a man satisfy these men with bread here in the wilderness?" Jesus asked them how many loaves they had, and they said, "Seven, and a few little fishes."

And he took the seven loaves and the fishes, and gave thanks, and broke them, and gave to his disciples, and the disciples to the multitude. There was plenty for all; and when they were through eating, they took up seven basketfuls of the broken bread and fish.

He sent the people away. Then with his disciples he took ship, and crossed over into the coasts of Magdala, a few miles from Capernaum.

Again the Pharisees came to him. This time they asked him to show them a sign from heaven.

How sad Jesus must have felt! for he knew their purpose. He sighed deeply, and said, "Why doth this generation seek after a sign? verily I say unto you, There shall no sign be given unto it, but the sign of the prophet Jonas."

Jesus was comparing his death and resurrection to the time when Jonah was within the great fish for three days and nights.

He also told them that in the evening when they saw that the sky was red, they took it as a sign that the next day would be fair; but if red in the morning, it would be bad weather.

Then he called them hypocrites, and said they could easily discern the face of the sky, but could not discern or understand the signs of the times.

Jesus and his disciples did not remain in this place long, on account of the way the Pharisees felt toward them. They again entered a ship and crossed over to the other side of the Sea of Galilee.

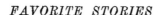

The Leaven of the Pharisees.

THE disciples forgot to take any bread with them when they left Magdala. When they found that it had been forgotten, and that they

were going into the desert again, Jesus said, "Take heed, and beware of the leaven of the Pharisees."

It seemed strange to the disciples that Jesus should warn them in this way just then, and they thought it must be because they had forgotten to take any bread with them. Then Jesus said: "Why reason ye, because ye have no bread? Do ye not yet understand, neither remember the five loaves of the five thousand, and how many baskets ye took up? Neither the seven loaves of the four thousand, and how many baskets ye took up? How is it that ye do not understand that I spake it not to you concerning bread, that ye should beware of the leaven of the Pharisees?"

Then they understood that Jesus did not mean bread when he spoke of the leaven of the Pharisees, but that he meant to beware of their doctrine or teaching.

There was another set of people whom Jesus warned the disciples against. They were called the Sadducees. These people did not believe in an oral law as the Pharisees did; and they did not believe that any one would ever live again after death. And so, of course, they did not believe in heaven, with its rewards for those who live and do right, nor in hell, with its punishments for those who do wickedly.

But Jesus did not say as much against the Sadducees as he did against the Pharisees; perhaps because the Pharisees made so much higher profession.

⊙✳⊙✳⊙✳⊙

A Blind Man Healed.

—:—

As Jesus went into the city of Bethsaida, they brought to him a blind man, and earnestly asked Jesus to heal him and give him back his sight. So Jesus took the blind man by the hand, and led him away from the town. Then, after he had spit on the man's eyes, and laid his hands upon them, he asked him whether he saw anything. The man looked up, and said, "I see men as trees walking."

Then Jesus again laid his hands upon the man's eyes, and made him look up. This time his sight was restored, and he could see clearly.

Once more Jesus made the request that nothing be said about his miracle which had just been performed. But such good news was hard to keep.

Later on they went north near the town of Cæsarea Philippi. And one day Jesus asked his disciples a question about himself. He said, "Whom do men say that I am?" And they said, "Some say that thou art John the Baptist; some, Elias; and others say that one of the prophets is risen."

Then he said unto them, "But whom say ye that I am?" Peter answered him, and said, "Thou art the Christ, the Son of the living God."

Jesus told Peter that God had revealed this to him, for that was the only way by which he could have known it.

From that time Jesus began to teach his disciples many things about his death and resurrection, and how many things he would have to suffer.

The things that he told them made them very sad; and once Peter said, "Be it far from thee, Lord: this shall not be unto thee." Jesus rebuked Peter sharply; for these things would have to take place, or Jesus would not fulfil his mission to this earth. And he also meant to teach them that it was very wrong to try to prevent some friend from doing what he felt was his duty, even though it might seem to be the path of trial and suffering.

He said that they must be willing to give their lives for the sake of the gospel if necessary, and that they must never be ashamed to tell others that they were Christians.

The Transfiguration.

—:—

A few days after the talk near Cæsarea Philippi, Jesus took Peter, James, and John up into a mountain to pray. The mountain was known as Mount Hermon, and it was very high. The disciples were tired after their long journey; and when they came near the top, they lay down, and soon fell asleep. But Jesus did not sleep. He had gone up into the mountain to pray; and as he prayed, no doubt he thought of the many things that were soon going to happen in Jerusalem, and prayed for strength to enable him to endure all that was to take place. And his heavenly Father sent him the help and strength he needed.

THE TRANS-FIG-U-RA-TION OF CHRIST.

At last Peter, James, and John awoke; and as they looked toward the part of the mountain where Jesus was praying, they saw a sight that filled them with wonder. There was Jesus; but he was changed, and his face was shining as brightly as the sun, and his raiment was as white as the snow. More than that, two men were with him, and they were speaking about the death of Jesus, which was to take place in Jerusalem. These men were Moses and Elias.

It was indeed a strange and grand sight. Peter wanted to say something; for he felt that he should like to have this sight continue there forever, as it was so beautiful.

What he did say was that it would be nice if they would build three tabernacles—one for Jesus, one for Moses, and one for Elias. But while Peter was still speaking, a bright cloud overshadowed them, and, behold, a voice out of the cloud said, "This is my beloved Son, in whom I am well pleased; hear ye him."

When the disciples heard the voice, they were frightened; and then Jesus was changed back to the way he had been before, and Moses and Elias disappeared from view, and Jesus said, "Arise, and be not afraid."

Jesus told them not to tell this vision to any one until after he had risen from the dead, and they did not tell it.

But they asked Jesus why it was that the prophets had said Elias must first come and restore all things, and that the Son of man must suffer many things, and be set at naught. Then Jesus told them that Elias had already come, and he said to them: "They have done unto him whatsoever they listed. Likewise shall also the Son of man suffer of them." Then the disciples understood that he spoke of John the Baptist.

Jesus Heals a Lunatic.

—:—

As Jesus and his three disciples came down from the mountain the next day, they found many people waiting for them. The Bible says that the people were amazed when they saw Jesus. The glory of God must have still been shining in his face.

Many ran to meet him, and among those who were in such haste was a man whose son was a lunatic.

Now, a lunatic is any one who is insane or a madman. This boy could not speak because he was possessed with a dumb spirit.

How much this father must have loved his poor boy, for he was his only child!

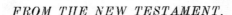

When he came to Jesus, he cried out: "Master, I beseech thee, look upon my son; for he is mine only child. And, lo, a spirit taketh him, and he suddenly crieth out; and it teareth him that he foameth again, and bruising him, hardly departeth from him. And I brought him to thy disciples, and they could not cure him."

Jesus was grieved that his disciples could not cast out the evil spirit; for he had given them power over all unclean spirits when he had sent them out to preach. And he said, "O faithless generation, how long shall I be with you?" Then turning to the father, he said, "Bring thy son hither."

The boy was brought forward; but as he was coming, the evil spirit threw him down upon the ground, and he wallowed, foaming.

Jesus asked the man how long his son had been in this condition, and he answered, "Of a child." And he said that many times the evil spirit had cast his son into the fire and into the waters to destroy him. And then he begged Jesus to have compassion and help them.

Jesus' answer was so precious. He said, "If thou canst believe, all things are possible to him that believeth." How glad the poor man must have been when he heard these kind words! With tears in his eyes, he said, "Lord, I believe: help thou mine unbelief."

Jesus then rebuked the evil spirit, and said, "Thou dumb and deaf spirit, I charge thee come out of him, and enter no more into him."

Once more the spirit threw the boy down as it had so many times before; but at the command of Jesus it came out, and the boy lay as one dead, and many of the crowd said, "He is dead."

But Jesus took him by the hand and lifted him up, and delivered him back to his father. What joy must have filled that father's heart when he knew his son was cured!

A Little Talk with His Disciples.

—:—

WHEN the disciples were alone with Jesus, they asked him why they were unable to cast the evil spirit out of the lunatic, and Jesus said it was because of their unbelief.

And Jesus told them that if they only had faith as a grain of mustard seed, which seed is very small, they could say to a mountain, "Remove hence to yonder place," and it would obey them. For he had given them such power that nothing was impossible for them.

Still, Jesus told them that this kind of spirit went out only by prayer and fasting.

What a beautiful lesson of faith the little mustard seed taught them! Although it was so very small, yet it was perfect. Our faith in Jesus may be small; but it must be perfect, if we expect it to become great. And, then, it also taught how small they were in themselves. All their greatness came from God.

At last Jesus left Cæsarea Philippi. This time he went around through the country of Galilee, and returned to Capernaum.

But he told his disciples that he had rather no one would know about it, and then he told them why. He said, "The Son of man is delivered into the hands of men: and they shall kill him; and after that he is killed, he shall rise the third day." And he said, "Let these sayings sink down into your ears."

They did not understand what Jesus meant, and they were afraid to ask him; but they thought many times about it.

The Tribute Money.

—:—

THE Roman king was very careful to see that all taxes were paid to him by all the Jews. And you remember that Mary and Joseph went to be taxed.

But there was still another kind of tax, or tribute money. This was a fixed sum of money, which would amount to about eighteen

PETER AND THE TRIBUTE-MONEY.   157

cents of our money. This was paid by every Jew in whatever part of the world he might live, and was claimed for the expenses of the temple services.

Now, it happened that one day while Jesus was in Capernaum, some one came to Peter and asked him whether Jesus were willing to pay tribute, and Peter answered yes.

But when Peter arrived at his house, he found that the. was no money either for him or for Jesus. He was about to speak of the matter; but before he had time, Jesus said that it was not necessary that they should pay this money, but that for fear some one might think they had done wrong and had not obeyed the laws of the land, it would be better to pay the money.

Then he said, "Go thou to the sea, and cast a hook, and take up the fish that first cometh up; and when thou hast opened his mouth, thou shalt find a piece of money: that take, and give unto them for me and thee."

Jesus knew that the Pharisees were eagerly waiting to find out something against him. And this matter was one that they could use to good advantage.

A Lesson on Humility.

—:—

On the journey down to Capernaum the disciples had talked much about the kingdom of heaven; and they wondered which of them would be the greatest.

You see they did not understand the words of Jesus concerning his death, his kingdom, and all the deep things of which he had spoken. Jesus did not intend that they should; but there was a time coming when they would know and understand all, and it was not far away. Then they would remember that their Master had told them, and their faith and confidence would be increased.

Jesus knew what they had said on the way, and so now he called the Twelve together and explained some things to them. He said that

if any one desired to be great in the kingdom of heaven, he would be the least, or servant of all.

And then he took a little child and stood it up in their midst, and explained that unless they were converted and became as little children, they could not even enter the kingdom of heaven.

THE LITTLE CHILD.

This was not the only time that the disciples had wondered who would be greatest in the kingdom of heaven. Jesus had often explained to them that his kingdom was different from the kingdoms of this world, where those who have the most money and influence are greatest; but it was so hard for them to understand about it.

Jesus went on to tell his disciples that those who showed kindness to little children were really doing a service to him, and that he would bless and reward them for the same.

And he also warned them against doing anything against a little child that could harm it, such as setting a bad example before it, or by any careless or wicked acts that would cause a child to fall into sin. It would be better for such, he said, that a millstone were hanged about his neck, and that he were drowned in the depth of the sea.

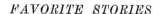

Offenses.

JESUS said, "Woe unto the world because of offenses." By offenses he meant the many wicked and sinful things the people were doing every day. He also said, "It must needs be that offenses come; but woe unto that man by whom the offense cometh!"

Jesus, perhaps, was again referring to his death, which was soon to take place at Jerusalem. And it was necessary that Jesus should be offended, treated cruelly, and put to death, in order that God's plan should be fulfilled, and that Jesus could become a sacrifice for the world.

But although it was necessary that these offenses should come, every person had a right to choose whether he would be the one to harm Jesus or not.

Offenses are still occurring every day, but we still have the right or privilege of choosing whether we will obey God or not. No one is obliged to do evil or offend God; but many do, and they will suffer for it, both in this life and in the life to come. Jesus said that if there was anything about his disciples that would make them want to do evil, they should get rid of it; for it was even better to enter into the kingdom of God with a hand or a foot cut off or an eye taken out, than to have all these members, and be cast into hell fire, as that fire could never be put out.

This lesson was also meant for us. We should never let anything remain about us that would hinder our serving God or keep us out of heaven. Oh! it means so much to serve the Lord, and to live so that we may know we are not offending him; but it is our privilege to live pure and holy lives even in this world.

Jesus said he had come to this earth to save the lost, and then he spoke the parable about the lost sheep. He said that if a man had a hundred sheep, and one of them should stray away from the rest, the man would quickly leave the ninety and nine, and go over the mountains in search of the one he had lost; and that when he had found it, he would be very glad, and would rejoice over it even more than he would over the ninety and nine that went not astray.

That, he said, was the way his heavenly Father felt about all his children. It was not his will that any of them should perish.

Forgiveness.

—:—

As the disciples listened to the words of Jesus, many things passed through their minds. His words seemed so deep and strange that he had often to explain their meaning. One time when Jesus was teaching them about their duty to forgive their enemies, Peter asked how many times they ought to forgive any one, and whether seven times would be enough. Jesus answered that they must forgive their brother not only seven times, but seventy times seven, if he trespassed against him so often; and then he spoke the following parable to show his meaning:

"Therefore is the kingdom of heaven likened unto a certain king, which would take account of his servants. And when he had begun to reckon, one was brought unto him, which owed him ten thousand talents. But forasmuch as he had not to pay, his lord commanded him to be sold, and his wife, and children, and all that he had, and payment to be made. The servant therefore fell down, and worshiped him, saying, Lord, have patience with me, and I will pay thee all.

Then the lord of that servant was moved with compassion, and loosed him, and forgave him the debt.

"But the same servant went out, and found one of his fellow servants, which owed him an hundred pence: and he laid hands on him, and took him by the throat, saying, Pay me that thou owest. And his fellow servant fell down at his feet, and besought him, saying, Have patience with me, and I will pay thee all. And he would not: but went and cast him into prison, till he should pay the debt.

"So when his fellow servants saw what was done, they were very sorry, and came and told unto their lord all that was done. Then his lord, after that he had called him, said unto him, O thou wicked servant, I forgave thee all that debt, because thou desiredst me: shouldest not thou also have had compassion on thy fellow servant, even as I had pity on thee? And his lord was wroth, and delivered him to the tormentors, till he should pay all that was due unto him. So likewise shall my heavenly Father do also unto you, if ye from your hearts forgive not every one his brother their trespasses."

More Disciples Instructed and Sent Out.

—:—

You have heard how Jesus called his twelve disciples together and gave them power to heal the sick people, and to do other wonderful things, and how he sent them out to the different cities to preach to the people. When Jesus saw how anxious the people were to hear the gospel, he said, "The harvest truly is great, but the laborers are few: pray ye therefore the Lord of the harvest that he would send forth laborers into his harvest." And he sent other disciples out as he had the Twelve. This time he appointed a much larger number of disciples than he did at first. There were seventy in all. He wanted them to go into as many different places as possible; so he did not send them out together, but sent just two to each place, into the cities and towns.

When he was sending them forth he said, "Behold, I send you

THE UNMERCIFUL SERVANT.

forth as lambs among wolves.'' He knew there would be many places where they would meet bitter persecution, and where they would need much help from the Lord.

This host of gospel workers did not go forth without being able to accomplish something. Jesus gave them the power that they would need. He knew there would be many people needing help, and many sick people who would be glad to be healed; so he gave them the power to heal the sick, just the same as he had given it to the twelve disciples who had been sent before this. He gave them not only power to heal the sick, but also power to cast evil spirits out of those who were possessed. Many people were truly made glad because he had given his power to others besides the twelve disciples.

He is a good and loving Savior, and wants to do all he can for those who will believe on his name. He has made a way whereby we can all share the same blessings and privileges that those did who walked with him here on this earth. He has promised these things to all who will believe; so if we are believers, we can come to him for help in sickness and trial, and in every way we may need his help.

Feast of Tabernacles.

—:—

THIS was a great feast kept by the Jews. Moses had commanded them to keep this feast in memory of their wandering in the wilderness; but Moses had called it the feast of the harvest, for it was to be kept near the end of the year. Now the time for this feast was near at hand; and the brethren of Jesus said to him, ''Depart hence, and go into Jerusalem, that thy disciples also may see the works that thou doest.''

Now, the brethren of Jesus did not believe that he was the Son of God, and this was why they said this. Jesus was sad when he heard them say this; for he knew how they felt toward him, and he was not ready to go up to Jerusalem yet. Then he said to them, ''My time is not yet come: but your time is always ready. The

THE SEND-ING OUT OF THE SEV-EN-TY.

world can not hate you; but me it hateth, because I testify of it, that the works thereof are evil. Go ye up unto this feast; I go not yet up unto this feast; for my time is not yet fully come.''

After this his brethren went up to Jerusalem to the feast. But Jesus remained in Galilee for a time, and then he, also, went up to Jerusalem; but he went secretly, for he did not wish his brethren to know where he was at the time.

On the way to Jerusalem, Jesus passed through a village of the Samaritans; but because Jesus was on his way to Jerusalem to attend the feast, the people of this town would not receive him. When James and John saw this, they said, ''Lord, wilt thou that we command **fire** to come down from heaven, and consume them, even as Elias did?'' The Samaritans, no doubt, had said unkind words to them, and the disciples thought they ought to be punished. But Jesus turned, and said to them: ''Ye know not what manner of spirit ye are of. For the Son of man is not come to destroy men's lives, but to save them. And they went to another village.''

At this place there were ten lepers. They were in a place far away from every one else; for a man who had the disease of leprosy was at once sent away from his home to keep his friends from taking the dreadful disease. When these men saw Jesus, they lifted their voices, and said, ''Jesus, Master, have mercy on us.''

Jesus heard them call for help, and he said to them, ''Go show yourselves unto the priests.'' 'And it came to pass, that, as they went, they were cleansed. And one of them, when he saw that he was healed, turned back, and with a loud voice glorified God, and fell down on his face at Jesus' feet, giving him thanks.'

Jesus was glad when he saw this one return, giving thanks for what had been done for him; but he was surprised that the other nine did not return also, and he asked, ''Where are the nine?'' We see the same things to-day. Many people receive help from God for both their bodies and their souls; but few of those who are helped, remember to give God the praise or thanks for the same. We should never forget to praise the Lord for his goodness to us.

Jesus at the Feast.

—:—

THE feast had already begun when Jesus reached Jerusalem. Many of the Jews were trying to find him: some because they believed he was a good man, and wished to hear him preach; and some because they wished to do him harm. For, you remember, it was because the Jews desired to kill him that he left Capernaum at different times. But although some of the Jews, and especially the Pharisees, longed to put Jesus to death, they were afraid to say very much against him, fearing those who were his friends.

Jesus' first act when he arrived in Jerusalem was to go to the temple and teach the people. They listened eagerly to his words, and they were astonished at his teaching; for they knew that he had never had the advantages of school-life and learning. But Jesus said to them, "My doctrine is not mine, but his that sent me"; and he said, "If any man will do His will, he shall know of the doctrine, whether it be of God, or whether I speak of myself."

Jesus once more taught the people by parables, in order that they might draw lessons from the things around them; and while he was teaching them, he said, "Why go ye about to kill me?" The people were surprised when he said this. They could not understand how he could know what was in their minds, and they answered: "Thou hast a devil. Who goeth about to kill thee?"

Although the people had such hatred in their hearts toward Jesus, he continued to preach to them. One day some one asked, "Is not this he whom they seek to kill?" The people wondered how he would dare to preach to them at such a time, and some asked whether he were really the Christ for whom they were looking.

Then cried Jesus in the temple, saying, "Ye both know me, and ye know whence I am: and I am not come of myself, but he that sent me is true, whom ye know not. But I know him, for I am from him."

Although they were so angry with Jesus, and wished so much to see him put to death, yet no one dared to do him any harm, for the time had not come for this. Many of the people, however, believed on him, and said, "When Christ cometh, will he do more miracles than this man doeth?"

Jesus continued to preach in the temple until the last day of the feast; and many said, "Of a truth this is a prophet," and others said, "This is the Christ."

On the last day of the feast the Pharisees sent officers to take Jesus and kill him; but when these officers heard Jesus' words, they could not do as they were commanded, and they returned without him. When asked by the Pharisees why they had done this, they answered that they had never before heard any one speak as Jesus spoke. Then the Pharisees asked the officers whether they, too, were deceived, and whether any of the leaders of Israel believed on Jesus. Then Nicodemus, the Pharisee who had gone to Jesus in the night to listen to his teaching, asked whether it were right to judge a man before they had heard what he had to say for himself. They knew that this was against their law; but they only mocked Nicodemus, and asked whether he, also, were a follower of Christ.

The Dispute with the Pharisees.

—:—

On the eastern side of Jerusalem was a mountain known as the Mount of Olives. Jesus, while in Jerusalem, often went to this place to pray and to rest; and he went there after the feast of the tabernacles had ended.

When he again returned to the temple, it was very early in the morning; and many people came in, and he sat down and taught them. As he was teaching the people, the Pharisees brought before him a woman who had led a very sinful life, and told Jesus that according to the law of Moses she ought to be stoned. They asked him what he would advise them to do. This they did in order that they might have something to bring against Jesus; but he pretended not to hear them. "He stooped down, and with his finger wrote on the ground, as though he heard them not."

But they continued asking him; so he, rising, said to them, "He that is without sin among you, let him first cast a stone at her." "And again he stooped down, and wrote on the ground."

"And they which heard it, being convicted by their own conscience, went out one by one, beginning at the eldest, even unto the last: and Jesus was left alone, and the woman standing in the midst. When Jesus had lifted up himself, and saw none but the woman, he said unto her, Woman, where are those thine accusers? hath no man condemned thee? She said, No man, Lord. And Jesus said unto her, Neither do I condemn thee: go, and sin no more."

Jesus once more began to preach to the people. He told them that he was the light of the world, and that all who followed him should not walk in darkness, but should have the light of life.

Once more the Pharisees began to contradict him and said, "Thou bearest record of thyself; thy record is not true."

Jesus answered, "Though I bear record of myself, yet my record is true: for I know whence I came, and whither I go; but ye can not tell whence I came, and whither I go." And he said that God had sent him from heaven to show them these things, and that even Abraham rejoiced to see this day, for he saw it, and was glad. But now they sought to kill him, because he had told them the truth, which he had heard from God. This Abraham did not do.

The Jews asked Jesus how it was that he had seen Abraham, who had been dead so many years; and Jesus answered, "Before Abraham was, I am."

"Then they took up stones to cast at him: but Jesus hid himself, and went out of the temple, going through the midst of them, and so passed by."

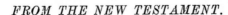

The Lawyer Instructed.

—:—

At one time a lawyer came and asked Jesus what he would have to do in order that he might inherit eternal life. Jesus referred him to the law of Moses, and asked him what it taught him to do; and

the lawyer answered, ''Thou shalt love the Lord thy God with all thy heart, and with all thy soul, and with all thy strength, and with all thy mind, and thy neighbor as thyself.'' Jesus then said, ''Thou hast answered right: this do, and thou shalt live.''

Now, the lawyer knew that he had not loved his neighbor as himself, and so pretending not to know what the commandment meant, he said to Jesus, ''Who is my neighbor?'' Jesus wanted to show him that he was not so ignorant as he tried to appear, and so he spoke a parable.

He said: ''A certain man went down from Jerusalem to Jericho. This man fell among thieves by the wayside who stripped him of his raiment and wounded him and departed, leaving him half dead. And by chance there came down a certain priest that way; and when he saw him, he passed by on the other side. And likewise a Levite, when he was at the place, came and looked on him, and passed by on the other side. But a certain Samaritan, as he journeyed, came where he was: and when he saw him, he had compassion on him, and went to him, and bound up his wounds, pouring in oil and wine, and set him on his own beast, and brought him to an inn, and took out two pence, and gave them to the host, and said unto him, Take care of him; and whatsoever thou spendest more, when I come again, I will repay thee. Which now of these three, thinkest thou, was neighbor unto him that fell among the thieves? And he said, He that showed mercy on him. Then said Jesus unto him, Go, and do thou likewise.''

Two Jews passed by the poor wounded man, but the good Samaritan showed him mercy. Jesus used the Samaritan to show this proud lawyer the lesson he wished him to learn—that he should show compassion without respect of persons. The Jews, you remember, despised the Samaritans, and had no dealings with them; but in spite of this fact the good Samaritan was the one who had compassion on the poor wounded Jew.

THE GOOD SAMARITAN.   171

In Bethany.

—:—

Jesus had spent some time in Jerusalem, and now he crossed over the river Jordan, and went into the country of Perea. We next find him in a small village called Bethany. This was not far from the Mount of Olives.

In Bethany was a home that Jesus often visited. It was called the home of Martha and Mary. There these two sisters lived with their brother Lazarus. Jesus was always a welcome visitor at their house.

These two sisters were much unlike each other. Martha was very active, and she took great pleasure in doing all she could to make others happy and comfortable. Mary, on the other hand, was of a quiet disposition, and to her there was no greater joy than to sit at the feet of Jesus and listen to his words. It seemed to Martha that her sister did not help her share the cares and responsibilities of the work enough; and one day when Mary was sitting as usual at the feet of Jesus while she herself was busy, she said to him, "Lord, dost thou not care that my sister hath left me to serve alone? bid her therefore that she help me." But Jesus knew that Mary was learning of the deep things of heaven, and so he said, "Martha, Martha, thou art careful and troubled about many things: but one thing is needful; and Mary hath chosen that good part, which shall not be taken away from her."

Jesus very much enjoyed Martha and Mary's quiet little home; yet he did not remain there long at a time, for we find that he was traveling about from place to place.

The Disciples Taught to Pray.

—:—

One time when Jesus was alone with his disciples, one of them said, "Lord, teach us to pray, as John also taught his disciples"; and then Jesus taught them this prayer: "Our Father which art in heaven,

"FRIEND, LEND ME THREE LOAVES."

173

Hallowed be thy name. Thy kingdom come. Thy will be done, as in heaven, so in earth. Give us day by day our daily bread. And forgive us our sins; for we also forgive every one that is indebted to us. And lead us not into temptation; but deliver us from evil.''

And then he taught them a lesson of importunity, which means that if God did not the first time they prayed give them the things they asked for, they should ask again and again until they received them.

To make this meaning clear to them, he spoke another parable. He said: ''Which of you shall have a friend, and shall go unto him at midnight, and say unto him, Friend, lend me three loaves; for a friend of mine in his journey is come to me, and I have nothing to set before him. And he from within shall answer and say, Trouble me not: the door is now shut, and my children are with me in bed; I can not rise and give thee. I say unto you, Though he will not rise and give him, because he is his friend, yet because of his importunity he will rise and give him as many as he needeth.''

Jesus did not want his disciples to think that their heavenly Father would not at once give them the things for which they asked him, nor that he would give them their request simply that they might not trouble him with their prayers; but he wanted them to understand that they must be in earnest when they asked for anything from God, and not stop asking until they received the thing for which they asked.

> When a favor, small or great,
>   You have asked from God on high,
> You'll receive it if you wait;
>   Do not leave with tear or sigh.
>
> God will help you, never fear;
>   For he is a God of love;
> But sometimes he'd have you wait,
>   Just your faith to better prove.

The Seventy Return.

—:—

THE seventy whom Jesus had sent out to preach to the people, and tell them that he was God's Son sent down from heaven to save the people from their sins, now returned. As Jesus welcomed them, their hearts were full of joy; and they began telling him at once of the wonderful miracles that had taken place. They said, "Lord, even the devils are subject unto us through thy name."

Jesus saw that there was danger of their becoming exalted, or thinking that they had cast the devils out through some great power in themselves. "And he said unto them, I beheld Satan as lightning fall from heaven. Behold, I give unto you power to tread on serpents and scorpions, and over all the power of the enemy; and nothing shall by any means hurt you. Notwithstanding in this rejoice not, that the spirits are subject unto you; but rather rejoice, because your names are written in heaven," or that they were chosen for so great a work.

Jesus would have them give God all the praise and glory for all the mighty works that had been done through them. But, still, their words had made Jesus very happy; for he said, "I thank thee, O Father, Lord of heaven and earth, that thou hast hid these things from the wise and prudent, and hast revealed them unto babes: even so, Father; for so it seemed good in thy sight."

Then turning to his disciples, he said, "Blessed are the eyes which see the things that ye see: for I tell you, that many prophets and kings have desired to see those things which ye see, and have not seen them; and to hear those things which ye hear, and have not heard them."

The names of the Seventy are not given; but the Lord had told them that their names were written in the Book of Life.

It was not so with all the Twelve, for one of that number was very wicked. It was Judas Iscariot. This disciple had had the same power to do great works that was given to the rest of the Twelve and to the Seventy; but his soul was full of evil, and he chose to do wrong rather than right,

All have this privilege. They are told to choose whom they will serve, Christ or Satan; and the choice they make decides what kingdom they will inherit, and also what kind of life they will lead.

A Man Born Blind is Healed.

—:—

It was a common belief among the Jews that afflictions came upon people on account of their sins. One day as Jesus passed along, he saw a man who was blind from his birth. This poor man had never looked into the faces of his father and mother; had never seen the sky at night, when the stars sparkled in its depths, nor the sun by day, when it lighted up the earth, and made everything around seem beautiful.

This poor man had never seen these things; and the disciples of Jesus asked, saying, "Master, who did sin, this man, or his parents, that he was born blind?" Jesus told them that they must not suppose that either the man himself or his parents had sinned more than others, but that the works of God should be made plain through him.

Jesus told them that he must hasten to do the works that God had sent him to do; for it would soon be night, and no more work could be done. He referred to the time when he would be taken away to die on the cross. After this he anointed the eyes of the blind man, and told him to go and wash in the Pool of Siloam. This the man did, and he could see the same as other people.

The news that the blind man could see, quickly spread abroad. The neighbors, who had known him so well, could hardly believe that it was the blind beggar who had sat and begged. "Some said, This is he; others said, He is like him; but he said, I am he." Then they asked him, "How were thine eyes opened?" "He answered and said, A man that is called Jesus made clay, and anointed mine eyes, and said unto me, Go to the Pool of Siloam, and wash: and I went and washed, and I received sight."

The news of the blind man's healing soon reached the ears of

the Pharisees.   They sent and had him brought before them, and
made him repeat the whole story of how he had been cured.

Now, it happened that the day on which the man had been healed

"ONCE I WAS BLIND, BUT NOW I SEE."

was the Sabbath; and the Pharisees said, "This man is not of God,
because he keepeth not the Sabbath-day."   But there was a division
among them; for some said, "How can a man that is a sinner do such
miracles?"   Then turning to the man who had been blind, they asked
him what he thought of the one who had opened his eyes; and he said,
"He is a prophet."

12

This was not the answer they wished to have him make, and therefore they were not pleased. They wanted to bring all the things against Jesus that they could. They tried to make themselves believe that the man had never been blind; so they sent for his parents.

When the parents came, the Pharisees asked, "Is this your son, who ye say was born blind? how then doth he now see? His parents answered them and said, We know that this is our son, and that he was born blind: but by what means he now seeth, we know not; or who hath opened his eyes, we know not; he is of age; ask him: he shall speak for himself."

Now, these parents spoke in this way because they were afraid of the Pharisees; for the enemies of Jesus had said that if any man did confess Jesus to be the Christ, he should be put out of the synagogue, and not allowed to join in the worship of God there.

Then the Pharisees called the man who had been blind, and told him to give God the praise, for Jesus was a sinner; but the man answered, "Whether he be a sinner or not, I know not: one thing I know, that, whereas I was blind, now I see. Then said they to him again, What did he to thee? how opened he thine eyes? He answered them, I have told you already, and ye did not hear: wherefore would ye hear it again? will ye also be his disciples?

"Then they reviled him, and said, Thou art his disciple: but we are Moses' disciples. We know that God spake unto Moses: as for this fellow, we know not from whence he is.

"The man answered and said unto them, Why herein is a marvelous thing, that ye know not from whence he is, and yet he hath opened mine eyes. Now we know that God heareth not sinners: but if any man be a worshiper of God, and doeth his will, him he heareth. Since the world began was it not heard that any man opened the eyes of one that was born blind. If this man were not of God, he could do nothing.

"They answered and said unto him, Thou wast altogether born in sins, and dost thou teach us? And they cast him out."

When Jesus heard what they had done, that is, that they had cast him out of their synagogue, he went with words of comfort, and asked the man if he believed in the Son of God. "He answered and said, Who is he, Lord, that I might believe on him? And Jesus said unto him, Thou hast both seen him, and it is he that talketh with thee. And he said, Lord, I believe. And he worshiped him. And Jesus said, For judgment I am come into this world, that they which see not might see; and that they which see might be made blind.

"And some of the Pharisees which were with him heard these words, and said unto him, Are we blind also? Jesus said unto them, If ye were blind, ye should have no sin: but now ye say, We see; therefore your sin remaineth."

The Sheep of Palestine.

GRASS grew in abundance in Palestine, and on account of the nice pasture very many sheep were raised.

In many places the Bible speaks about sheep, and of their being animals that are very apt to go astray if they do not have a shepherd, or person to take care of them. Therefore each flock of sheep had its own shepherd to lead it about from one pasture to another.

This was very necessary; for the sun becomes very hot there, and in the summer it does not rain, and the grass becomes dry and brown in many places. Then the shepherds have to pick out those valleys where there is still some moisture, and where there is good grass, or else their sheep will die.

We read in the Bible a good deal about men who lived in olden times and who were shepherds. Abraham was a shepherd, and he had many sheep, for which he cared very tenderly. So, too, Isaac was a shepherd, and his son Jacob had many sheep, and was a rich man. His sons were shepherds also, and they used to guide their flocks to places where there was good pasture.

Later on we find that Moses was a shepherd; and for forty years he led his flocks in the wilderness, and watched over them and cared for them with the most tender love.

It was while he was watching over his sheep that God spoke to him out of the burning bush, and told him that he must go down to Egypt and deliver the children of Israel from their cruel bondage in Egypt.

THE SHEPHERD LEADING HIS FLOCK..

Moses obeyed God and went down, and in this way became the leader of Israel to the land of Palestine.

Even King David was a shepherd, and he risked his life at different times to save his sheep.

In one of his Psalms he says: "The Lord is my shepherd; I

THE SHEPHERD AND THE LAMBS.

shall not want. He maketh me to lie down in green pastures: he leadeth me beside the still waters. . . . Yea, though I walk through the valley of the shadow of death, I will fear no evil: for thou art with me; thy rod and thy staff they comfort me.''

David wanted to express his confidence in God; for he felt that God would be just as good to him in every time of need as he himself was willing to be to his own sheep.

The sheep become so acquainted with their shepherd that they know his voice as soon as they hear it, and they will not follow any one else.

The sheep-cote or fold spoken of in the Bible was the place where the sheep were led at night for protection from the wild animals. An old house, a cave, or some place that had a high wall around it, was usually chosen.

The sheep or lamb was a common sacrifice among the Jews, who kept the law of Moses. It was very suitable for this purpose, on account of its innocence, mildness, submission, and patience.

Many times, to reach the sheepfold, they were forced to climb up a steep, narrow, and rocky path. The sheep did not mind this; but all followed their shepherd, who was leading them carefully over the rough places.

○✸○✸○✸○

The Good Shepherd.

—:—

THERE was another great feast in Jerusalem. This time it was the feast of the dedication, and it was in the winter.

This feast was kept in memory of the time when the Jews reconsecrated the temple after it had been profaned more than one hundred years before the birth of Jesus. It usually lasted eight days. The Jews would light one light on the first day, two on the second, and so on until the eighth day, when they lighted eight. It was often by them called the ''feast of lights.''

This was a time of great merry-making among them, and business of all kinds went on as usual.

HE SHALL GATHER THE LAMBS
IN HIS ARMS
AND CARRY THEM IN HIS BOSOM

THE
GOOD
SHEPHERD

GUNSTON

Jesus came to this feast, not to take part in their amusements, but to preach to the many people who would be present.

One day Jesus walked in that part of the temple known as Solomon's Porch, and the Jews gathered round him with the question, "How long dost thou make us to doubt? If thou be the Christ, tell us plainly."

Now, Jesus had told them many times before, but they did not believe him; so he said: "I told you, and ye believed not: the works that I do in my Father's name, they bear witness of me. But ye believe not, because ye are not my sheep."

Now, Jesus had never lived the life of a shepherd, yet he knew what it meant to be a shepherd, and he also knew all about the habits of sheep; and now he used them as an example to show the people the meaning of his words.

You know, in all the parables, Jesus gave examples from the things about him.

Now, in his talk in the temple he went on to say: "My sheep hear my voice, and I know them, and they follow me. My Father gave them me; and no man is able to pluck them out of my Father's hand. I am the good shepherd; the good shepherd giveth his life for the sheep."

And Jesus compared the kingdom of heaven to a sheepfold, and said that he was the door. If any, he said, wished to enter, they must enter by the door, or they would be as thieves and robbers who try to climb up over the wall or to enter by some other wrong way.

Jesus said that he had other sheep, who were not of that fold; that those he would bring; and that there would be one fold and one shepherd. He was speaking of the Gentiles, who were considered as lost sheep; and he meant that they would have the same privileges that the Jews enjoyed.

Those who loved Jesus knew perfectly well what he meant by what had been said. But the Pharisees said, "He hath a devil, and is mad; why hear ye him?" Some one asked whether a devil could open the eyes of the blind, but the Pharisees only became more angry.

At last their hatred and anger was so great that they took up stones to throw at Jesus.

Then Jesus asked them for which of his good works they were going to stone him. They answered that it was not for any good work, but because he, being a man, made himself equal with God.

Jesus said, "Is it not written in your law, I said, Ye are gods?" He then asked them how, if this was true, they could say he blasphemed because he said that he was the Son of God. And he said that the works alone which he did, were enough to convince them that what he said was true.

When Jesus saw that they were determined to kill him, he escaped out of their hands.

Grief in the Home at Bethany.

—:—

ON account of the great persecution by the Pharisees, Jesus was obliged to leave Jerusalem again. We next read about him on the other side of the river Jordan, in that part of the country where John at first baptized the people.

Many of the people gathered around him to hear his wonderful words. Many, also, of the men there believed on him, remembering how John had pointed him out as the Messiah, and had told them to prepare for his coming.

But a sad event took him back for a short time quite close to Jerusalem.

In the little home in Bethany where Jesus had so often visited, Lazarus was taken very sick.

His loving sisters, Martha and Mary, at once thought of their friend Jesus, and sent him word that their brother was sick. They believed that if Jesus were only there, he could heal their brother, whom he loved so tenderly.

Jesus was grieved when he heard of their trouble; but he was very busy at the time, and did not feel that he could leave the people.

He said, "This sickness is not unto death, but for the glory of God, that the Son of God might be glorified thereby." So he remained two days longer in the same place where he was. On the third day he said to his disciples, "Let us go into Judea again."

His disciples were much surprised when they heard him say this, and reminded him of the late persecution of the Jews, and of how they had sought to stone him; and they even tried to persuade him not to venture.

But Jesus told them there was no danger, for God would protect them; and then he said, "Our friend Lazarus sleepeth; but I go, that I may awake him out of sleep."

The disciples did not understand that Jesus meant that Lazarus was dead, for he had said the words so quietly, and they said, "Lord, if he sleep; he shall do well."

Then Jesus told them plainly, "Lazarus is dead. And I am glad for your sakes that I was not there, to the intent that ye may believe." And then he said, "Let us go unto him."

The disciples still felt that for Jesus to go to Bethany would surely mean death, for he would be so near his enemies; but Thomas said, almost in despair, "Let us also go, that we may die with him."

Jesus Returns to Bethany.

—:—

THE sisters in Bethany surely felt that Jesus had forsaken them in their hour of grief. How they must have longed to see him!

When Jesus reached Bethany, he found the household full of sadness. Lazarus had died, and had been buried. Many friends and kind neighbors had come to try to help comfort the two sisters.

Among those who had come, were many Jews, who were helping to do the things necessary to be done at such times.

Some one brought the news to Martha that Jesus was coming, and she went at once to meet him; but Mary sat quietly in the house.

For ye
shall go out
with Joy,
and be led forth
with Peace:

Isaiah LV,12

As soon as Martha came to where Jesus was, she said, "Lord, if thou hadst been here, my brother had not died."

Jesus told Martha that her brother would rise again; but she thought he was speaking of the time when he would rise in the resurrection at the last day, and she said that she knew he would rise then.

But Jesus explained to Martha that he was the resurrection and the life, and said, "He that believeth in me, though he were dead, yet shall he live: and whosoever liveth and believeth in me shall never die." Then he asked her whether she believed, and she said that she believed he was the Christ, the Son of God, who should come into the world.

Jesus did not care to go to the crowded house; so Martha returned alone, and called her sister secretly, and told her Jesus had come, and wanted to see her.

Now, Martha knew that many of the Jews were in the house, who had come to comfort them, and that if they were to find out that Jesus was near, they might do him harm.

As soon as Mary heard the joyful news that Jesus was near, she arose quickly, and went to the place where Martha had talked with him.

Some of the Jews saw Mary leave the house in such haste, and thinking that she was going to her brother's grave to weep, they followed, that they might be able to say comforting words to her. Although these Jews had such hatred for Jesus, some of them had tender hearts, and they pitied these two sisters.

Mary was weeping when she came to Jesus, and she fell down at his feet saying the same words that Martha had said just a short time before, which were, "Lord, if thou hadst been here, my brother had not died."

When Jesus saw her weeping, and also saw the pitying tears on the faces of the Jews who were with her, he was very sorrowful, and groaning, he asked where they had laid Lazarus. They said, "Lord, come and see."

Jesus knew how much these two sisters loved their dear brother, and how lonely they were now, and he wept with them.

Some of the Jews, when they saw Jesus weeping, said, "Behold how he loved him!" and others said, "Could not this man, which opened the eyes of the blind, have caused that even this man should not have died?"

○✦○✦○✦○

Lazarus is Raised from the Dead.

—:—

WHEN Jesus and the mourners had come to the grave, which was a small room cut out of the side of a rock, with a large stone or slab for the door, he groaned again. Then he commanded that the stone be taken away.

Now, Lazarus had been dead four days; and when Martha heard the words of Jesus, she said, "Lord, by this time he stinketh." Jesus reminded her of the words he had spoken to her such a short time before—that if she would believe, she should see the glory of God.

When the stone had been taken away from the grave, Jesus looked up to heaven, and said, "Father, I thank thee that thou hast heard me." Then he cried out with a loud voice, "Lazarus, come forth."

And then—what a sight! The dead man bound in his grave clothes, and with a napkin over his face, stood before them. Jesus said, "Loose him, and let him go." Those standing around never forgot this scene. It was one they would always remember.

What joy must have filled the hearts of Martha and Mary as they received their dear brother back! All their sorrow had vanished, and there was no more need of comforting words being spoken to them. So their friends left, and went back to Jerusalem.

Many believed on Jesus because of this great miracle; but some hated him still more, and tried to do him harm.

Those who hated him went as fast as they could to the Pharisees, and told them what a great miracle had just been done.

When these Pharises heard the news, they knew that there was no one among them that could do such great miracles as Jesus had done. Their hearts were full of fear, lest the people, when they heard these wonderful things, would all believe on Jesus.

Then they gathered together, and held a council to make a plan to kill Jesus. They thought that Jesus would really be made their king, and that they would lose both their place and nation.

But one of them, whose name was Caiaphas and who was high priest, told them plainly that they knew "nothing at all." He then

LAZ-A-RUS RAISED FROM THE DEAD.

"prophesied that Jesus should die for that nation; and not for that nation only, but that also he should gather together in one the children of God that were scattered abroad. Then from that day forth, they took counsel together for to put him to death."

Jesus once more left them, and went to a small town called Ephraim, where few people were living. It was near the wilderness. Here he stayed for some time.

Beyond Jordan.

—:—

For some time Jesus and his disciples remained near the wilderness of Ephraim. Then we find that he crossed over the river Jordan into the country of Perea. Here Jesus spent some time in teaching the people, and in healing many who were afflicted.

One poor woman had been afflicted for eighteen years. Her body was bent over, and she could not straighten herself.

When Jesus saw this woman, he called her to him and said that he would heal her. Then when he had laid his hands upon her, she was at once made straight, and she began to praise God for his goodness.

Now, there were Pharisees even in that part of the country, who were anxiously looking for something that they could use against Jesus; and as this woman had been healed on the Sabbath-day, they thought that was a good point.

The ruler of the synagogue spoke about it first. He said to the people, "There are six days in which men ought to work: in them therefore come and be healed, and not on the Sabbath-day."

Jesus asked if there was any one there who would not give his cattle a drink on the Sabbath-day, or who thought that this woman who had been such a great sufferer for eighteen years ought not to have been healed, simply because it was the Sabbath-day? The people were ashamed when he had said these things, and they began to praise God for his goodness, and for all the glorious things that Jesus had done.

Then Jesus repeated some of his parables concerning the kingdom of heaven. And he went from one village to another teaching the people.

In answer to the question of one as to who would be saved and enter into the kingdom of heaven, Jesus said, "Strive to enter in at the straight gate: for many will seek to enter in, and shall not be able." And he said that when once the door of the kingdom was closed there would never be any other way to enter. Many, he said, would try, and would say, "We have eaten and drunk in thy presence, and thou hast taught in our streets"; but the Lord would answer them, "I know you not whence ye are; depart from me, all ye workers of iniquity."

Then there would be great sorrow among them; for they could see those from the east, from the west, from the north, and from the south received into the kingdom of God, but they themselves would be shut out forever.

Journeying Toward Jerusalem.

—:—

Now the time for the great feast of the Passover was near at hand, and Jesus once more prepared to return to Jerusalem.

He knew that this was his last visit to the city he loved so well. How full of sadness and pain at this time his heart must have been! but he did not hesitate for a moment.

Even the cruel words of one of the Pharisees which were thrust at him did not cause him to turn back; for he knew all that was going to take place, and he knew also that God would strengthen him for the same.

When he came in sight of Jerusalem, great sorrow filled his heart; and he said: "O Jerusalem, Jerusalem, which killest the prophets, and stonest them that are sent unto thee; how often would I have gathered thy children together, as a hen doth gather her brood under her wings, and ye would not! Behold, your house is left unto you desolate: and verily I say unto you, Ye shall not see me, until the time come when ye shall say, Blessed is he that cometh in the name of the Lord."

How true were these words! Jesus had come to them to be their king; they would soon reject him; and then there would never be any way for them to see him again, unless they could believe that he had been sent to them from above.

How strange it was that the people could not understand! and yet when we look about us, we can see the same unbelief to-day.

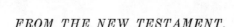

Jesus is the same king that he was then; but ah! how few there are who have accepted him, or who believe that he is the Son of God!

Very many believe that there is a God. This they can not help, for they see the many things which God has created. His great and wonderful works are seen in everything about them.

But then, to believe that Jesus was God's Son is quite another thing. They look upon Jesus as an ordinary man, just as the Jews did in days of old. This is because their hearts are full of unbelief; and if he were here among them, they would no doubt treat him in the same manner that the Jews did hundreds of years ago.

He is coming again. But the next time he comes, he will not remain long with us. He is coming to gather those together who do believe on him, and then he will take them home to heaven with him. There they will see what his kingdom is like, and they will be in it.

At the Pharisee's Table.

—:—

MANY times Jesus had told his disciples of the way he would have to suffer and of his death, but they never understood him.

They expected he might have to suffer many things, but, still, they believed that some time he would set up his kingdom at Jerusalem, and they also expected to become great.

Jesus knew how they felt regarding his kingdom, and for this reason he continued to teach them, and gave many lessons from the things they saw around them and from their daily lives.

He sometimes repeated a parable, but nearly always gave them a new one, each with deeper meanings, as they were more able to understand them now.

One day as they were traveling toward Jerusalem for the last time, a Pharisee invited them to eat at his table. It seems that this Pharisee had prepared a great feast, and had invited many guests that they might watch all Jesus' words and actions.

While Jesus was at the feast, a man who had the dropsy came to

13

him to be healed. Jesus never turned away any one who was sick, or afflicted in any way; but he knew that the Pharisees were watching him, and that it was the Sabbath.

At other times he had been reproved by them for doing merciful acts on the Sabbath-day. So now, before healing this man, Jesus turned to the Pharisees, and asked, "Is it lawful to heal on the Sabbath-day?"

As they did not answer, Jesus healed the man, and he went away rejoicing.

He then asked who would stand by and see one of his animals fall into a pit, and because it was the Sabbath-day would not help it out.

This was a question they did not like to answer, for they knew that they would not in such a case wait until the next day.

Jesus had noticed that many of the people who came to the Pharisee's feast had tried to get into the best rooms and seats. Then he gave them a little lesson on this line to show how wrong it was to do this.

He said: "When thou art bidden of any man to a wedding, sit not down in the highest room; lest a more honorable man than thou be bidden of him; and he that bade thee and him come and say to thee, Give this man place; and thou begin with shame to take the lowest room. But when thou art bidden, go and sit down in the lowest room; that when he that bade thee cometh, he may say unto thee, Friend, go up higher: then shalt thou have worship in the presence of them that sit at meat with thee."

This must have been quite a reproof to those proud Pharisees, but it was a good lesson for the disciples as well.

And Jesus went on to say that when any one prepared a feast he ought to invite the poor people who were unable to return the invitation, and said that the Lord would bless and reward them in heaven for such kindness.

I will instruct thee and teach thee in the way which thou shalt go: I will guide thee with mine eye.

The Great Supper.

—:—

WHILE still in the home of the Pharisee, Jesus told the people a story about a certain rich man who made a great feast or supper. This man invited many of his friends and relatives to the feast; and when everything was prepared, he told his servant to go and tell the guests that all was ready and that they should come.

But all the company who had been invited, began to make excuses. One said, "I have bought a piece of ground, and I must needs go and see it: I pray thee have me excused."

Another said, "I have bought five yoke of oxen, and I go to prove them: I pray thee have me excused."

And still another said, "I have married a wife, and therefore I can not come." And so they continued until all had asked to be excused.

When the servant came and told his master what the people had said, the master was very angry, and disappointed. He told the servant to go out into the streets, and invite the poor people and all who were lame and blind. When the servant had done as his master said to do, he returned, and said, "Lord, it is done as thou hast commanded, and yet there is room."

Again the servant was sent forth, and this time told to bring in any of the people he met until the house was filled, but not to allow any of those who were first invited to taste of the supper.

Now, the man who gave the supper meant God, and the supper itself, the good news of the gospel. The servant meant those who went out to preach to the people, and who tried to get them to live good lives and go to heaven as their reward.

The men who were first invited were the Jews; for the gospel was preached to them first, and they would not believe it.

And the men who were brought into the supper afterward, meant the people of other nations who have heard the gospel since that time and obeyed it.

The command to bring them in out of the streets and lanes was

THE GREAT SUP-PER.

to show that the poor as well as the rich are invited to come and be saved.

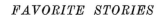

The True Disciple.

WHEN Jesus had left the home of the Pharisee, he told those who were with him what it meant to be true disciples.

He said they must not love any of their friends more than they loved God. They must even be willing to leave their homes and friends, and go out among the people and try to get them saved.

This would, many times, be very hard to do; but they must be willing to go, if God asked them to go.

He called it bearing their cross. He did not tell them then about the cross he was going to bear; but they remembered these words, and understood them later.

Jesus wanted them to know that it meant a great deal to be a Christian. He compared any one seeking salvation to a man who started to build a tower. This man began and laid a nice foundation, and told his friends what a beautiful tower he meant to build. But, lo, when he had only half finished it, he found it would cost so much money that he could not complete it, and he was forced to leave it half done.

Then those who came to see the tower would say, "This man began to build, but was not able to finish."

How much better it would have been for the man had he carefully counted the cost of the building before he began; for he not only wasted his time and money, but gave those who wished to mock him a chance to do so.

We see many about us to-day who forget to count the cost. They think what a beautiful life they could live as a Christian, and they make a start. But ah! they forgot to count the cost. They found that they were not willing to do what Jesus asked them to, and that they could not bear to give up the pleasures of the world.

So they went back into the world, only to see their old friends smile and say, "This man began to build, but was not able to finish."

The Lost Sheep.

—:—

AMONG the Jews was a class of people who were more hated and despised than any others.   They were the publicans, or tax-gatherers.

The Jews were obliged to pay taxes to the Romans, and these publicans were men who went about over their country collecting the money for the Roman king.

THE LOST SHEEP.

Much as the Jews hated the Romans, they hated still more those of their own people who went about collecting taxes.

In some cases, too, these tax-gatherers deserved to be looked down upon; for many of them were in the habit of charging more than the right amount of tax, and keeping the extra amount for themselves.

For this reason the Jews classed them with a set of people then known as "sinners," and they thought that any one who had respect for himself would never have anything to do with such people.

But Jesus did not feel so about them. He knew that in every condition of life there were some who would be glad to follow him. He had even chosen one of these publicans to be his disciple. Matthew was his name, and he was one of the Twelve.

At different times Jesus had eaten with publicans, and for this the Pharisees found much fault with him.

On the way to Jerusalem, as the crowds gathered around Jesus to listen to his words, many publicans were among them. The Pharisees tried to use this against Jesus, and to have their friends look down on him; but Jesus knew their purpose, and again spoke a parable.

He said: "What man of you, having an hundred sheep, if he lose one of them, doth not leave the ninety and nine in the wilderness, and go after that which is lost, until he find it? And when he hath found it, he layeth it on his shoulders, rejoicing. And when he cometh home, he calleth together his friends and neighbors, saying unto them, Rejoice with me; for I have found my sheep which was lost."

And then he explained that God and the angels rejoiced in the same manner when one sinner became a Christian.

The joy in heaven, he said, would be much greater over that person who was lost and who had been found than it would be over ninety and nine just persons, or those who were living good lives.

Sinners were the kind of people God sent his dear Son Jesus into the world to save.

The Lost Piece of Money.

WHEN Jesus had finished the parable of the lost sheep, he spoke another. This one was about a woman that had ten pieces of silver.

THE LOST PIECE OF MONEY.

One day the woman lost one of the pieces, and it worried her very much.

She at once left her work, and lighting a candle, she went to see if she could find it.

Each room was carefully swept, and every piece of furniture moved, and at last she found it. Oh, how glad she was!

As soon as possible she called her friends, and told them that she had found that which had been lost, and asked them to rejoice with her, for she was so happy.

By this parable Jesus meant that God loved every one; but that those who were the deepest in sin and lost would be sought most carefully, and that when found, there would be great rejoicing in heaven.

God is good! His tender mercy
  Is bestowed on all mankind:
E'en the lowest, vilest sinner
  May be cleansed, and pardon find;
May have all his wicked actions
  Swept forever from his view,
And with Jesus, his dear Savior,
  Live a life most pure and true.

All the angels up in heaven,
  Robed in garments pure and white,
Will rejoice and praise Jehovah,
  When beholding such a sight;
And how glad will be the Savior,
  Who with heart so full of love,
Left his home, fulfilled his mission,
  That he might God's great love prove.

Oh, the thanks converted sinners
  Ought their God each day to give,
That he showed them grace and favor,
  And permitted them to live!

Dear one, if you're still a sinner,
Don't delay, no longer wait;
Time is speeding—heed the warning—
Soon, ah soon! 'twill be too late.

The Foolish Young Man.

—:—

THE heart of Jesus still ached for the poor lost sheep of Israel.

As he looked about him and saw these poor sinful people, he longed to show them their great need of a Savior, and how much God loved them, even though they were poor outcasts among their own people.

And he wanted to assure them that if they would repent of their sins, God would be willing to forgive them, and would receive them into his kingdom.

Jesus loved to teach in parables, and many lessons he taught the people in this way.

Now that he might make his meaning very plain, he told them a parable of a certain man who had two sons.

One of them was very obedient; that is, he did everything he thought his father would wish him to do. And he loved his home very much, and each day did all he could to make it more beautiful.

As his father had plenty of everything and gave him the privilege to enjoy all things as if they had been his own, the life of this young man was very happy.

But it was not so with the other son. He was what we would call "a wild young man." All his desire was to have a good time, no matter how much it cost. He did not care for his home, nor for the life that he led there.

So one day he went to his father, and said, "Father, give me the portion of goods that falleth to me."

No doubt his father was grieved when he heard his son say this, but he divided all that he had between his two sons.

Not very long after that the younger son gathered together all that belonged to him, and went a long way from home, and led a gay life.   Little did he think of or care for the future.

As long as his money lasted, he had many friends that were glad to be with him, and to help him enjoy the pleasures of life. Together they feasted, drank wine, and spent much money.

But at last there came a day when the money was all gone.   The foolish boy had spent every penny.

THE WAYWARD SON.

Then, to make matters still worse, a great famine arose in the land.   Nothing would grow, and the people all around were seeking for something to eat, that they might not perish, or die from hunger.

Then the friends of the young man left him, as such friends always do when there is no more money for them to use.

Had he been careful of the portion his father gave him, he would now have needed every penny. But he had nothing to eat, and he was in great want.

Then he went and hired himself out to a man in that land who kept swine. This man told him to go out into the field and take care of the swine.

What a fall this was to the proud young boy who had never known any hardships or trouble! Day after day, alone, hungry, and disgusted with himself, he sat in the fields caring for the swine. No companions were with him, except these dirty beasts.

At last he became so hungry that he would have been glad even to eat the food which was thrown to the swine, but he did not even have the privilege of doing this.

⚬✸⚬✸⚬✸⚬

The Prodigal's Return.

BUT God caused that the young man's sorrow should turn out for his good. He now had time to stop and think. All his sinful life arose before him, and he could now see how very foolish he had been.

He saw that all the sinful pleasures which he had tried so hard to enjoy had only brought him sorrow and pain.

Then his thoughts began to go back to the home that he had left, and to the kind father who had so tenderly watched over him in his youth. And as he thought on, he knew that even the servants in his father's house were better off than he was now, even though he was a son.

He said, "How many hired servants of my father's have bread enough and to spare, and I perish with hunger!"

When he remembered how lovingly his father had always treated him, he thought that if he would return home, and tell him how wicked a life he had lived and that he was very sorry, perhaps his father would forgive him.

And he thought, "If my father will only take me back, I will gladly take the place of a servant.'' He did not wait any longer, but he rose and went home.

How sad his poor father must have been all this time! No loving letters had been written by this wayward son, and the father knew from the past that his son was wasting all the money he had been given. But he loved him, and longed to see him again.

One day as he was looking in the direction that his son had gone, he saw him coming. Oh, how glad the father was!

Poverty had made a great change; but the father knew his son, and ran to meet him. Ragged and dirty as he was, his father threw his arms about him and kissed him.

Then the son began to confess his sins. He said, ''Father, I have sinned against heaven and in thy sight, and am no more worthy to be called thy son.'' But his father would not let him go any farther, for he saw that his son was sorry for all his evil life.

He told his servants to bring out the best garments they had in the house and put them on his son, and to hasten and prepare food for him to eat.

○✺○✺○✺○

The Brother's Jealousy.

—:—

ALL fathers are not so good and kind as was the father of this wayward son you have been reading about. Some would have said, ''I will wait and see whether you really mean what you say and are sorry.'' While others would have turned away from a son who had brought such shame and disgrace upon the family.

But Jesus wanted to show the great and loving kindness of his heavenly Father.

Then Jesus went on to say that the father of the wayward boy had a great feast prepared, and invited their friends to it, that they might rejoice because his son had returned. He even ordered the servants to kill and prepare the fatted calf for the feast.

Now, the elder brother was in the field, and he did not know of his **brother's return**. As he came near the house, he heard the music

Luc 15, 11. 32.

and dancing. And he called one of the servants, and asked what it meant.

The servant answered, ''Thy brother is come; and thy father hath killed the fatted calf, because he hath received his son safe and sound.''

When the brother heard this, he became very angry, and would not go in. When his father heard that his elder son was outside, he went and begged him to go in. He told him that it was right they should be glad the prodigal son had come back again, and that it was right they should rejoice over him; for he had been as one dead, and he was now alive again; he had been lost, and now he was found.

But the elder brother could not feel that way about it. In the first place, he did not have a forgiving spirit, and now jealousy had so filled his heart that he believed himself greatly wronged.

He told his father that he had been with him many years, and had been faithful in everything; and that yet he had never been given even one little kid that he might make a feast and invite his friends; but that just as soon as the son returned who went away and wasted with bad companions all he had, the best calf they had on the place was killed.

The father was very sorry when he heard his son speak thus. He reproved him by saying, ''Son, thou art ever with me, and all that I have is thine.''

The parable was very plain. Jesus wanted to show the Pharisees how wrong it was for them to object to the publicans and sinners having the chance to receive forgiveness of their sins. He also wanted to show them how jealous and wicked their hearts were, and how much they themselves were in need of pardon and forgiveness.

God is love, and he wants all to come to him and enjoy the good things he has in store for them. But they must all receive it in God's own way.

There is not a man or child in all the world who is so bad that God will not forgive him, and receive him back as his own son, if he will only be sorry for the wrong he has done, and will try to do better.

God will hear the prayers of such people, and will bless them when they pray, and will help them through temptations.

The Unjust Steward.

—:—

ANOTHER parable that Jesus spoke was about a certain rich man. This man did not care to look after his own affairs; so he hired a steward, or man to look after them for him.

All went well for a time; but one day some one came and told the rich man that the steward was wasting his goods.

The master at once began to inquire into the matter, and soon found that the report was true. He called the steward, and asked him what he meant by such dealings; but the steward could only confess his wrong.

His master was very angry with him, and said he could be no longer steward.

When the steward saw that he was really removed from being steward, and that he could no longer live in the home of his master, he wondered what he could do to save himself from starvation. He said to himself: "What shall I do? I can not dig: to beg I am ashamed." At last he thought of a plan.

He decided to go to his master's debtors that had been unable to pay their full accounts, and to get what each one could pay. Then he would cancel the rest of each bill.

In this way he would make to himself friends of his master's debtors, so that when he should lose his stewardship they would receive him.

So he called to see each one, and asked how much they were owing his master. The first one said, "A hundred measures of oil." The steward told him to sit down quickly and write fifty.

He then asked another, "How much owest thou?" and he was told a hundred measures of wheat. The steward said he might write sixty; and so he went around among them all.

When his former master heard what had been done, he praised the steward for his wisdom.

Now, Jesus wished to show the people that they were all debtors to God, and also that they were stewards placed over the things belonging to God.

By the master's praising the unjust steward, Jesus did not mean that the man was pleased because his goods were wasted, but that he praised him for wisely looking out for himself.

This is just what Jesus meant that the people must do; that is, look out for themselves, and see that they have a place to stay in the future, when they can not dig and to beg would be of no service to them.   That time is after death.

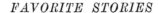

The Rich Man and the Beggar.

—:—

BECAUSE of the parable of the unjust steward, the Pharisees found much fault with Jesus.   For Jesus had said, "Ye can not serve God and mammon: for a man will either hate the one, and love the other; or else he will hold to the one, and despise the other."

Now, the Pharisees, although they tried to appear as if they loved God very dearly, were very covetous; that is, they were greedy, and wanted to become great and rich.

Instead of going and putting the Lord's money to a good work, they tried to justify themselves.   But Jesus told them plainly that God knew their hearts, and that that which was highly esteemed among them was an abomination before God.

Then Jesus told them the parable of the rich man and Lazarus. This was not Lazarus, the brother of Martha and Mary, but was a poor beggar.

Jesus said there was a man who was very rich.   He was clothed in beautiful clothes, made of the finest linen, and each day he had the choicest of food to eat.

And there was also a beggar whose name was Lazarus.   This

THE UNJUST STEWARD

poor man was all covered with sores, and was not able to do any-thing to support himself. But he thought that if he could only have some of the crumbs that fell from the rich man's table, he would be so thankful; so he had his friends carry him to the rich man's gate.

Here he lay, with the hope that the rich man would see him, and would give him something to eat; but in this he was disappointed.

The rich man never acted as if he saw him. But the dogs were his companions, and we read that they came and licked his sores as he sat at the gate.

At last the beggar's sufferings were ended by death's coming to his relief. And the angels carried him to Abraham's bosom. There was very little display at his funeral; for he was nothing but a poor beggar, and he filled only a pauper's grave. Jesus did not even mention his funeral, but we know that the world would not make much ado over the death of one they thought so little of. But God loved him, and he had a soul just as well as the rich man.

We can imagine we see the pleasure of the rich man when he realized that the poor despised beggar was dead, and so would trouble him no more by sitting at his gate; for it certainly was not a very pleasant sight to him.

After a while the rich man also died; and he had a grand costly funeral, for Jesus said he was buried. No doubt many friends mourned for him, and did all they could to show their respect.

But Jesus went on to say that instead of this man's being carried by the angels to Abraham's bosom as the beggar was, he found him-self in terrible torments. As he lifted up his eyes, he saw Abraham afar off, and Lazarus in his bosom. Then he cried and said, "Father Abraham, have mercy on me, and send Lazarus, that he may dip the tip of his finger in water and cool my tongue; for I am tormented in this flame of hell.

"But Abraham said, Son, remember that thou in thy lifetime re-ceivedst thy good things, and likewise Lazarus evil things: but now he is comforted, and thou art tormented. And besides all this, be-tween us and you there is a great gulf fixed: so that they which would

THE RICH MAN AND THE BEGGAR.   213

pass from hence to you can not; neither can they pass to us that would come from thence."

When the rich man saw that there was no chance for him to escape the punishment for his sins, he asked Abraham to send Lazarus back to his father's home to warn his brethren, and to tell them what awful trouble he was in. For he said that he had five brethren who were living as carelessly as he had lived, but that if they could know what he was suffering, perhaps they would repent, and not come to that terrible place of torment.

Abraham answered that they had the words of Moses and the prophets, which were enough. The rich man replied, "Nay, father Abraham: but if one went unto them from the dead, they will repent. And he said unto him, If they hear not Moses and the prophets, neither will they be persuaded though one rose from the dead."

In this way the Pharisees were again reproved, and made to see their standing in God's sight; but, as in the parable, it only hardened their hearts.

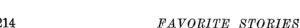

How the Kingdom of God will Come.

—:—

THE Pharisees had been hearing so much about the kingdom of God that at last they asked when it would come. Jesus answered, "The kingdom of God cometh not with observation: neither shall they say, Lo here! or, lo there! for, behold, the kingdom of God is within you."

Jesus meant that the kingdom of God was not something which they could see or point out to their friends, and say, "This is the place where our king sits on his throne." No, indeed!

Jesus wanted them to understand that the kingdom of God was in heaven. There God sits upon a throne, and rules his people with a law of love. Those dwelling in this kingdom are any and all who love and obey his commands. Jesus was going to return to heaven when he had finished his work upon the earth. After that he would

be teacher and guide to his people, and God would turn the kingdom over to the care of his Son.

Then turning to his disciples, Jesus told them that great suffering would come upon them all, but that they must be prepared for it, and not be frightened or discouraged when it came; for he would have to die, that God's plan to save mankind from sin might be fulfilled.

And then Jesus spoke of the way he was going to come for his people at the end of the world; for he was coming for them, and would take all his people up to heaven with him. Every one, he said, must be ready for that time because no one knew just when it would be, except God, and there would be no time to prepare after he came. They must live so pure and holy that they would be ready to receive him at any time.

Many warnings, he told them, would be sent out among the people; but they would all be sent before that time. His appearing would be as unexpected as the lightning which flashes in the sky.

However, Jesus said, it would be as it was in the days of Noah— many would hear about his coming, but they would be careless, and would pay no attention to the warnings they had heard. They would think they had plenty of time, as the people did then; but as the flood came and destroyed all but a few souls, just so Jesus would come again, and gather those who were ready and waiting for him.

He also said that he might come in the night when the people were asleep. Two men might be sleeping side by side in one bed. One would be expecting him, and would have been living a good life; but the other would be wicked. Jesus would take the good man, but would leave the bad one.

And he said: "Two women shall be grinding together; the one shall be taken, and the other left. Two men shall be in the field; the one shall be taken, and the other left."

These words were spoken that they might understand how necessary it was to live pure and holy lives, in order that their hearts be fit places to set up his kingdom. Also, that they might know how uncertain life is, and that the end of the world is coming.

The Widow and the Unjust Judge.

—:—

ANOTHER parable was spoken by Jesus to show the people how they ought to live and the great necessity of prayer.

He said, "There was in a city a judge, which feared not God, neither regarded man." There were many judges of this kind in those days and are still, who do not fear God, nor care for the real welfare of those who come to them for help. They were glad to help the rich who paid them much money, but the poor were left to suffer.

Now, in this same city where the unjust judge lived, was also a widow. This widow had an enemy that was causing her much trouble; and she came to the judge very often, begging him to punish her enemy. But the widow was poor and had no money, and he did not care to be bothered with her case.

But day after day the widow came asking him to help her. The judge would have been glad to have her leave his house and go away, but this he saw she would not do.

So one day he said within himself, "Though I fear not God, nor regard man; yet because this widow troubleth me, I will avenge her, lest by her continual coming she weary me."

Hear what the unjust judge said. He was doing what the woman asked him to do only that he might stop her coming. But Jesus had a much deeper meaning to bring out of this parable.

If this man, who was unjust, and who had no mercy or pity in his heart, could be moved by the widow's coming to him so often, how much more will God, who is so good and merciful, give to his children what they ask him for.

Jesus said, "I tell you that he will avenge them speedily." So, children, if you go to God in prayer, and ask him for anything, do not think that because he sometimes makes you wait he will not grant your request; for he will.

Sometimes he sees that it is for our good to wait for an answer to our prayers; but if we are in real earnest, as was the widow, he will answer.

The Two Men in the Temple.

—:—

"Two men," Jesus said, "went up into the temple to pray; the one a Pharisee, and the other a publican."

The lives of these two men had been very different in the sight of the world.

THE PHARISEE AND THE PUBLICAN.

The Pharisee, on the one hand, had lived a good life; that is, had not done the things that their law commanded them not to do. Yet within his heart were many desires to do the things the law condemned.

The publican, on the other hand, had broken the law many times; and he knew that he had done wrong, and that he was a great sinner.

Now, these men had gone to the temple for the same purpose—

to pray to God.   When the Pharisee began, he looked over at the publican, and began his prayer something like this: ''God, I thank thee, that I am not as other men are, extortioners, unjust, adulterers, or even as this publican.''

Then he told what he did.   He said, ''I fast twice in the week, I give tithes of all that I possess,'' etc.

But the publican knew how wicked he had been, and oh, how sorry he was!   He would not even lift his eyes up toward heaven; but he beat upon his breast, saying, ''God be merciful to me a sinner.''

Which of these prayers do you think pleased God most?   It was the prayer of the one who felt that he was a sinner in God's sight, and who was sorry for his sins.

Jesus said, ''I tell you, this man [the publican] went down to his house justified rather than the other: for every one that exalteth himself shall be abased; and he that humbleth himself shall be exalted.''

Jesus Blesses Little Children.

—:—

THE people brought little children to Jesus, that he might put his hands on them and bless them.

For some reason, the disciples did not think this was the proper thing to do, and they found fault with the mothers for bringing their children.   Perhaps it was because Jesus was very tired and they felt that he needed rest.

The disciples would have sent the dear little children all away; but when Jesus saw what they were doing, he was much displeased and reproved them.

And Jesus said, ''Suffer the little children to come unto me, and forbid them not; for of such is the kingdom of heaven.''   Oh, what sweet words these were! and how happy the dear mothers of these children must have been!

Some of the children may have been very ragged and dirty, for many are in those Eastern countries; but Jesus loved them all the

CHRIST BLESSING THE CHILDREN.

219

same, and he would not turn any away before he had put his hands upon them and blessed them.

Jesus certainly must have loved little children dearly. He knew that they would soon grow to be men and women, and that the lessons taught them in their childhood would always be remembered. Then, too, when the older people died, the children would have to take their places, and become the disciples of Jesus.

When Jesus said, "Of such is the kingdom of heaven," he meant that every one who was in that kingdom must have a heart as pure and innocent as a little child's; that if one's heart were not pure, one could in no wise enter heaven.

How happy you ought to be, children, that Jesus used you as an example of those who are to reign with him above in his kingdom!

The Rich Young Man.

—:—

ONE time a rich young man came to Jesus, and said, "Good Master, what shall I do that I may inherit eternal life?" Jesus asked why he had called him good; for none, he said, were really good except God.

Jesus then told the young man that if he wished to enter heaven he should keep the commandments. The young man said that he had done this from his youth up.

When Jesus saw what a noble young man he was, and what a good life he had always led, he loved him. But one thing was lacking— the young man loved his riches.

Jesus saw this, and told the young man to go and sell all his possessions and give to the poor. In this way the young man would be laying up treasures in heaven. Then Jesus told him to take up his cross, and become his disciple.

This was not the advice that the young man was expecting to hear, and it made him sorrowful. He was not willing to give to the poor, although he had so much money, and he went away with a very sad heart.

When he had gone away, Jesus turned to his disciples, and said: "How hardly shall they that have riches enter into the kingdom of God! It is easier for a camel to go through a needle's eye, than for a rich man to enter into the kingdom of God."

When the disciples heard this, they were astonished, and said, "Who then can be saved?" Jesus was expecting them to say this, and tenderly looking at them, he said, "With men it is impossible, but not with God: for with God all things are possible."

Peter said to Jesus, "Behold, we have forsaken all, and followed thee; what shall we have therefore?" Jesus answered that all who had given up friends and homes for his sake would receive a hundred-fold more in this life, and would inherit everlasting life.

The Parable of the Laborers.

—:—

AGAIN Jesus spoke a parable to represent what the kingdom of heaven was like, for it seemed so very hard for them to understand just what it was.

He said that the kingdom of heaven was like a man who owned a large vineyard.

A vineyard is a place were grapes are grown, and there were many grapes raised in that part of the country; and as Jesus was always drawing lessons from the things around him, he this time used the vineyard as an example.

Jesus said that when the owner of this vineyard saw that the grapes were ripe, he also saw that he would need help in picking them. So he went out very early in the morning to hire laborers for his vineyard. He told all the laborers that he would pay them a penny a day for their work; and they went into the vineyard, and began at once to pick the grapes.

About nine o'clock he went out again, and saw some standing

idle; and he told them to go into his vineyard, and he would pay them for their work.

Again he went out, about mid-day and about three o'clock, and hired more help.

And about five o'clock he went out, and found some standing idle; and he asked them why they had been idle all the day. They answered, "Because no man hath hired us."

The man told them that if they would go and work in the vineyard, he would pay them what was right.

When evening came, the man called his steward, and told him to go and pay all the laborers for their work in his vineyard, beginning with those whom he had hired last.

The steward did as he was told, and paid each man a penny. When those who had been hired very early in the morning saw the others receiving a penny each, they supposed that they would receive more when the steward came to them, but no—each man received a penny.

Those who had worked so long and hard were not satisfied when they saw this, and they went to the owner of the vineyard, and said, "These last have wrought but one hour, and thou hast made them equal with us, which have borne the burden and heat of the day.

"But he answered one of them, Friend, I do thee no wrong: didst not thou agree with me for a penny? Take that thine is, and go thy way: I will give unto this last, even as unto thee. Is it not lawful for me to do what I will with mine own? Is thine eye evil because I am good?"

This parable taught the people that there was much work for God's people to do. The rich man represented God; his vineyard, the world; and the fruit in the vineyard, the souls of men. The laborers were the disciples and ministers of Christ.

The time of day that they were hired represents the time of life when a person hears the voice of God calling him to come and give his heart to him. And their wages are the reward God has for every one of his children.

THE LABOURERS IN THE VINEYARD.

God pays all his children alike, whether they were hired or called in the morning or late in the day of their lives.

Solemn Thoughts.

—:—

ONE day, while on their way to Jerusalem, Jesus took his disciples away from the crowds that were following them, and told them for the third time about his coming death and resurrection.

As Jesus told them how he was going to have to suffer, great fear came upon them. They loved Jesus so dearly, and the thought of his sufferings made them afraid.

Jesus told them that he would be delivered up to the chief priests, who would say that he was worthy of death.

Then he told them that the Gentiles would mock him, and scourge him, and even put him to death; but that the third day after he was crucified, he would rise again. And he would go up into heaven, he said, where he would prepare his kingdom for all the good people on the earth.

The disciples had never understood the deep meaning of the words of Jesus. Neither did they understand him now.

Two of the disciples, James and John, talked the matter over with their mother.

Like most mothers, their mother felt that she should like to see her two sons well favored in the kingdom of God; and not understanding the depth of its meaning, she went with them to Jesus, and asked him to grant a certain request.

Jesus asked what her request was; and she answered, ''Grant that these my two sons may sit, the one on thy right hand, and the other on the left, in thy kingdom.''

Jesus told her plainly that she did not know how great a request she had asked. Then turning to the two sons, he asked, ''Are ye able to drink of the cup that I shall drink of, and to be baptized with the baptism that I am baptized with?'' They answered, ''We are''—

CHRIST AND THE MOTHER OF ZEB-E-DEE'S CHILDREN.

but oh, how little they knew of what was to come upon Jesus!

Jesus told them that they should indeed drink of the cup that he was going to drink of, which meant the cup of sorrow and persecution; but that to seat the one on his right hand and the other on his left, he had no right to do. God, he told them, would give that place to those for whom he had prepared it.

When the other ten disciples heard of the request, they talked about James and John, and thought they should have known better than to ask such a thing. Then, too, Jesus had told them that those desiring to be first were very likely to be last.

Jesus was displeased when he heard what the other ten had said about James and John; so he once more called them all to him, and explained matters more clearly.

He said that in worldly matters it was the custom to look up to princes and kings, and to do them as great honor as possible, but that it was not so in spiritual things.

If any, they were told, would be great in the kingdom of heaven, he should be minister or servant of all the others. Then he said, "Even the Son of man came not to be ministered unto, but to minister, and to give his life a ransom for many."

The City of Jericho.

—:—

THEY did not have much time to spare, as the time for the feast of the Passover was near at hand. The river Jordan had been crossed, and they were near the city of Jericho.

There had been a large and beautiful city by the name of Jericho destroyed shortly after the children of Israel had entered the land of Canaan. At that time a curse was pronounced upon the one who in after years might rebuild that city. Josh. 6: 26.

This was not undertaken until many years had passed by; but in 1 Kings 16: 34 we read of a man by the name of Hiel, who did rebuild Jericho.

Years afterward, under the Romans, Jericho became a place of importance, and it was full of costly treasures.

In the days of Elisha the water was very bad; and the people came to the old prophet, and asked him to heal the waters. 2 Kings 2: 19-22.

Elisha had them bring him some salt. This he took and put into the spring that was near the city; and God healed the water, and made it good for the people to drink. This spring may still be seen near Jericho, and it is called the "Ain es Sultan."

Jericho was not far from the place where John the Baptist baptized Jesus, and it was right on his way from Perea to Jerusalem. At different times he had visited the place; and the people had become acquainted with him, and they knew of his great power to heal.

The scene must have been a beautiful one, as Jesus came near the city. Many different kinds of beautiful trees grew near the spring Ain es Sultan, and the gardens and fields were so fair and sweet.

But there was a sight that made him feel very sad. There before him sat a poor man who was blind, and who got his living from the people by begging of them as they passed by.

Blind Bartimeus.

—:—

THE blind man near Jericho did not see Jesus, for he was not able to see any one; but he heard the great noise of the people passing, and he wondered what it meant. Some one told him that it was Jesus of Nazareth passing by.

Oh, what joyful news that was to the poor man! He had heard of Jesus and of his power to heal, and he believed that he would heal him. He began to cry very loud, and said, "Jesus, thou son of David, have mercy on me."

When Jesus heard the cry, he stood still, and commanded that the man be brought near him; and some of the multitude went at once to bring him. They told the man that Jesus had sent for him, and said to be of good comfort, for he would help him.

The poor man was in such haste to go to Jesus that he rose at once, and cast aside his outer garment, that it might not hinder him.

When Jesus saw him, he said, "What wilt thou that I should do unto you?" The blind man answered, "Lord, that I might receive my sight."

Jesus said, "Receive thy sight: thy faith hath saved thee." Then he touched the eyes of the blind man, who was instantly healed.

The man's heart was full of joy and praise to the one who had done such a great work for him, and he followed on with the crowd that was with Jesus.

The Man in a Tree.

—:—

Soon after the blind man's healing, Jesus entered Jericho. Now there was living in this city a man by the name of Zaccheus. This man was a publican, or tax-gatherer, and he had become very rich. Much of his money may have been gained by being dishonest and taking more money from the people than he had any right to take. But, however that may have been, many knew that he was a publican. and he was hated by the Pharisees. Jesus knew all about him, too.

Now, Zaccheus was a very small man; but he had heard about Jesus, and had a great desire to see him. Knowing that he could not see above the heads of the people as they passed by him, he climbed up into a sycamore-tree. Here he could see Jesus, of whom the people were telling such wonderful things.

Safely hiding in the tree, not thinking of a kind word or look from the Savior, was this little man. How great must have been his surprise to see Jesus, as he passed beneath the sycamore tree, look up at him, and then to hear him say, "Zaccheus, make haste, and come down; for to-day I must abide at thy house."

There was no delay or questions asked. Zaccheus came down as soon as possible, and took Jesus home with him. He could not tell why Jesus had honored him this way, but great joy filled his heart on account of it.

"ZACCHEUS, COME DOWN."   229

When the people saw that Jesus had gone to the publican's house, they found fault with him and said, "He has gone to be guest with a man that is a sinner." But they had spoken against him in this way many times before.

Zaccheus was very glad to have Jesus with him in his home, and he at once began to talk in such a way that Jesus could see he was very anxious to do what was right. He said, "Behold, Lord, the half of my goods I give to the poor; and if I have taken anything from any man by false accusation, I restore him fourfold."

Jesus was pleased with the way Zaccheus talked; for he saw that the poor publican, who was so looked down upon, really wanted to live right. Not only was he willing to give much to the poor around him, but he wanted to make his wrongs right. And Jesus said unto him, "This day is salvation come to this house."

How unlike the young ruler who came to Jesus to learn how he might inherit eternal life! He had not been willing to give up his riches, and he had gone away sorrowful. But Zaccheus gave up his goods of his own free-will. And Jesus made him an heir to heavenly possessions.

○✸○✸○✸○

Parable of the Ten Pounds.

—:—

AFTER the visit with Zaccheus, Jesus continued his journey; and another blind man was healed before he left Jericho.

Then he spoke a parable about a nobleman that had become heir to a kingdom; but he was obliged to go a long way from his home to gain possession of it. For this reason he had to leave his home property in the care of servants.

He, therefore, gave to each of his ten servants money to use while he was away. He gave each of them one pound, and said, "Trade ye herewith till I come."

Some of these servants did not like the nobleman, and they decided, after he had gone, that they would do just as they pleased.

Many days passed by, but at last the nobleman returned. He

THE PARABLE OF THE TALENTS.

231

had been successful in getting the kingdom, and he was very rich. No doubt he had a nice reward or present for each of his servants; but most of all, he wanted to know how they had used the money he had given them.

He commanded them all to come into his presence. The first servant said, "Lord, thy pound hath gained ten pounds." The master was glad when he heard this, and he said, "Well, thou good servant: because thou hast been faithful in a very little, have thou authority over ten cities." The second servant had not done so well, yet his pound had gained five pounds; and the master made him ruler over five cities.

But when the third servant came, he said, "Lord, behold, here is thy pound, which I have kept laid up in a napkin: for I feared thee, because thou art an austere man: thou takest up that thou layest not down, and reapest that thou didst not sow."

How surprised his master was at the words of this servant! He could see how they had been talking about him in his absence. "And he saith unto him, Out of thine own mouth will I judge thee, thou wicked servant. Thou knewest that I was an austere man, taking up that I laid not down, and reaping that I did not sow: wherefore then gavest not thou my money into the bank, that at my coming I might have required mine own with usury? And he said unto them that stood by, Take from him the pound, and give it to him that hath ten pounds."

The other servants were surprised when they heard their master's command to give the pound to the one who had ten pounds; but he said: "Unto every one which hath shall be given; and from him that hath not, even that he hath shall be taken away from him. But those mine enemies, which would not that I should reign over them, bring hither, and slay them before me."

The meaning of this parable is very plain. God is preparing a kingdom for his people. Jesus is the nobleman, and he has given his servants money or talents to use. If they will not use them, he will take their talent, and give it to some one who will.

Let us be very sure we are using our talents, and not laying them aside in a napkin.

○✶○✶○✶○

Six Days before the Passover.

——:——

THE feast of the Passover had not yet been held. It was six days before the time set to hold it, and Jesus went once more to visit the home of Martha.

How glad they must have been to again see Jesus! They loved Jesus, not only because they believed he was God's Son, but because he had called their brother back from the grave. And they wanted to show him their love in every way they could.

A man named Simon, who was once a leper, but who had been healed, invited Jesus to come to his home. This man prepared a nice supper, and invited to come to his house at that time many guests who were anxious to see Jesus.

Perhaps the feast was prepared at Simon's house because there was more room than at Martha's house; but Martha waited upon the guests herself, and Lazarus was there with them.

Many of the people came not for Jesus' sake only, but also that they might see Lazarus. When the Pharisees saw this, they thought it would be best to kill Lazarus, as well as Jesus, for many were believing on Jesus because of him.

While Jesus was eating, Mary, who was always anxious to show her love, came quietly up to him, and taking a box of very costly ointment, she poured it on his head and feet. And then, stooping down, she wiped his feet with her hair. The house was at once filled with the rich perfume, and all present realized what she had done.

One of the disciples, whose name was Judas Iscariot, did not think it was proper and right for Mary to do this. He considered it a great waste of money on Mary's part, but he did not understand.

Then another thing, Judas did not have true love for Jesus; in his heart he hated him. Now, Judas carried the bag which contained the money that was given to the disciples. Judas, having all the care of this bag, often took money from it for himself that he ought not to take and thus became a thief, and he was anxious to see much money go into the bag.

He did not care for the poor; but he said, "Why was not this ointment sold for three hundred pence, and given to the poor?"

Mary had not meant to be extravagant or wasteful, and she did not mean to neglect the poor; but she wanted to show her love for the Savior by anointing him.

When Jesus heard the words of Judas, he was grieved; for he knew the thoughts that were in this wicked man's heart. Then he said: "Let her alone; why trouble ye her? she hath wrought a good work on me. For ye have the poor with you always, and whensoever ye will, ye may do them good: but me ye have not always.

"She hath done what she could: she is come aforehand to anoint my body to the burying."

And then Jesus said that wherever the gospel should be preached in after-years, this kind act of Mary's would be told as a memorial of her.

Jesus Rides upon a Young Colt.

—:—

Now the time had come for which they had so long been looking. Hundreds of years before this God had said that Jesus, the King of the Jews, should come one day to Jerusalem riding on a young colt.

Jesus knew the time had come, so he sent two of his disciples to a village that was quite close. There, Jesus said, they would find, tied beside its mother, a colt upon which no man had ever ridden.

This colt he told his disciples to bring to him. And he said that if any man found fault with them, or asked why they were taking the colt, they should say, "Because the Lord hath need of him."

You may be sure the two disciples went as fast as they could, as they had been hoping and longing for this time to come; for they still believed that Jesus would some day take his place upon the throne in

MARY ANOINTING THE FEET OF JESUS.

Jerusalem. In the village, just where Jesus had told them to look, they found the young colt and its mother tied.

Just as they were untying the colt, some one asked what they were going to do with the colt; but when the disciples said, "The Lord hath need of him," he said no more, but let them go.

Then they brought the colt to Jesus; and when they had spread

JESUS RIDING ON THE COLT.

some of their outside garments over its back, Jesus sat upon it.

And many of the people in the great crowd that was following, took off their long, loose outer garments that were worn in those days, and spread them upon the ground for Jesus to ride over.

Sometimes they do this now in Eastern countries, to show their respect for any one.

JESUS ENTERING JERUSALEM.   237

Others of the people cut branches off the trees, and laid them in the way, and then sang beautiful songs. These are some of the words: "Hosanna to the Son of David. Blessed is he that cometh in the name of the Lord; Hosanna in the highest."

The Pharisees did not enjoy the singing, and the words were anything but pleasant to them. Some even asked Jesus to have his disciples keep quiet; but Jesus answered that if they should keep quiet, the very stones around them would cry out.

As the crowds moved along, they talked about the way Lazarus had been raised from the dead.

It was hearing about this that had excited them so much, and had made so many come out to meet Jesus. And now they would soon enter the beautiful city.

Entering Jerusalem.

—:—

THEY were now very close to Jerusalem. As they came to a certain part of the Mount of Olives, they could see the beautiful city. There stood the wonderful temple straight before them.

As Jesus looked, such sorrow filled his heart that he wept. He could see the great and bitter scene which was before him—that one of his disciples would turn away from him, and go to his enemies, who would pay a few pieces of money to get that disciple to betray his Master; and then he could see how these enemies would finally crucify his own body.

But Jesus did not weep for himself. He wept for the Jews because they loved their sins, and hated their Savior. Jesus knew how God would punish them, and how their beautiful city would be destroyed in a few years by the Romans, who would burn the temple, and kill many of the people. This was surely enough to cause Jesus to weep.

He had taught them so long, and worked so many miracles among them, and still they did not trust him. He would have been glad to

protect them against all the harm and danger that he saw was ahead of them; but they would not let him.

Then Jesus entered Jerusalem, still riding upon the colt.

When he came to the temple, he went inside and remained until evening. Then he took his disciples, and returned to Bethany.

A Lesson on Faith.

THE following morning, as Jesus was returning to Jerusalem, he was very hungry. Quite a distance ahead of him, and near the path he was traveling, he saw a fig-tree.

When he came to it, he found that it had no fruit on it, and he said to the tree, "Let no fruit grow on thee henceforward forever." And presently the fig-tree withered away.

It seemed strange that Jesus would speak thus; but it was not because he was angry with the tree for not having fruit on it, but because he wanted to teach his disciples a lesson of faith, and how much they would be able to do if they would only trust God and believe his promises.

When the disciples saw that the tree really had withered away, they could hardly understand how it was; and Peter spoke to Jesus about it.

The answer Jesus made was so precious. He said, "Have faith in God; for verily I say unto you, If ye have faith, and doubt not, ye shall not only do this which is done to the fig-tree, but also if ye shall say unto this mountain, Be thou removed, and be cast into the sea, it shall be done.

"And all things, whatsoever ye shall ask in prayer, believing, ye shall receive."

The disciples had great need of lessons like this. Jesus wanted them to have such a perfect trust and faith in God that they would not be afraid to ask him for anything they were needing, and that they would not be afraid to ask for others too.

This same promise is for all God's people to-day. They can have anything they ask for, if they truly believe that God will give it to them.

Some one might say, "What if they asked for something they ought not to have?"

God's children would not do that. They would very soon see that it was not God's will for them to have it, and of course would not believe that they would receive it.

Jesus in the Temple.

—:—

JESUS found the temple, which had been built only as a place in which to worship God, in a very sad condition.

Many of the people had returned who had been in the habit of using the temple as a place to make money, by selling sacrifices to those who came to the feast. Jesus two years before this had driven them out, and overthrown their tables, and now he did the same again. He did not give them time to remove any of their goods, but cast them out as quickly as possible.

And he said, "Is it not written, My house shall be called of all nations the house of prayer? but ye have made it a den of thieves."

The people now had the chance to accept Jesus if they would; but it was as he had said it would be—they rejected him. Only a few lame and blind people came to Jesus as he was teaching in the temple. These he healed, and sent away happy.

But some little children sang the songs that they heard as Jesus rode up to the temple, and they kept singing them. Their words were, "Hosanna to the Son of David."

Some of the Pharisees who were watching Jesus all the time to find something that they could use against him came up to Jesus, and said, "Hearest thou what these say?"

Jesus answered by asking them whether they had never read the words from the Bible, "Out of the mouth of babes and sucklings thou hast perfected praise."

In the evening, he, with his disciples, left the city, and went out to spend the night in the Mount of Olives; but he returned to the temple early the next morning.

More people came out to hear him, and some listened with real interest. But the same spirit of faultfinding was in the Pharisees. When he had been preaching for a good while, some of them came and said, "By what authority doest thou these things? and who gave thee this authority?

"And Jesus answered and said unto them, I will also ask of you one question, and answer me, and I will tell you by what authority I do these things.

"The baptism of John, was it from heaven, or of men? answer me.

"And they reasoned with themselves, saying, If we shall say, From heaven; he will say, Why then did ye not believe him?

"But if we shall say, Of men; they feared the people: for all men counted John, that he was a prophet indeed.

"And they answered and said unto Jesus, We can not tell. And Jesus answering saith unto them, Neither do I tell you by what authority I do these things."

Then Jesus told them a story about a man who had two sons. One day this man went to one of his sons, and told him to go and work in his vineyard. At first the son said he would not go; but afterwards he was sorry that he had refused, and he went and did as his father had told him.

The father also told his other son to go and work in his vineyard. This son said he would go, but did not keep his word.

Then Jesus asked which of these sons did the will of his father, and the Pharisees answered, "The first." This, Jesus said, was the way it would be in the kingdom of God. The publicans whom they hated so much would go into the kingdom before they themselves would; for they believed that Jesus had been sent from heaven, but these Pharisees believed not.

The Vineyard of the Lord.

—:—

THERE was a man who planted a vineyard, Jesus said, and set out a nice hedge all around it, to protect it from wild beasts and thieves. And he built a tower and a winepress, that nothing would be lacking.

Then he gave it in charge of some husbandmen that he employed to take care of it, and went away into a far country, where he remained a long time.

When the time drew near for the fruit to be ripe, he sent his servants to the husbandmen, that they might receive from them the fruits of the vineyard. But instead of delivering the fruit to the servants, they treated them shamefully. They beat one, killed another, and stoned another.

But the owner of the vineyard did not stop with this. He sent other servants, more than at the first; and they were treated in the same manner as the first.

Last of all he sent his son, saying, "They will reverence my son."

But when the husbandmen saw the son, they said among themselves, "This is the heir; come, let us kill him, and let us seize on his inheritance. And they took him, and killed him, and cast him out of the vineyard."

Then Jesus asked the Pharisees what they supposed the lord of that vineyard would do to those husbandmen when he came home.

They answered, "He will miserably destroy those wicked men, and will let out his vineyard unto other husbandmen, which shall render him the fruits in their season."

They did not at first realize that the parable was spoken against them; but they might have known it, for it was very plain.

The people of Israel were God's vineyard, and the hard-hearted Pharisees were the cruel husbandmen. The servants sent to bring the fruit were those dear honest people who loved God with all their hearts and obeyed his commands, and the son, or heir, was Jesus, God's Son.

Then Jesus asked them whether they had never read in the Bible:

THE PARABLE
OF THE
VINEYARD

ST MARK XII.

"The stone which the builders rejected, the same is become the head of the corner. Whosoever shall fall upon that stone shall be broken: but on whomsoever it shall fall, it will grind him to powder."

When the Pharisees heard this, they understood that the parable had been spoken against them; for Jesus had ended it by saying, "The kingdom of God shall be taken from you, and given to a nation bringing forth fruits thereof."

Be Ye Ready; or, The Parable of the Ten Virgins.

—:—

A little band I have in mind,
Just ten in all, of virgins kind;
Each holds a lamp within her hand,
And in two groups they meekly stand.
    Why are they here?
    The night's so drear;
'Twould seem their hearts would fill with fear.

They all expect a friend to come,
They're all invited to his home;
There'll be a marriage feast, you see;
To meet him they must ready be.
    'Tis long to wait;
    Here at the gate
They all sink down in sleepy state.

At last a sudden cry arose;
What did it mean? All eyes unclose.
"The bridegroom's come!" Ah! this is why
They heard the sudden midnight cry.
    They haste and trim
    Their lamps, now dim;
They must prepare to welcome him.

Five had their lamps soon burning bright,
Their rays sent forth a ruddy light;
The lights of five grew dim so fast

THE WICKED HUSBANDMEN.

245

'Twas plain to see they could not last:
    If they could get
    Some oil, as yet,
Perhaps, the bridegroom might be met.

Of course, it was a foolish thing,
These five should all forget to bring
Oil for their lamps; so to the wise
They hastened with these pleading cries:
    "Our lights are gone!
    Of oil we've none!
Divide, or we'll be left alone!"

The wise, for fear their own might fail,
Said, "Nay, go buy where it's for sale."
They hastened, but ere they returned,
The bridegroom came, they after learned.
    He'd found the wise
    With full supplies;
His coming caused them no surprise.

He took them in, his feast to share,
Then closed the door with utmost care.
The foolish came, and speaking thus,
Said, "Lord, lord, open unto us."
    The lord said, "Nay,
    You now must stay
Where there'll be weeping night and day."

Ah! watch and pray and ready be,
Lest some day likewise you should see
The Lord's appearance in the skies,
And have to go for fresh supplies.
    Christ warns us all,
    Both great and small,
To ready be at his last call.

THE FOOLISH VIRGINS.

247

Plots Laid by the Pharisees to Entrap Jesus.

—:—

THE Pharisees saw that Jesus always had an answer for all their questions, and that they could not entangle him in his talk. Then they made a plot whereby they thought that perhaps they could get him to say something which would give offense either to the people or else to the Romans.

They chose men who would pretend to be only common people, but who were really spies, to go to Jesus and ask him some questions. Then they intended to go to the governor and tell him the words of Jesus, and thus work mischief.

They chose the subject which had always caused them so much trouble—whether it were right to pay tribute money. They said, "Tell us therefore, What thinkest thou? Is it lawful to give tribute unto Cæsar, or not?"

Cæsar was the Roman emperor who had conquered the Jews. He was the one who compelled the Jews to pay taxes; but he protected them from other nations, who might have done them harm.

The Pharisees knew that if Jesus said it was not right to pay the taxes, he would be arrested by the Romans; but that if, on the contrary, he said it was right, the people would lose all confidence in him; for they still hoped that Jesus would be their king, and would deliver them from the Romans.

Jesus understood their motive for asking the question, and he said, "Why tempt ye me, ye hypocrites?" Then he asked them to show him a penny. When they brought it, he said, "Whose is this image and superscription?" And they answered, "Cæsar's." On one side was a picture of Cæsar, and on the other side were words which meant, "Greatest High Priest." These were called his image and superscription, and were what Jesus referred to.

So Jesus said, "Render to Cæsar the things that are Cæsar's, and to God the things that are God's."

When the Pharisees heard these words, they marveled or won-

dered at the wisdom of Jesus, and they left him and went away.

They understood that Jesus meant that while they were under the Roman emperor it was right for them to acknowledge him as their rightful ruler, and that it was certainly their duty to pay him the tribute he required. Thus their plot to entangle Jesus in his words was entirely overthrown.

After this some of the Sadducees came to Jesus and asked some questions concerning the law of Moses. These were the people who did not believe in the resurrection of the dead.

They, too, asked Jesus foolish questions, in order that he might be placed under arrest; but when Jesus answered all their questions with heavenly wisdom, they could not help saying, "Master, thou hast well said." And after that they did not dare ask him such simple questions.

When the Pharisees and Sadducees had been put to silence, a lawyer ventured to ask a question. He said, "Master, which is the greatest commandment in the law?"

"Jesus said unto him, Thou shalt love the Lord thy God with all thy heart, and with all thy soul, and with all thy mind.

"This is the first and great commandment.

"And the second is like unto it, Thou shalt love thy neighbor as thyself.

"On these two commandments hang all the law and the prophets."

The lawyer answered, "Well, Master, thou hast said the truth: for there is one God; and there is none other but he: and to love him with all the heart, and with all the understanding, and with all the soul, and with all the strength, and to love his neighbor as himself, is more than all whole burnt offerings and sacrifices.

"And when Jesus saw that he answered discreetly, he said unto him, Thou art not far from the kingdom of God."

Then Jesus warned the people against the Pharisees; for they made strict rules for other people, but what they did themselves was only to be seen of men and to be well spoken of. Their works, he taught, would not amount to anything in the sight of God.

He told the people that they were to listen to the words of the Scribes and Pharisees, for they were the words of the law of God; but that they must not act like them.

Jesus pronounced many dreadful woes upon the Pharisees for their hypocrisy and disobedience. And then, thinking of the people whom they led astray and of the beautiful city that was soon to be destroyed for their sins, he cried out: "O Jerusalem, Jerusalem, thou that killest the prophets, and stonest them which are sent unto thee, how often would I have gathered thy children together, even as a hen gathereth her chickens, under her wings, and ye would not! Behold, your house is left unto you desolate."

The Widow's Offering.

—:—

WITHIN the temple was a place called the treasury. This was the place where the people put their offerings or money for the poor people and for the care of the temple.

Jesus was very tired when he had finished his talk with the Pharisees, and his heart was very full of sorrow.

He went and sat down near the treasury, and sat there watching the people as they came to offer their gifts.

Many of those who were rich cast large sums of money into the treasury; but there was a poor widow, who had only two mites.

This was a very small amount of money; but as she had no more, she was not ashamed to offer what she had.

Jesus saw what the widow put into the treasury, and he was pleased, for he knew what a great sacrifice she had made to spare even that amount.

He called his disciples to him, and said, "Verily I say unto you, That this poor widow hath cast more in, than all they which have cast into the treasury."

Why did Jesus say this? It was because she, being very poor, had cast in all the money she had. She was perfectly willing to give

THE WIDOW'S OFFERING.   251

it to the Lord, for she had faith to know that he would not let her suffer.

The rich who had cast so much money into the treasury perhaps looked with disdain upon the little, humble offering of the widow; but they had cast in of their abundance, and would never miss their offerings.

So we see that God is not pleased so much with the amount of our offering as he is with the sacrifice we have made to spare it.

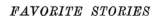

A Voice from Heaven.

THE hour when Jesus was to be sacrificed for the sins of the people was now close at hand.

Although he was God's Son, and had all power to save his own life, he did not want to do it; for it was for this purpose that he had been born into the world.

But Jesus had a body like ours. It shrank from pain and suffering, although it endured so much; and now as he saw the time fast approaching, he said: "Now is my soul troubled; and what shall I say? Father, save me from this hour: but for this cause came I unto this hour. Father, glorify thy name.

"Then came there a voice from heaven, saying, I have both glorified it, and will glorify it again."

The people who were standing near Jesus, heard the voice, and they wondered what it was, for they could not understand the words. Some said, "It thundered"; and others, "An angel spoke to him."

Then Jesus told them that it was God's voice, and said, "This voice came not because of me, but for your sakes." Then he spoke of his death and resurrection, and warned them to prepare to meet him when he came to the earth again to gather his people together and then return with them to heaven, where they would reign with him in his kingdom.

The Pharisees could not understand nor believe what he said, for

their sinful lives had blinded their eyes. But there were a good many who did believe that he was the Christ; and to such he said: "He that believeth on me, believeth not on me, but on him that sent me. And he that seeth me seeth him that sent me."

Then Jesus, with his disciples, left the temple to go to the Mount of Olives, where they had been staying during the feast of the Passover. When they had passed out of the temple, the disciples spoke of the great and beautiful stones that were in the building; and as they were admiring them, Jesus said: "Seest thou these great buildings? There shall not be left one stone upon another, that shall not be thrown down."

When they had reached the Mount of Olives, they could see the beautiful temple in the distance, and four of the disciples, Peter, James, John, and Andrew, asked Jesus when all the things of which he had been telling them were going to happen. In answer he said, "Take heed lest any man deceive you. For many shall come in my name, saying, I am Christ; and shall deceive many."

He told them that many troubles were in store for them, and for all the Jews. Great armies, he said, would rise up against the Jews, Jerusalem would be destroyed, and there would be distress on every hand.

There would be wars and rumors of wars, and earthquakes, famines, and pestilences. And he warned them to take heed to themselves; for they would be persecuted, put in prison, and have to suffer many things.

But all these things would only turn to them for a testimony. When they were brought before kings, God would teach them what to say, and they who heard their words would realize that their wisdom must be from above.

In all their troubles they should not be forsaken; and more than this, after the Son of man had been crucified and he had risen and gone to heaven, he was going to come to get all those who were watching for his coming.

No man, he told them, could know just when that time would be, but every one must watch.

Jesus reminded them of the way Noah had warned the people so faithfully in his time, and of how they would not heed his warnings and at last the flood came and drowned them.

Scenes of the Judgment Day.

—:—

LITTLE did the children of Israel think the night they were delivered from the bondage of Egypt that their deliverance and the Passover feast would have so great a meaning.

They could not understand that year after year a feast was to be kept in honor of that time, as long as they continued to be a nation.

Neither did these Jews, at the time when Jesus was with them, realize that their being a separate and a favored nation was nearly at a close, and that the sacrifice which was to be offered at this feast would be the Lamb of God, and that this offering would be remembered as long as the world should last, as the true sacrifice that "taketh away the sin of the world."

Jesus had always kept this feast, and now the time was near at hand when he would go to a place alone with his disciples and eat it. But before this time, Jesus gave his disciples an idea of what the judgment-day would be like.

He said that day would be at the end of the world. Then all nations would be gathered together, and the Son of man would be seated upon his throne in heaven, with all the holy angels around him.

Then the people would be divided as a shepherd would divide his flock. All the sheep would be placed on the right hand, and all the goats on the left.

The sheep represented the people who loved God, and believed that he had sent Jesus into the world to save them from their sins. The goats were those who did not believe this, and those who treated Jesus so shamefully in this life.

When the people were all divided, then Jesus, who would be sitting upon his throne, would say to those on his right hand: "Come, ye blessed of my Father, inherit the kingdom prepared for you from the foundation of the world:

"For I was an hungred, and ye gave me meat: I was thirsty, and ye gave me drink: I was a stranger, and ye took me in:

"Naked, and ye clothed me: I was sick, and ye visited me: I was in prison, and ye came unto me."

In surprise, these would ask when they had seen Jesus in any of those conditions, and he would answer them, "Verily I say unto you, Inasmuch as ye have done it unto one of the least of these my brethren, ye have done it unto me."

Then Jesus would turn to those upon his left hand, and say: "Depart from me, ye cursed, into everlasting fire, prepared for the devil and his angels:

"For I was an hungred, and ye gave me no meat: I was thirsty, and ye gave me no drink:

"I was a stranger, and ye took me not in: naked, and ye clothed me not: sick, and in prison, and ye visited me not."

Then these, like the others, would be filled with surprise, and they would ask, "Lord, when saw we thee an hungred, or athirst, or a stranger, or naked, or sick, or in prison, and did not minister unto thee?"

Then would he answer them, Verily I say unto you, Inasmuch as ye did it not to one of the least of these, ye did it not to me."

And then these would go away into everlasting punishment, but the righteous into life eternal.

Judas among the Rulers.

Now the day for the feast of unleavened bread was close at hand; and the rulers of the city gathered together to talk the matter over, and to decide how they could go about it to kill Jesus. But they said it must not happen on the feast-day, for they feared there would be an uproar among the people.

The high priest that year was named Caiaphas, and it was at his house that these rulers had gathered. Most of them were Pharisees, but one among them was—ah, how can I say it?—a disciple of Jesus. Yes, it was Judas Iscariot.

You remember that he was a thief, and that he found fault with Mary for using the precious ointment so freely a short time before this. He had gone there to see what these wicked men would give him if he would betray his Master.

The men were glad when they heard his errand, and they promised to pay him thirty pieces of silver if he would deliver Jesus into their hands.

Never since the world began has a worse or more bitter crime been committed. It would have been far better if that man had never been born.

The rulers decided that it would be best to take Jesus as quietly as possible. Now that they had the promise Judas had made them, their minds were greatly relieved. And Judas left them.

What must have been the feelings that filled the heart of this disciple as he left the house of the high priest?

Alone with His Disciples.

—:—

WHEN the day arrived that they were to eat the Passover, the disciples came to Jesus, and asked him where he should like to have them go to prepare it.

Jesus told them that he would eat the Passover in Jerusalem, and that they might go there to prepare it.

He chose Peter and John to go, and said that soon after they entered the city a man bearing a pitcher of water would meet them. They were to go to this man, and tell him that the Master wished to eat the Passover at his house. Then the man would receive them kindly, and would give them a large upper room in which to prepare the feast.

Peter and John did just as Jesus told them to do, and found everything as he had told them they would. The man gladly gave them his best room.

And when all was ready, they sent for Jesus and the remainder of the Twelve, and they sat down together. When supper was thus prepared, Jesus rose, laid aside his long upper garment, and took a towel and girded himself.

Now, it was the custom of the people to wash their feet after having been out in the dusty roads. Jesus knew this, but that was not his reason for washing his disciples' feet. He wanted to teach them the great lesson of humility and love, and give them an example that they might follow.

When he had poured water into a basin, he began to wash each of his disciples' feet. Ah, what a humble place it was for Jesus to fill!

When he came to Peter and was about to wash his feet, Peter said, "Lord, dost thou wash my feet?" Jesus answered, "What I do, thou knowest not now; but thou shalt know hereafter."

Then Peter said, "Thou shalt never wash my feet"; but when Jesus said, "If I wash thee not, thou hast no part with me," Peter answered, "Lord, not my feet only, but also my hands and my head." Jesus told him that it was necessary to wash only his feet; for he was not washing them because they were dirty, but for the lesson he wished them to learn.

When their feet had all been washed, Jesus put on his garment and sat down again, and then explained to them the meaning of what he had done. He said: "Know ye what I have done to you? Ye call me Master and Lord: and ye say well; for so I am.

"If I then, your Lord and Master, have washed your feet, ye also ought to wash one another's feet.

"For I have given you an example, that ye should do as I have done to you.

"Verily, verily, I say unto you, The servant is not greater than his lord; neither he that is sent greater than he that sent him,

17

"If ye know these things, happy are ye if ye do them."

Jesus said this was a very solemn time to him. As it would be the last time they would have the privilege of sitting down together as they were then, he told them again of his love and of God's love.

Then Jesus spoke of the wicked deed that Judas was about to do, and said that he had told them what was to come to pass, that they might remember his words after the things had happened. Then he told them plainly that one of them would betray him.

The other disciples wondered whom he could mean, and one of them ventured to ask. Jesus answered, "He it is, to whom I shall give a sop, when I have dipped it. And when he had dipped the sop, he gave it to Judas Iscariot."

Judas at once rose to go; and Jesus said to him in a low voice, "That thou doest, do quickly."

How wretched Judas must have felt when Jesus said this. Still, he was the only one who knew his Master's meaning. The others saw him leave; but they supposed he was going out to buy something for the feast, or else to give something to the poor.

The Lord's Supper Instituted.

—:—

As soon as Judas had passed out, Jesus said, "Now is the Son of man glorified, and God is glorified in him." And then he called his disciples "little children," and said he was going to be with them only a little while longer. They would wonder many times, he said, where he had gone, and would seek him; but they would be unable to find him, for he was going back to heaven.

He told them that to be his true disciples after he was gone, they must love one another even as he had loved them. If they did this, all men would know they were his disciples.

Then, when he had taken bread and blessed it, he broke it in pieces, and handed a piece to each of his disciples, saying, "Take, eat; this is my body."

JESUS TEACHING HUMILITY.

259

And when he had taken the cup and had given thanks, he gave it to them, saying, "Drink ye all of it; for this is my blood of the new testament, which is shed for the remission of sins."

Jesus meant that the bread represented his body, which was soon to be slain for the people, and that the wine represented his blood, which he would shed on the cross.

He wanted them to understand just why he was slain, and to remember it for years after, or always, until he came back to this earth for them, when he would take them home with him to heaven.

And this is why the Lord's Supper is kept by God's people to-day—that they may keep in remembrance the time when the Lamb of God was slain, and remember him as their Passover.

It was never necessary after that day to offer a little lamb as a sacrifice to keep in remembrance the deliverance from the bondage of Egypt. The bondage of sin is what God's people are delivered from to-day, and it is through the death of Jesus that they are delivered.

Peter's Fall Foretold.

—:—

THEN Jesus said that it was written in the Bible, "I will smite the Shepherd, and the sheep of the flock shall be scattered abroad." This very night, he said, this scripture would be fulfilled. They would all be offended because of him, and would leave him to suffer alone.

But after all his suffering was over, he would return, and go before them into Galilee.

When Peter heard Jesus say this, he said, "Though all men shall be offended because of thee, yet will I never be offended." Jesus said to him, "Verily I say unto thee, That this night, before the cock crow, thou shalt deny me thrice." Peter answered, "Though I should die with thee, yet will I not deny thee." And the other disciples said the same thing.

Then Jesus said to Peter, "Satan hath desired to have you, that he may sift you as wheat: but I have prayed for thee, that thy faith fail not: and when thou art converted, strengthen thy brethren."

Peter could not understand why Jesus would say such things to him, and he answered, "Lord, I am ready to go with thee, both into prison, and to death." But Jesus wanted to prepare Peter for what was coming.

Then Jesus comforted his disciples by saying: "Let not your heart be troubled: ye believe in God, believe also in me. In my Father's house are many mansions: if it were not so, I would have told you. I go to prepare a place for you. And if I go and prepare a place for you, I will come again, and receive you unto myself; that where I am, there ye may be also. And whither I go ye know, and the way ye know."

Thomas said, "Lord, we know not whither thou goest, and how can we know the way?" Jesus replied, "I am the way, the truth, and the life." And then he explained many things to them. And he said: "If ye shall ask anything in my name, I will do it," and, "If ye love me, keep my commandments."

Prayer in the Name of Christ.

—:—

THE disciples had been taught to pray before this, and the prayer Jesus taught them is generally known as "The Lord's Prayer"; but now Jesus said that he was going to his Father in heaven, and that whatever they wanted, if they would ask the Father in his name, he would give it to them.

He said that until this time they had never asked anything in his name, but that now if they would ask, they should receive; for the Father, he said, loved them because they had loved his Son.

And he said, "I came forth from the Father, and am come into the world: again I leave the world, and go to the Father."

When Jesus had spoken thus, his disciples said that they believed they could understand his words now, and that they believed he had come from God.

Once more Jesus told them of the sorrows they would have to pass through, but said, "Be of good cheer; I have overcome the world," and then he prayed for them. That was really the Lord's prayer. It may be found in the seventeenth chapter of John.

After this they rose, and left the house where they had eaten the Passover, and went as usual to the Mount of Olives.

There was a garden on this mount, known as the Garden of Gethsemane. Jesus had often spent the night in this place, and it was here that Jesus now led his disciples.

The Midnight Agony.

—:—

WHEN they had come to the Garden of Gethsemane, Jesus told some of his disciples to sit down and rest while he went farther on to pray.

Three of the disciples, however, Jesus chose to go with him. They were Peter, James, and John, the same disciples that went up into Mount Hermon with him when he was transfigured before them.

Now that he was suffering so much, he felt that he should like to have these three with him. He said to them: "My soul is exceeding sorrowful, even unto death: tarry ye here, and watch with me. And pray that ye enter not into temptation."

Then "he went a little farther, and fell on his face, and prayed, saying, O my Father, if it be possible, let this cup pass from me: nevertheless, not as I will, but as thou wilt."

After a time he returned to the three disciples, but he did not find them watching. It was now very late in the night, and they who only a few hours before had been so willing to suffer anything for Jesus were so tired that they had fallen asleep.

He said to Peter, "What! could ye not watch with me one hour? Watch and pray, that ye enter not into temptation." Then he ex-

"O my Father, if it be possible, let this cup pass from me."

cused them by saying, "The spirit indeed is willing, but the flesh is weak," showing by this that he remembered that their bodies were very tired.

CHRIST IN GETHSEMANE.

Going away again, he prayed, "O my Father, if this cup may not pass away from me, except I drink it, thy will be done."

Then he came again, and finding them asleep, he went away the third time, and prayed the same words. And his agony became so great that his sweat was as it were great drops of blood falling down to the ground.

When he came to them the third time and found them sleeping, he said: "Sleep on now, and take your rest: behold, the hour is at hand, and the Son of man is betrayed into the hands of sinners. Rise up, let us go; lo, he that betrayeth me is at hand.''

All this time Judas had been plotting and planning with the Pharisees to find some way to betray his Master, and this had been one cause of the fearful suffering of Jesus. But the great cause was the awful weight of sin that was resting upon him. The sins of the whole world were pressing upon his soul. He had no sins of his own to bear; for he was holy, harmless, and undefiled.

Oh, how we ought to thank our heavenly Father for permitting his dear Son to suffer such things for us. It was the only way by which we could be saved from sin, and become pure, as was the first man, whom God formed and placed in the Garden of Eden.

Jesus is Made Prisoner.

—:—

WHEN Jesus came to his three disciples the third time, he saw not far away a multitude coming toward him. Jesus knew why they were coming, and he could have escaped as easily as he had done many times before; but the time had come for him to suffer, and he quietly stood still.

At the head of the multitude was one of the twelve disciples, even Judas, and he led them straight to the place where Jesus was. Now, the Pharisees did not know exactly which was Jesus; so for fear they would make a mistake, Judas had given them a sign. He had said, ''Whomsoever I shall kiss, that same is he; take him and lead him away safely.''

When they reached the place, Judas hurried forward, and going up to Jesus, he said, ''Hail, Master,'' as if he were very glad to see him. Then he kissed Jesus. Jesus called him ''friend,'' and said, ''Wherefore art thou come?''

What a sorrowful look Jesus must have given him! but all he said was, ''Judas, betrayest thou the Son of man with a kiss?'' Then the Pharisees came forward, and took Jesus as their prisoner.

The disciples who had been so overcome with sleep such a short time before were now fully awake. They saw what had happened to their beloved Master, and their hearts were filled with terror at the sight of the armed soldiers.

Now, Peter had a sword; and when he saw what had really taken place, he drew it, and cut off the right ear of the servant of the high priest.

When Jesus saw this, he was grieved; and he told Peter to put away his sword at once, and said, "Shall I not drink the cup which my Father hath given me?"

He also said: "Thinkest thou that I can not now pray to my Father, and he shall presently give me more than twelve legions of angels? But how then shall the Scriptures be fulfilled?"

"I was daily with you in the temple teaching," he said to those who had come to arrest him, "and ye took me not: but the Scriptures must be fulfilled."

Turning to the servant, whose name was Malchus, Jesus reached out his hand and touched the bleeding ear, and it was instantly healed. Even to the last, the works of Jesus were works of mercy and peace. Then the soldiers bound Jesus.

When the disciples saw that they were in danger of being taken also—what did they do? Did they stand by their loving Master? Ah, no! Every one of them fled. Even Peter, who had said he would never leave Jesus, but if necessary would die with him, and John, whom Jesus had loved more than the rest for his gentle and loving ways, ran with the others.

Jesus was then led back to the city of Jerusalem, to the house of Caiaphas the high priest. There the Pharisees and the chief men of the city were gathered together waiting to see what would happen.

JUDAS BETRAYING JESUS WITH A KISS.

Peter Denies His Master.

—:—

WHEN Peter saw that Jesus had really been taken, he no doubt remembered that he had said he would never leave Jesus, even if he were to die for him; still, he was too fearful in his heart to keep his promise.

THE DENIAL OF PETER.

But he did long to know how things were going, and what was to be done with Jesus; so he followed the crowd afar off.

Another disciple, who was probably John, followed also; and when they came to the high priest's house, they asked permission to go inside and warm themselves by the fire, for it was cold.

This other disciple was well known in the house of the high priest, while Peter was a stranger; but both were allowed to go inside.

As they entered, a damsel asked Peter whether he were one of those who had been with Jesus; but he said, "No; I am not."

Soon after this, as Peter was warming himself by the fire, another one of the maids saw him; and when she came to the place where he was, she asked him whether he were not one of those who had followed Jesus of Nazareth. But he denied it again, and said, "I know not, neither understand I what thou sayest."

After a while some who had heard him speak before said to him, "Surely thou also art one of them; for thy speech betrayeth thee. Thou art a Galilean."

Then a relative of Malchus', the high priest's servant, asked, "Did not I see thee in the garden with him?" When Peter heard this, he answered angrily that he knew nothing of what they were talking.

Just then he heard a cock crow. At once he remembered the words of Jesus—that before the cock crowed he would three times deny his Master. He then looked toward the place where Jesus was standing, and saw that Jesus had turned around and was looking at him.

What must have been Peter's thoughts then? We know that his heart was filled with sorrow, for he went out and wept bitterly.

Poor Peter! his repentance was sincere and lasting. He had not denied his Master from any such reason as had prompted Judas.

Jesus freely forgave Peter, and made him strong and very useful in his service afterwards.

But what about Judas? Did he become sorry? Ah, yes! But you shall hear about him later.

Jesus before the Council.

As soon as possible after the arrest of Jesus, the council met, and tried to find such false testimony against Jesus as would warrant putting him to death; but they found none.

Many were willing to act as false witnesses, but they did not agree with one another.

The high priest then asked Jesus of his disciples and of his doctrine. "Jesus answered him, I spake openly to the world; I ever taught in the synagogue, and in the temple whither the Jews always resort; and in secret have I said nothing. Why askest thou me? ask them which heard me, what I have said unto them: behold, they know what I said.

"And when he had thus spoken, one of the officers which stood by struck Jesus with the palm of his hand, saying, Answerest thou the high priest so? Jesus answered him, If I have spoken evil, bear witness of the evil: but if well, why smitest thou me?"

Now Jesus was still bound. Then how very unkind and cruel it was for them to strike him; but Jesus did not resent it. He felt no anger toward them.

After a long time they found two false witnesses who seemed to agree on the same thing. You know a witness is one who has seen or heard another do or say something, and he simply tells what it was.

These witnesses said that they had heard Jesus say, "I am able to destroy the temple of God, and to build it again in three days." But even they did not perfectly agree in the matter.

All this time Jesus had remained quiet, and made no answers to the charges brought against him.

The high priest wondered very much at this, and he asked Jesus what he had to say for himself; but Jesus still remained silent. This was very displeasing to the high priest, for he had hoped that whatever Jesus would say might in some way be turned against him. So he asked Jesus a question that required an answer.

He said, "Art thou the Christ, the Son of God?" Jesus answered, "I am: and ye shall see the Son of man sitting on the right hand of power, and coming in the clouds of heaven."

When the priest heard Jesus say this, he asked the people what they thought of his words; and because they considered them to be blasphemous, they said he was worthy of death.

The great council of the chief priests and elders had now con-demned Jesus to death; but still other steps must be taken before they would dare kill him. The Roman governor, Pontius Pilate, had to be consulted.

Then those soldiers and servants who were standing about began to spit in the face of Jesus; and when they had covered his eyes, they struck him with their hands, saying, "Prophesy unto us, thou Christ, Who is he that smote thee?"

As soon as possible in the morning Jesus was led away to the hall of judgment to appear before Pilate.

Jesus before Pilate.

—:—

THE chief priests and Pharisees would not enter the judgment-hall with Jesus; but remained outside for fear of being "defiled," and thus made unfit to eat the Passover. They were very particular about observing outward forms and ceremonies, but in their hearts they were far from God.

When Pilate saw that a prisoner had been brought, he went out-side and asked the people what they had to say.

They had nothing to bring against Jesus that would make him worthy of death according to the law of the Romans; so they said he was a malefactor, or evil-doer, and was worthy of death.

Then Pilate said, "Take him and judge him according to your law." But the Jews answered, "It is not lawful for us to put any man to death."

Pilate returned to the hall where Jesus was, and asked him, "Art thou the King of the Jews?"

Jesus asked Pilate how he happened to ask him this question, and inquired whether some one had not told him to ask it. Pilate answered, "Am I a Jew? Thine own nation and the chief priests have delivered thee unto me: what hast thou done?"

Then Jesus answered, "My kingdom is not of this world: if my kingdom were of this world, then would my servants fight, that I should not be delivered to the Jews: but now is my kingdom not from hence.

"Pilate therefore said unto him, Art thou a king then? Jesus answered, Thou sayest that I am a king. To this end was I born, and for this cause came I into the world, that I should bear witness unto the truth. Every one that is of the truth heareth my voice.

PERSECUTING JESUS.

"Pilate saith unto him, What is truth? And when he had said this, he went out again unto the Jews, and saith unto them, I find in him **no fault at all.**"

The Pharisees became more fierce than ever when they heard these words from Pilate, and they said, "He stirreth up the people, teaching throughout Jewry, beginning from Galilee to this place."

Pilate asked whether Jesus was a Galilean; and when the people said yes, he at once sent him to King Herod, who was the ruler of Galilee, and who happened to be at Jerusalem at that time.

Now, Herod had long wished to see Jesus; for he had heard many things about the wonderful miracles which he did, and he hoped that at this time he might see him perform some miracle. But Jesus would not work any miracles to please the curiosity of a wicked man, neither would he answer the questions Herod asked him.

When Herod saw this, he and his men mocked Jesus; and when they had put a purple robe upon him, such as was worn by kings, he sent him back to Pilate.

Herod and Pilate had been enemies, but through the trial of Jesus they became friends again.

Pilate's Wife Has a Dream.

—:—

After King Herod had sent Jesus back to Pilate, the chief priests and rulers of the Jews were called together. And Pilate said to them: "Ye have brought this man unto me, as one that perverteth the people; and behold, I, having examined him before you, have found no fault in him concerning those things whereof ye accuse him. No, nor yet Herod: for I sent you to him; and lo, nothing worthy of death is done unto him."

Pilate really wished to release Jesus, because of a dream which his wife had. The dream had troubled her very much, and she had sent a message to her husband, saying, "Have thou nothing to do with that just man: for I have suffered many things this day in a dream because of him."

Pilate said that if it were necessary he would chastise or punish him, but that he did not want to put him to death.

Now, it was a custom of the Jews that every year at the feast of the Passover one prisoner should be set free, and the people had the right of choosing who it should be. Pilate reminded them of this custom, and asked whether it would not be all right to release Jesus.

When they heard this, they cried out all at once, "Away with this man, and release unto us Barabbas."

Now, Barabbas was a murderer and a robber. This, Pilate knew, and he also knew that the Jews had no just accusation to bring against Jesus; so he asked, "What will ye then that I shall do unto him whom ye call the King of the Jews?" Then the horrible cry arose, "Crucify him, crucify him!"

As soon as the crowd of people became quiet, Pilate asked, "Why, what evil hath he done?" But they cried out louder than before, "Crucify him!"

The Sentence.

—:—

PILATE from the first had been unwilling to say that Jesus must die; but he was afraid of the fierce crowd around him that was screaming those terrible words: "Crucify him, crucify him!"

Again he tried to persuade them to let Jesus go free, but they demanded that he give them Barabbas. They would rather endure suffering from the hand of that wicked murderer than spare the life of one who never did any sin and whose deeds were all deeds of kindness and love.

When Pilate saw that they were determined to put Jesus to death, he told them that they must bear all the blame. This they said they would gladly do, and then Pilate washed his hands as a sign that he was free from all guilt in the matter—but was he?

Ah! he was not innocent in God's sight, and his actions were those of a coward.

When Pilate delivered Jesus to them, he said, "Behold your king." But the people cried out: "Away with him, crucify him. We have no king but Cæsar." Then Jesus was delivered into their hands.

PILATE WASHING HIS HANDS.

They now had Jesus, and also the power to do all the wicked things that they had often longed to do. God permitted it, because it was necessary that Jesus should die, that through the shedding of his precious blood the way of salvation might be opened for all the people in the world.

When the Pharisees really had Jesus in their power, they did many things to make him suffer.

After his back had been made bare, and he had been scourged, the soldiers who had charge of him replaced the purple robe that Herod had put on him. Then when they had made a crown out of thorns, they placed it upon his head, and mocked him by saying, "Hail, King of the Jews!" and many struck him with their hands. Oh, how shameful to treat God's righteous Servant, our loving Redeemer, in this way! but these evil men had hearts like stone. They had no pity for Jesus. They hated him because they were wicked, and he was good.

Another Scene.

About the time when the soldiers were mocking Jesus, another terrible event was taking place not far off.

When the chief priests and elders had gained the consent of Pilate to crucify Jesus, they left the judgment-hall; but the matter was so on their minds that they met in the temple to talk it over.

All at once some one appeared before them. It was Judas the traitor. Oh, how wretched he was! He could now fully realize what he had done, and his heart was filled with terror. How he wished that he could undo the wicked deed he had committed so short a time before.

He had heard that they had condemned Jesus to death, and now he had sought for the Pharisees, to see whether they would not change their plans; but it was too late.

He could see their hard looks; yet he ventured to say, "I have

JUDAS TRYING TO UNDO THE WRONG HE HAD DONE.

277

sinned in that I have betrayed innocent blood." But they harshly answered, "What is that to us? see thou to that."

The last time Judas had stood before them, he had come to bargain for the sum of money he was to receive if he would betray his Master. And he had agreed to do the terrible deed for thirty pieces of silver. This was about equal to fifteen dollars and thirty cents. Now this money that he had once coveted so greedily had become hateful to him. He could not even bear the sight of it.

So he threw it down upon the floor in front of the chief priest, and then went away and hanged himself.

Poor Judas! He had added another terrible deed to the one already committed. He had taken the life which he considered his own, but which really belonged to God.

How much better it would have been had he hastened to Jesus, and begged him to forgive him, even though he could not undo the harm he had done! He had heard his Master say, "Him that cometh to me I will in no wise cast out," and, "Come unto me, all ye that labor and are heavy laden, and I will give you rest."

Although Judas was sorry for his evil deeds, yet he did not love Jesus, and that was why he would not go to him.

When Judas had gone away, and the Pharisees saw the money still lying there, they took it up, and wondered what they could do with it. They could not put it in the treasury, because it was the price of blood. But when they had talked the matter over, they decided to buy with it some ground in which to bury strangers. They therefore bought the potter's field, and it was always spoken of as "The field of blood."

One of the prophets had years before prophesied that all this should happen. He had said: "They weighed for my price thirty pieces of silver. And the Lord said unto me, Cast it unto the potter: a goodly price that I was priced at of them. And I took the thirty pieces of silver, and cast them to the potter in the house of the Lord."

DEATH OF THE BE-TRAY-ER JU-DAS IS-CAR-I-OT.

279

Bearing His Cross.

—:—

THERE was no time lost by the Pharisees after Pilate had given them permission to crucify Jesus. After placing a crown of thorns on his head, and putting a reed or wand in his hand, they mocked him by calling him king of the Jews. Then they took the purple robe off him, and dressed him in his own clothing, and led him away to a place called Golgotha or Calvary.

Now, Jesus had eaten nothing since he had eaten the last supper with his disciples. Since then, think of the suffering he had endured—first in the Garden of Gethsemane, where his sweat was as great drops of blood; then the suffering before the high priests, as well as before King Herod, and then Pilate's scourging. After all this he was commanded to carry his own cross, upon which he was going to be crucified. Was it strange that he sank beneath that heavy load?

When Jesus sank to the ground under the heavy weight of the cross, they laid hold of a man named Simon, who had just come from the country, and made him carry it the rest of the way.

Among the crowd of people who followed were many women; and when they saw Jesus fall, they wept loudly. Jesus heard them, and turning toward them, he said, "Weep not for me, but weep for yourselves, and for your children." For many troubles, he said, were to come upon them, and they would even wish they had never been born.

Jesus knew that God would send a fearful punishment upon the people for their cruel treatment of his beloved Son.

When they had reached Golgotha, some one gave Jesus vinegar and gall to drink. This seems to have been for the purpose of deadening pain; but when he had tasted, he refused to drink it.

Jesus had often spoken to his disciples about bearing the cross. He did not simply mean a cross of wood; for there were many other things that might come upon them fully as hard to bear as the cross that Jesus bore. They were to be willing to bear just as patiently as he was bearing his trials now any suffering that might come upon them.

We all have a cross to bear. Let us bear it in the right way.

CHRIST CAR-RY-ING HIS CROSS.

The Crucifixion.

—:—

At last they came to the place where Jesus was to be crucified. This place was called both Golgotha and Calvary, and it was only a little way from Jerusalem.

Then came the sad and terrible scene of the crucifixion. They placed the dear, patient Jesus upon the cross, and drove great nails through his hands and feet, so that he would hang upon it until he died. Oh, the agony he must have suffered! And, dear children, he bore all that pain for you, and for every one who would believe that he was God's Son.

Two men who had been condemned to die, were led out to be crucified with Jesus. They, too, were nailed to crosses, just as Jesus had been—one at his right hand and the other at his left.

But these were bad men. They were thieves, who were being put to death for the wicked things they had done; while Jesus was innocent, never having done anything wrong.

Now, persons who were crucified did not die quickly; they sometimes lived for many hours after they were nailed to the cross.

While Jesus was hanging upon the cross, and suffering such bitter pain many of the Pharisees walked past him, repeating all the hard things they had said before.

Some said, "Ah, thou that destroyest the temple, and buildest it in three days, save thyself, and come down from the cross."

Others said: "He saved others; let him save himself, if he be the chosen one of God. Let Christ, the King of Israel, descend from the cross, that we may see and believe."

Now, Pilate had written a title, and placed it above the head of Jesus upon his cross. The writing was, "JESUS OF NAZARETH, THE KING OF THE JEWS."

The Jews were not at all pleased with the writing, for it called him really their king. Some of them went to Pilate, and said, "Write not, The king of the Jews; but that he said, I am the King of the Jews." But Pilate would not change what he had written.

THE CRU-CI-FIX-ION   283

This title was not only written so that the Jews could read it, but written in three different languages, which were the Greek, the Latin, and the Hebrew. In this way all present might be able to read it, and know that this was the King for whom they had looked, and might note the treatment he was receiving.

The soldiers were obliged to stay and watch until the end came. While they were waiting, they sat down and divided among themselves Jesus' clothes.

His loose outer garment was divided into four parts. But his under garment was made in one piece, and it could not be divided. So they said, "Let us not rend it, but cast lots for it, whose it shall be."

Many years before, King David had prophesied that they should do this. He had said, "They parted my garments among them, and cast lots upon my vesture."

The Penitent Thief.

THE thieves who were being crucified with Jesus, heard the many bitter remarks that were made by the Pharisees. These remarks made an impression upon them both, but in different ways.

One of them repeated some of the words he had heard. "If," said he, "thou be the Christ, save thyself and us." What a remark for one to make who had such a short time to live!

The other thief, when he heard the remark, wondered how any one in their condition could speak so, and he said, "Dost not thou fear God, seeing thou art in the same condemnation?"

And he reminded him of their past lives, which had been so sinful, and said that they deserved their punishment, but that Jesus had never done anything amiss.

Then turning to Jesus, he said, "Lord, remember me when thou comest into thy kingdom."

Jesus was glad when he heard the poor man speak in this way.

His answer was so precious—"Verily I say unto thee, To-day shalt thou be with me in paradise." He had not replied to any of the other questions asked him, but instead prayed that God would forgive those who asked them.

Perhaps this alone convinced the thief that Jesus was really the King, and that if so, his kingdom must be somewhere. It certainly did not seem to be there. Then, perhaps he had listened to Jesus when he had been teaching the people in the past.

But whatever the thief had seen or heard, he now believed that Jesus was God's Son and his Savior.

Looking down from the cross, Jesus saw his own dear mother. Oh, how she must have been suffering! Others had come with her, that they might be with Jesus until the very last. Among these was the disciple whom Jesus had always loved so much. The Bible does not tell his name, but we believe it was John.

When Jesus saw this disciple, he looked at his mother, and said, "Woman, behold thy son!" and to the disciple he said, "Behold thy mother!" "And from that hour that disciple took her unto his own home."

Then it suddenly grew dark, and there was darkness everywhere for several hours.

The Death of Jesus.

—:—

As the awful hours rolled on, which were increasing the sufferings of Jesus, it seemed to him at last that even God had forsaken him. In his agony he cried out, "My God, my God, why hast thou forsaken me?" What must have been his sufferings in both mind and body? No one can ever picture them as they were. But they were nearly ended.

Some one, seeing how much he was suffering, held to his mouth a sponge which had been dipped in vinegar, and he drank.

When Jesus had received the vinegar, he said, "It is finished"; and he bowed his head, and died.

"What was finished?" do you ask? God's plan of salvation was finished. Jesus, the Lamb of God, had become the sacrifice for sin. Through his death every one might be saved; and more than that, he had promised his disciples that when all was finished, he would go to heaven, and would send a Comforter, or Holy Spirit, that would teach them, and keep them from feeling like committing sin.

Jesus did as he had promised, as you will soon see.

But we first must find out what happened at the time Jesus died. There were terrible sounds all around. The earth opened in places, and rocks were broken in pieces; graves were opened, and many who had died before this time were awakened, and arose after the resurrection of Jesus.

But the strangest thing that happened was that the vail of the temple which hung in front of the holiest place, was torn from top to bottom.

From the time of Moses until the death of Jesus it had not been lawful for any one to enter this part of the temple, except the high priest when he went to offer sacrifices for the people, and even then his life was in danger.

But now Jesus had been offered up as a sacrifice for the sins of the people, and God was going to set up his altar in men's hearts.

By the death of Jesus, then, the old Jewish law passed away, together with the awful curse of sin that had rested upon all mankind from the time of Adam. Jesus took all this load of sin upon himself, in order that all who truly repented and believed it would be as pure and free from sin as Adam was when God created him. In this way Jesus became the Savior of the world.

When those who were standing around saw all that happened at the death of Jesus, many said, "Truly this man was the Son of God."

The Burial.

—:—

ON account of the next day being the Sabbath, it was thought best not to let the bodies remain on the cross over night. For this reason the

THE BURIAL OF JESUS.

Pharisees sent to Pilate to know whether they might hasten death by breaking the legs of those on the cross, and whether they might take the bodies away.

Having gained Pilate's consent, they returned; and the soldiers broke the legs of the thieves who had been crucified with Jesus.

When they came to Jesus, they found that he was dead already, and they did not break his legs. But one of the soldiers pierced his side, and there came out a stream of blood and water.

There was a prophecy in the Bible about this treatment of the body of Jesus. It read thus: "A bone of him shall not be broken." And in another place it read, "They shall look on him whom they pierced."

And then came the preparation for the burial of Jesus.

Among the Pharisees were two men that had not consented to the death of Jesus; but they were not able to prevent the fierce crowd from doing the wicked deed.

One of these was Joseph of Arimathea. He was a good man, and was looking for the kingdom of God. He had been convinced through the sermons of Jesus of what this kingdom was; and although he had been unable to save the life of Jesus, he determined to see that he was at least properly buried.

He was a brave man; but for fear that the Jews would overthrow his plans, he went quietly to Pilate, and asked that he might take the body down from the cross and bury it.

Pilate was surprised when he heard that Jesus was dead, and he sent a soldier to see if it were really true. When he learned that Jesus was dead, he gave the body to Joseph, who carefully took it down from the cross, and wrapped it in a clean linen cloth.

The other Pharisee that did not consent to the death of Jesus, was Nicodemus. This was the same man that had gone to Jesus one night about three years before to learn of him the way of salvation. He had not forgotten the words spoken to him that night; and although he did not have the courage to boldly follow him in life, he now wished to help Joseph bury his body.

Nicodemus brought a mixture of costly spices and ointment, for he longed to do something to show his respect.

There was a garden close by, where a new tomb had been made.

The tomb had never been used to bury any one in, so here they carried the body of Jesus, and laid it away carefully.

The tomb had been cut in the side of a great rock, in which there was but one opening, and against this opening or door they rolled a large stone.

There were two women who watched carefully to see where Jesus would be buried. These were Mary Magdalene and Mary, the mother of Joses, who was one of the disciples of Jesus.

When all was done that they could do, they returned home to prepare for the Sabbath; but the women intended to return early on Sunday morning, as soon as the Sabbath had ended. Their laws were very strict concerning the seventh day, which was the Sabbath; and all the Jews were expected to observe them.

How sad must this Sabbath have been to the disciples in Jerusalem, and to the three friends of Jesus in Bethany. Jesus had told them all many times before about his betrayal and his cruel death; but it had seemed hard for them to realize that what he told them would ever be true. They could not understand why such things would ever have to take place.

Now it had happened just as Jesus had said, and they were left alone. Jesus would never deliver them from the hands of the Romans, as some of them had once hoped; but he would deliver them from a greater bondage—from one to whom they had been slaves for hundreds of years. That one was Satan.

The Tomb is Guarded.

—:—

JESUS had many times spoken of rising from the dead on the third day, but the disciples had never paid much attention to the words. If they remembered them now, it was with little thought that any such thing would come to pass.

The Pharisees, however, remembered very clearly what Jesus had said; so they hurried away to Pilate, and said: "Sir, we remember

that that deceiver said, while he was yet alive, After three days I will rise again. Command therefore that the sepulcher be made sure until the third day, lest his disciples come by night, and steal him away, and say unto the people, He is risen from the dead: so the last error shall be worse than the first.''

Pilate gave them permission, and said, ''Ye have a watch: go your way, make it as sure as ye can.''

So they went and closed up the tomb so that no person could enter or go out of the tomb without breaking the seal. They also placed a guard of soldiers around the tomb, to prevent any one from coming near it.

When the Pharisees felt that all had been done that was necessary to keep the body of Jesus in the tomb, they went away to their homes.

But what happened that night? ''Behold, there was a great earthquake; for the angel of the Lord descended from heaven, and came and rolled back the stone from the door, and sat upon it. His countenance was like lightning, and his raiment white as snow. And for fear of him the keepers did shake, and became as dead men.''

The mocking crowd had told Jesus to come down from the cross if he were really the Christ, as he said he was; but Jesus was suffering that shame for a purpose. Now the time had come for him to rise from the grave, and no man could have any more power over his body.

○✸○✸○✸○

Morning of the Resurrection.

—:—

Very early in the morning of the first day of the week, after the Sabbath was past, the women that had watched where they buried Jesus, returned to the tomb. They brought sweet spices with them, expecting to anoint the body of him whom they loved so well, and thereby show their respect and affection.

They knew nothing of the soldiers that had been placed at the tomb, nor of the angel that had appeared to them. Neither did they know that they would not find the body of Jesus within the tomb where it had been left.

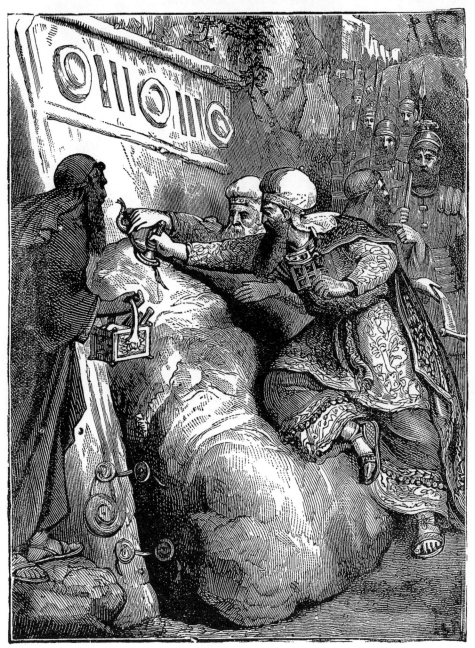

SEALING THE TOMB.

Some of their friends were with them. On the way they began to wonder who would roll away the stone for them; but when they reached the place, they found that the stone had already been removed.

The angel was still there; and when the women saw him, they were frightened. But the angel said to them: "Be not affrighted: ye seek Jesus of Nazareth, which was crucified: he is not here: for he is risen, as he said. Come, see the place where the Lord lay. And go quickly, and tell his disciples that he is risen from the dead; and, behold, he goeth before you into Galilee; there ye shall see him: lo, I have told you."

This was indeed a wonderful message. The hearts of the women were full of joy at the prospect of once more seeing Jesus. But they were still trembling from fear.

As they were hurrying away from the sepulcher to tell the disciples, behold, Jesus met them. And he said in his old familiar voice, "All hail."

Mary Magdalene had been so anxious to see the body of Jesus again that she had gone very early, and ahead of the rest, to the tomb. It was still dark when she reached the place.

When she saw that the tomb was empty, and that Jesus was not there, her heart was full of grief; for she supposed that some one had taken the body away. She did not pay any attention, if she heard the words of the angel. But she might not have heard them then.

With a sorrowful heart she left the place, and went as quickly as possible to find Peter and John. She told them that the Lord had been taken away from the tomb, and that they could not find where he had been laid.

When they heard this, Peter and John ran at once to the tomb; but when they reached it, they found things just as Mary had said. They saw the linen clothes, and the napkin that had been wrapped about his head; but the body was gone.

All at once they remembered what Jesus had said about rising from the dead on the third day, and they believed that his words had

been fulfilled.　With thankful hearts they hurried back to tell the rest of the disciples.

JESUS REVEALS HIMSELF TO MARY.

　　Mary had returned to the tomb as soon as possible, and she stood at the door, weeping.　She did not go inside, but she stooped down and looked inside.　What a sight she saw!　There were two beautiful angels dressed in white.   One was sitting where the head and the other where the feet of Jesus had lain.

They spoke to her and said, "Woman, why weepest thou?"   She answered, "Because they have taken away my Lord, and I know not where they have laid him."

Mary did not wait to hear their answer, but turned around toward the garden.   There she saw a man standing.   He asked her the same question that the angels had asked.

Supposing that he was the gardner, she answered his question by saying, "Sir, if thou have borne him hence, tell me where thou hast laid him, and I will take him away."

This man whom she was speaking to was none other than Jesus for whom she was looking; but she did not know him.

Jesus wanted to say something which would be comforting and which would show her that he was not dead, but alive.   But one word was enough.

"Mary!" said Jesus.   And she knew at once that it was Jesus who spoke to her.   "Master!" she exclaimed, and threw herself at his feet, and worshiped him; but he told her to go and tell the disciples that she had seen him.

Other Things that Happened.

—:—

Now what do you suppose the soldiers did after they found that Jesus had really left the tomb, and that they had no power over him any longer?   Part of them went to the city, and told the Pharisees all that had happened.

The Pharisees called a meeting at once; and when the matter was talked over carefully, they decided that the best thing to do was to say very little about what had taken place.

They told the soldiers that they would pay them a large sum of money if they would tell the people a lie.   This was that his disciples had come to the tomb at night and had stolen the body of Jesus while they (the soldiers) were asleep.

The soldiers took the money, and did as they had agreed to do. And many believed that it was true; that is, the enemies of Jesus believed it was true, but those who loved him knew very well that the soldiers' report was false.

THE ANGEL AT THE TOMB.

In the afternoon of the same day that Jesus rose, two of his disciples were walking toward the village of Emmaus. This place was about six miles from Jerusalem.

As they walked along, they were very sorrowful. They had heard the report that Mary Magdalene had brought, and then the many other reports; but it was so hard to believe that Jesus had really risen.

As they were trying to decide how the matter could be, a stranger caught up with them. This stranger was really Jesus, but they did not recognize him.

CHRIST WITH THE TWO DISCIPLES.

He appeared to be going in the same direction, and he soon began to talk with them, and he asked why they were so sad. They were surprised that even a stranger had not heard of the death of Jesus; but as he did not seem to know, they told him all that had happened.

The stranger listened to them for some time in silence, and then he began to talk to them in a wonderful way. He explained to them all that had been written in the Bible about the Messiah, and how, long before, the prophets had said he would have to die for the sins

of the people.   And he said, "Ought not Christ to have suffered these things, and to enter into his glory?"

By this time they had reached the village of Emmaus, and the stranger seemed to be going farther; but the disciples had received such comfort from his words that they invited him to remain with them over night.

He yielded to their wishes, and agreed to share their evening meal, which they were soon ready to eat.

Jesus took up the bread, and when he had blessed it, he broke it in pieces as he had so often done before, and then it seemed as though their eyes were opened.   They knew that this stranger was really none other than their beloved Master.   But just as they realized who it was, he vanished from their sight.

And they remembered how they had enjoyed hearing him talk to them on the way, and they rose, and hurried back to Jerusalem to tell the other disciples.

When they reached Jerusalem, they found that the disciples there were rejoicing also.   Jesus had appeared to Peter, and they were still talking about it.   As they continued to talk, they suddenly saw that Jesus was standing in their midst; and he said, "Peace be unto you."

They were at first very much frightened; but Jesus told them not to be afraid, but to come and feel his hands and his feet.   To convince them still more of the reality of his physical resurrection, he ate some food in their presence.

Then they were glad; and Jesus reminded them that he had often said these things were going to happen, but that they did not understand them.   But now his words were fulfilled, and they could not help believing them.

He told them that they must now go and preach to the people in all parts of the world, and tell them to enter the kingdom of God. He said that they must begin at Jerusalem, and that every nation in the world must hear the good news; and "he that believeth not," Jesus added, "shall be damned."

Then he said: "Peace be unto you: as my Father hath sent me,

even so have I sent you. And these signs shall follow them that believe; In my name shall they cast out devils; they shall speak with
new tongues; they shall take up serpents; and if they drink any deadly
thing, it shall not hurt them; they shall lay hands on the sick, and
they shall recover.''

He then told them to wait there at Jerusalem until they received
power from on high; for they should receive the Holy Ghost, who
would guide them, and teach them what to do and say.

What Thomas Said.

—:—

ALL the disciples except two had seen Jesus. These were: Judas
the traitor, who had hanged himself; and Thomas, who was not with
the others when Jesus came.

When the other disciples again saw Thomas, they said, ''We have
seen the Lord.'' But he would not believe them. He thought they
must have been mistaken, and he said, ''Except I shall see in his
hands the print of the nails, and put my finger into the print of the
nails, and thrust my hand into his side, I will not believe.''

Nothing of importance happened until a week had passed. Then
while they were all gathered together in a room by themselves, Thomas
being present this time, Jesus once more appeared in their midst.
The doors had all been shut as before, and just as suddenly as the
other time Jesus stood before them, and said, ''Peace be unto you.''

Jesus at once looked over at Thomas, for he knew Thomas had
doubted what the other disciples had said. Jesus told him to come
near him, and then said, ''Reach hither thy finger, and behold my
hands; and reach hither thy hand, and thrust it into my side; and be
not faithless, but believing.'' Thomas did not doubt any longer, but
said, ''My Lord, and my God!''

Jesus said, ''Thomas, because thou hast seen me, thou hast believed: blessed are they that have not seen, and yet have believed.''

DOUBTING THOMAS.

The Disciples Go Fishing.

—:—

ONE evening some time after Thomas had seen Jesus, some of the disciples decided to go fishing. Peter was the first to propose it;

"IT IS THE LORD."

for he said, "I go a fishing." Six others said they would go with him, and it was not long until they were out in a boat upon the Sea of Tiberias.

They had a net to fish with, for in those days that was the principal way of fishing. It was not a good night for fishing; and when morning came, they had caught nothing.

Just as it began to get light enough to see, they saw a man standing on the shore not far from them. He called out to them, "Children, have ye any meat?" and they answered, "No."

Then the man on the shore said that if they would cast their net on the other side of the boat, they would find fish. This they did, and they caught so many fish in the net that it seemed ready to break.

Until then the disciples did not know that it was Jesus who was talking to them; but when John saw the multitude of fishes, he said to Peter, "It is the Lord."

They were not far from the shore, and they landed as quickly as possible, dragging the great net of fishes. Peter, however, could not wait for the rest; so he jumped into the sea, and swam ashore.

When they reached the land, they drew out the net, and counted their fish. They had one hundred and fifty-three; and though there were so many, yet the net was not broken.

They found a fire of coals, and fish laid upon it, and also some bread. And Jesus said for them to come and dine with him. It was a solemn meal that they ate.

When the meal was over, Jesus turned to Peter, and said, "Simon, son of Jonas, lovest thou me more than these?"

Perhaps Jesus wanted to remind him of one evening not very long before this, when Peter told Jesus that he loved him so well that he would give his life for him if necessary; but when in the midnight hour, he, with the rest of the disciples, left their Master in the hands of the soldiers.

But Peter had suffered much on account of his actions then, and had been very sorry. He was more humble now, and realized his own weakness, and said nothing about loving Jesus more than the other disciples did. He only answered, "Yea, Lord; thou knowest that I love thee." Jesus said to him, "Feed my lambs."

Then, a second time, Jesus asked the same question; and Peter answered, "Lord, thou knowest that I love thee." Jesus said again, "Feed my sheep."

Once more Jesus asked the question. Peter was grieved that he should think it necessary to ask the question three times; but it was three times that Peter had denied Jesus. The third time Peter answered Jesus, he said, "Lord, thou knowest all things; thou knowest that I love thee." And once more Jesus said kindly, "Feed my sheep."

And then he said, "Verily, verily, I say unto thee, When thou wast young, thou girdedst thyself, and walkedst whither thou wouldest: but when thou shalt be old, thou shalt stretch for thy hands, and another shall gird thee, and carry thee whither thou wouldest not."

Jesus was speaking of what was to happen to Peter in the future. He had a great work for Peter to do, and he said to him, "Follow me." Three years before, Peter had heard these same words, and he had risen, and left all to follow the meek and lowly Jesus. Now again he heard the call of his Master, and all through the remainder of his life he tried to follow in the footsteps of the Lord, until at the last he even gave up his life upon a cross.

When Peter rose to follow Jesus, after he had listened to what the Lord had said concerning his work and death, he noticed one of the other disciples following them. This was the one who had always been so dear to Jesus on account of his faithfulness and his loving acts. Jesus had not just at this time said to the other disciples, "Follow me," and so Peter wondered, and asked what would happen to this disciple. In answer Jesus said, "If I will that he tarry till I come, what is that to thee? follow thou me."

"Then went this saying abroad among the brethren, that that disciple should not die: yet Jesus said not unto him, He shall not die; but, If I will that he tarry till I come, what is that to thee?"

Carried up into Heaven.

AFTER this the eleven disciples went into Galilee to a certain mountain where Jesus had appointed to meet them, and he met them there. About five hundred other disciples were there.

Jesus told them that God had given him all power, both in heaven

JESUS ASCENDING INTO HEAVEN.

303

and on earth.   Once more he told them to go out and teach people everywhere the way to be saved from their sins, and how to get to heaven.

He commanded them to baptize the people in the name of the Father, and of the Son, and of the Holy Ghost.

Jesus told them to teach all that he had taught them, and to remember all the things he had commanded them to do; and he promised that he would always be with them, even to the end of the world.

Once after this, Jesus appeared to James, and then to all the apostles while they were in Jerusalem.

The last thing he did was to lead them up on the Mount of Olives as far as Bethany.   Here, with uplifted hands, he blessed them, after which he was carried up into heaven, and a cloud received him out of their sight.

"And while they looked steadfastly toward heaven as he went up, behold, two men stood by them in white apparel; which also said, Ye men of Galilee, why stand ye gazing up into heaven? this same Jesus, which is taken up from you into heaven, shall so come in like manner as ye have seen him go into heaven."

They were filled with great joy at the thought, and they returned to Jerusalem to await the coming of the Holy Spirit.   They rejoiced, knowing that their Lord had conquered death, and had made it possible for every one to be saved from sin and to live a pure and holy life here, and then after this world passed away, might dwell with and serve God forever.

The Story of the Apostles.

—:—

AFTER Jesus had ascended into heaven, the disciples all returned to Jerusalem to wait there for "the promise of the Father."   They would often meet in an upper room, where they spent the time in prayer and praise to God.

Often many others met with them, among whom was Mary, the

mother of Jesus, and even some of his brethren. They loved to meet and wait on the Lord together in earnest prayer.

One day there were about one hundred and twenty persons in this happy company. After they had been together some time Peter stood up and began to talk to them. He spoke of one of their number who was not with them, and who never would be with them again. That was the wicked Judas, who had been a guide to those who took Jesus.

He also spoke of what had happened at the death of Judas. The thing, however, that was most upon his mind was the importance of choosing some one to fill this disciple's place—some one who would be ready to go out with them to preach to the people. He quoted two verses from the Psalms of King David, where this very thing had been spoken of. It was this: "Let his habitation be desolate, and let no man dwell therein: and his bishopric [office] let another take." The first part of this had come to pass in the death and burial-place of Judas, and now the last part was to be fulfilled.

Peter said he believed that the Lord would be pleased to have them choose some one of the men who had traveled with them ever since the time when John baptized Jesus in the river Jordan until the day he ascended into heaven.

The disciples were willing to do this; so they chose two men— Joseph called Barsabas and Matthias. But the disciples wanted God to decide which of these two should be the apostle. So when they had prayed, they cast lots, and asked God to choose for them. The lot fell to Matthias, and he was numbered with the eleven apostles.

It was right that they should seek God's direction in this matter, for it was part of God's work. It is also well for us to look earnestly to God for guidance in moral and religious matters, and even in other things when we have any duty before us that seems difficult or hard. We might think that we knew what was best and right to do, but we do not always know. God alone can direct us aright. Therefore let us ask him for all the help and wisdom we may need.

God's Church.

—:—

THE Passover and the day of Pentecost were two seasons kept by God's people at that time in memory of two very important events. The first was their deliverance from Egypt, and the second was when God gave them the law at Mount Sinai, fifty days afterward.

God taught his people in those days many deep lessons from the things that occurred in their lives from time to time.

These things were called types, shadows, and figures, meaning that they were only as pictures of what was going to take place in the future. Many of these types have a very deep meaning for the Christian to-day, but most of them were hidden until after the death of Jesus.

The way that God delivered his people from the bondage of Egypt at the time when the Passover lamb was slain, is a type of the salvation that came to the people of God through the death of Jesus, the Lamb of God.

The things received by the children of Israel at Mount Sinai were also a type of the blessings and commands that have come to the children of God through the gift of the Holy Spirit.

Jesus had promised to send this gift to his true followers. He had told them to wait at Jerusalem until the Holy Spirit was given, and at last the time had come for Jesus to fulfil his promise.

Just fifty days had passed since he, as the true passover, had been slain, and now the day of Pentecost was fully come. They were all together in one place. ''And suddenly there came a sound from heaven as of a rushing mighty wind, and it filled all the house where they were sitting. And there appeared unto them cloven tongues like as of fire, and it sat upon each of them. And they were all filled with the Holy Spirit, and began to speak with other tongues, as the Spirit gave them utterance.''

The Holy Spirit had come to stay with and in the people of God until the end of time.

After the giving of the law at Mount Sinai, fifty days after the first Passover, God taught his people how he wanted them to worship him under the old dispensation, or before the birth of Jesus. He gave them a real system; that is, he told them just what laws they must observe, and what sacrifices they must offer, as long as they continued to be a nation.

RECEIVING THE HOLY GHOST.

They had a sanctuary, or house of God; a priesthood; sacrifices; and ordinances, or certain things that they must do.

Now at the coming of the Holy Spirit from heaven, fifty days after the true Passover, God properly set in order the system of worship and sacrifice that Christians were to observe until Jesus came to take all who love him to his heavenly kingdom; where they will worship and serve God forever.

Under the old testament form of worship, there was a sanctuary, or house of God, in which God dwelt among the people. Under the new testament there is also a sanctuary, or house of God. It is the bodies of all who love Jesus, the Son of God. The Bible explains it thus: "Ye are the temple of the living God, as God hath said, I will dwell in them, and walk in them; and I will be their God, and they shall be my people."

These Christians form the church, or house of God. No one can join this church. They must be born of God to get into it. This, you remember, is what Jesus was trying to explain to Nicodemus. And then, you remember the story about the sheepfold. Jesus said, "I am the door: by me if any man enter in, he shall be saved." So, you see, we get into God's church through Jesus, the door, when we get saved from our sins. Then our names are written by Jesus in his Book of Life. After that, there is nothing that is able to take us out of God's church, except sin.

The old testament priesthood, or body of priests, was a type of the new testament priesthood. They offered the sacrifices and gifts in the tabernacle and temple of God.

All the children of God are now a holy priesthood, and Jesus is their great high priest. They offer sacrifices to God all the time. These sacrifices are praise, righteousness, and good works.

Under the old testament there were certain ordinances connected with the worship of God. So, also, under the new testament God has told us to keep certain ordinances. Some of these are baptism, the Lord's supper, and feet-washing.

Well, let us go back to the disciples when the Holy Spirit was poured out upon them. There were a great many Jews in Jerusalem who had come from other countries to be present at the Passover. They spoke many different languages; and so, in order that they might hear the gospel, the Holy Spirit gave the gift of tongues to the disciples, who at once began to preach as the Holy Spirit led them.

The People are Astonished.

—:—

As the apostles continued to preach, the news was spreading rapidly, and a multitude soon were listening to their words.

They were astonished at the way the apostles explained the Bible; but the part which surprised them most was that they could all understand what they heard, for each one heard the truth explained in his own language.

Many knew the apostles, and that most of them had never been at school much in their lives. For this reason they knew that God must be giving them the words, and they could not help believing what they heard.

Of course there were some who said things about the disciples that were not true. They even said that the disciples had drunk too much wine, and that they did not realize what they were saying.

But Peter stood up and told them that these men were not drunken as they supposed, for men did not get drunk so early in the morning; but that God had sent down his Holy Spirit, as he had promised.

Peter then explained to them about Jesus of Nazareth, who had worked so many miracles among them. And he reminded them of how shamefully they had treated Jesus, and had even crucified him.

This same Jesus, Peter said, God had raised up, and he was now sitting on a throne up in heaven. This Jesus had made known the ways of life, and now he had given them power to go out and tell the people everywhere how to get saved and be prepared to live with him in the next world, or heaven.

Telling the Glad News.

—:—

MANY were glad when they heard the words spoken by the apostles on the day of Pentecost; for they could understand now that Jesus was the Savior for whom they had been looking.

Many things that were said, however, brought sadness to their hearts; for they remembered how Jesus had been treated such a short time before. Some were so sorry that they came up and asked what they should have to do in order to be forgiven.

Peter answered, "Repent, and be baptized every one of you in the name of Jesus Christ." Then God, he said, would forgive them, and also give them the gift of the Holy Spirit, as he had to the disciples; for it was promised not only to them, but to their children after them, and to all who afterwards would believe.

There was a great work done for God that day. About three thousand people believed on account of what they had seen and heard.

When this great meeting had ended, the disciples went out among the people, and visited everywhere. They explained all about Jesus— that he was the Savior for whom they were looking—and many were glad, and believed that the things which they heard were true.

A Great Case of Healing.

—:—

ONE day as Peter and John were going up to the temple, they saw a man lying near the gate that was called Beautiful. This man had been lame all his life, and he was now past forty years of age. He was so poor that he had to live on what people kindly gave him. For this reason all knew him as a beggar.

But this poor man had friends, and every day they carried him up to the gate of the temple, where he could ask alms of the people.

As Peter and John were passing him, he asked help from them; but he expected that they would give him money. Peter stopped as he was passing the lame man, and looking straight into his eyes, said, "Silver and gold have I none; but such as I have give I thee: In the name of Jesus Christ of Nazareth rise up and walk."

Now the man had been born with weak bones in his ankles and feet. He had never been able to stand; but when Peter said "Arise," he took hold of the lame man's hand, and the weak ankle-bones became strong, and he, leaping up, stood, and walked, and entered with them into the temple.

A great many people were already in the temple; and when they saw what had happened, they were astonished. Those who were not close enough to see him healed, knew that he who was leaping and praising God in the temple was the same person that had so often begged money of them.

Then they looked at Peter and John, thinking they were very great men, because of the lame man's healing. But Peter and John did not want to be praised; for they knew that Jesus had done the healing, and they wanted him to receive the praise. So they said: "Ye men of Israel, why marvel ye at this? or why look ye so earnestly on us, as though by our own power or holiness we had made this man to walk? The God of Abraham, and of Isaac, and of Jacob, the God of our fathers, hath glorified his Son Jesus; whom ye delivered up, and denied him in the presence of Pilate, when he was determined to let him go. But ye denied the Holy One and the Just, and desired a murderer to be granted unto you; and killed the Prince of life, whom God hath raised from the dead; whereof we are witnesses. And his name through faith in his name hath made this man strong, whom ye see and know: yea, the faith which is by him hath given him this perfect soundness in the presence of you all. And now, brethren, I wot [know] that through ignorance ye did it, as did also your rulers. But those things, which God before had showed by the mouth of all his prophets, that Christ should suffer, he hath so fulfilled." Acts 3: 12-18.

Peter then urged the people to repent of their sins, and be converted, that God might not remember against them the cruel treatment of his Son.

The Wonderful Name of Jesus.

You remember, I told you of some people who were called Sadducees. They, together with the Pharisees, had been the most bitter enemies of Jesus.

The Sadducees did not believe in the resurrection of the dead; and so when they heard Peter say that Jesus had risen from the dead, they became very angry.

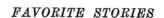

It was nearly night, but they took both Peter and John to prison. There they were left until the next morning, when they were brought before the high priest.

Peter and John were not at all discouraged; for Jesus had told them that they would have to suffer many things, and this was only the beginning.

Peter had shrunk from suffering a few weeks before—had even denied his Master! Not so now. He boldly stood and answered all questions; for the high priest had asked him, who had given him power to heal.

Peter said that if it was for the healing of the poor lame man that they must answer, he would tell them plainly that by the name of Jesus Christ, whom they had crucified, these things had been done. Jesus, Peter told them, was the stone which they had tried to destroy, but he had become the head of the corner.

By this, Peter meant that God would give salvation only to those who came to him in the name of Jesus, his Son. All other blessings, too, were now to be received in the same way. That is why, children, we must always say "for Jesus' sake" or "in Jesus' name" when we pray and ask God for any blessing. These words are often only a form to some people, but we should feel in our hearts what we say.

When the high priest and rulers of the city saw how boldly these two disciples stood up and answered their questions, they were surprised. And, too, they could not help seeing that a great miracle had been done on the lame man; but they were determined not to believe in Jesus themselves, and they intended to do all they could to keep others from believing.

Such hatred was in their hearts that they would have enjoyed punishing Peter and John; but this they did not dare to do, on account of the people who had seen the miracle.

They at last decided that perhaps if they would threaten the disciples, and tell them not to preach in the name of Jesus, the trouble might be stopped. This was done; but Peter and John were as bold as ever, and they said: "Whether it be right in the sight of God to

hearken unto you more than unto God, judge ye? We can not but speak the things which we have seen and heard.'' God had told them to speak, and they were going to obey.

But as the judges could find against them nothing for which they could be punished, they threatened them again, and then let them go.

Peter and John hurried home to their friends, and told them all that had happened during the night and in the morning. And then they all got down to pray, and to thank God for his wonderful goodness and blessings.

They ended their prayer by asking God to give them even greater boldness, and to help them to speak all the things that he wished them to speak. They asked him to show his power by healing the sick and by working many miracles, and to help them always to tell the people that the work was done in the name of Jesus.

God answered their prayer by shaking the place, and by filling them with more power and boldness to preach his word.

Selling Their Possessions.

A GREAT many people believed in Jesus now. Three thousand had turned to him after Peter's first sermon on the day of Pentecost, and five thousand had believed after Peter's second sermon in the temple. This made eight thousand people—quite a multitude. They were all very happy. Those who were rich gave to the poor, and all shared alike.

One rich man, named Barnabas, sold his land, and brought the money and laid it at the apostles' feet, to be used as they thought best. Barnabas was a good man, and you will soon hear more about him; but first I will tell you about a man who was a believer, but who was not so good.

You see, some of these believers could not help believing, because of the many miracles that had been done among them. They wanted to get to heaven when they died, but they were not willing to sacrifice all they had in this life.

God wants his people to be willing to give up everything they may have in this life if he asks them to do so. In some cases he may ask them to do this, and if he does, they should do it willingly, as did Barnabas.

SHARING THEIR POSSESSIONS.

Now I will tell you about the other man. His name was Ananias. He saw the great work that was going on, and felt a desire to do something to help it. His desire must have been to seem as generous as Barnabas, and to get the people to praise him.

It seems he sold his land, but afterward did not like to part with all the money. So he and his wife, whose name was Sapphira, agreed to keep part of the price. He then took the rest, and laid it at the apostles' feet as if it had been all he had.

What happened then ?   Do you think the apostles knew what Ananias had done?   They did know, for God told them.

So when Ananias laid down the money, how surprised he must have been to hear Peter say, ''Ananias, why hath Satan filled thine heart to lie to the Holy Ghost, and to keep back part of the price of the land?''   And Peter went on to say that the land and money had all belonged to Ananias, and that it had been in his power to use it as he thought best; but that when he had decided to deceive God's people, by pretending to give all his money and then not doing so, he had lied to God, and not to them.

As soon as Ananias heard Peter's words, he fell down dead.   Some young men took his body and wrapped it in linen cloths, and took it out and buried it.   When the people saw what had happened to Ananias, they were filled with fear, and they realized what a terrible thing it was to try to deceive God.

Another Sudden Death.

—:—

SAPPHIRA did not know what had happened to her husband, and she was not frightened.   She knew what they had decided to say if asked any questions; for it would take away so much of the praise if the apostles knew they had given only part.

About three hours after her husband's death she came in.   Perhaps she was expecting to be thanked and praised, but she was not expecting what came.

Peter wanted to test her, to see if she, too, would try to deceive the Lord.   He said, ''Tell me whether ye sold the land for so much?'' And she answered, ''Yea, for so much.''   Then Peter asked her why she had agreed with her husband to tell this lie and tempt the Spirit of the Lord.   He told her what had just a short time before happened to her husband, and said that the same thing was going to happen to her.

When Peter said this, Sapphira fell down dead; and the young men who had just returned from burying her husband buried her also.

The people who had been so frightened over the death of Ananias were now still more frightened.

Children, let this little story ever be a warning to you. Speak the truth, no matter how much you are tempted to do otherwise.

There are different kinds of lies. Some are very innocent in appearance. There are others so small that we wonder why they are uttered at all. Then, there are others that are spoken when the truth would serve the same purpose a thousand times better. These are the kind of lies that are generally spoken by polite or society people.

Such lies as these are not thought to amount to much, for they are not spoken to do any one harm. But they do amount to a great deal in God's sight. God wants every one to speak the truth at all times.

Another thing, God keeps a record of all the lies, small or great, that are spoken.

Although every one does not die suddenly, as did Ananias and Sapphira, yet they will die some time, and will have to meet God. They will hear him read off all their deeds, both good and bad. In this way, God will know where each one belongs—on his right hand, or on his left.

But, children, if at some time you have told things which were not true, do not think that God does not love you. He loves you just as much as he ever did; and if you will go to him as the prodigal son went to his father, you will find he will forgive you, and blot out everything he had in his book against you. He will never remember these things again, and you can begin to live a new life from that moment.

But if you ever do anything wrong after that, God will keep a record of it until you are sorry and ask him to forgive you.

THE DEATH OF SAPPHIRA.

The Doors of the Prison Opened.

—:—

AFTER the sudden death of Ananias and his wife, the work of the Lord went on rapidly; and the people looked upon Peter almost as they had upon Jesus a short time before, for many were being healed. But Peter was very careful to tell them often that they must give Jesus the praise for everything that was done.

People from all parts of the country came to be healed, and there were so many that Peter could not lay his hands on them all. Some were brought and laid upon beds or couches in such a way that the shadow of Peter while passing would fall upon them.

When the high priest and the Sadducees saw what a multitude was following the apostles, and also knew that no such miracles had ever been done by any one else, except Jesus, they decided that it would never do to let these men go on in this way. So once more they were taken to prison. But they were not to stay in this prison long, not even one whole night. An angel came while it was still dark, and let them out.

When the angel opened the doors, he said, ''Go, stand and speak in the temple to the people all the words of this life.'' So, as soon as it was light, they went to the temple and began to preach as usual.

They may have had time to go and tell their friends of the angel, and how he had delivered them; but whether they did so or not, the high priest knew nothing of their escape from prison until the next morning.

The next morning when the council met to decide what to do with their prisoners, they sent officers to the prison to bring them. What a surprise was awaiting them! Their prisoners were gone. The doors were locked, and the keepers of the prison standing before them; but when they went inside, they could not find any one.

They hurried back and told the high priest and the judges that they could not find the prisoners. The judges were very much astonished. They could not think what had become of the apostles, and they were very much worried over the matter.

While they were trying to decide what to do, some one entered, and said, "Behold, the men whom ye put in prison are standing in the temple, and teaching the people." This was another surprise.

Officers went at once to bring the apostles before the council; but these officers did not dare to be rough with them, for fear of being stoned.

As soon as the high priest saw the apostles, he said, "Did not we straitly command you that ye should not teach in this name?" And he said that the apostles had not only disobeyed him in that, but were filling the minds of all the people in Jerusalem with the idea that the council was guilty of killing Jesus.

The apostles were not frightened, and Peter answered, "We ought to obey God rather than men"; and he told them why they dared to preach in the name of Jesus.

The judges became so angry that they would have been glad to do anything to the apostles, and they tried to get something against them that would make them worthy of death.

O✴O✴O✴O

Gamaliel's Advice.

—:—

AMONG the judges was a man who was very wise, and whom all the people greatly respected. This man's name was Gamaliel. When he saw how things were going, he had the apostles sent out, and then he told the council what he thought was the best thing to do.

He warned them against doing anything in a hurry, and reminded them of certain men that had been in their city before. The name of one was Theudas, and the other, Judas of Galilee. Each of these men had pretended to be some one great; but both had been slain, and their work had come to naught.

And he said that it would be the same with these men if their works were not of God, and that if the work they were engaged in was of God, nothing could stop it.

This was good advice, and they all agreed to do as Gamaliel had said. But before letting the apostles go, they beat them, and warned them not to speak any more in the name of Jesus.

The apostles did not mind the beating, but were glad that God counted them worthy to suffer shame for his name's sake. Every day they went into the temple, and there preached the many wonderful things that Jesus had taught them. The sick and suffering were healed, and many people became not only believers, but real disciples of Jesus.

Because the Twelve had to be out teaching the people so much, it was decided best to appoint seven good men to stay at home and attend to things there. Stephen and Philip were among the seven that were chosen, and they were called deacons. Now there was a Philip among the apostles, and one among the deacons.

Stephen.

—:—

STEPHEN was a good man, full of faith and power. He did many wonderful works and miracles among the people, but the enemies of Jesus hated him.

Many wise men came to Stephen to dispute or argue with him; but when they heard his many wise words, they were surprised, and they wondered where his wisdom came from.

At last, wishing to bring him before the council, they paid some men to tell lies about him and say that he had spoken against Moses and against God. When the people heard the lies these men told, they believed them, and went and caught Stephen, and brought him before the council.

False witnesses then came in, who said they had heard Stephen say that Jesus of Nazareth would destroy their city, and change the customs of Moses; but they had twisted the meaning of Stephen's words. He had never said that Jesus was going to destroy Jerusalem, but that he had prophesied it would be destroyed. The Romans were going to do it, and God was going to let them because of the wicked unbelief of the Jews. God himself had brought in the Christian dispensation, and the old religious customs were soon to pass away.

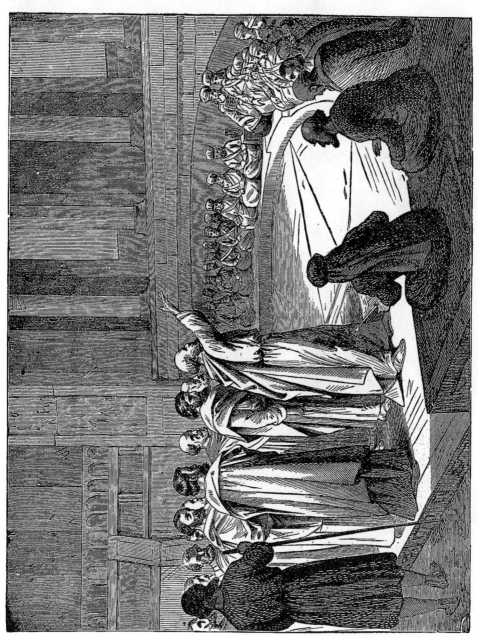

STEPHEN BEFORE THE COUNCIL.

After these things had been spoken, the judges all looked at Stephen, and they were surprised to see that his face shone like the face of an angel, it was so bright and glorious. But this did not cause the wicked judges to change their plans.

The high priest asked Stephen if these things were true. In answer, Stephen made a long speech. He began away back when God

MARTYRDOM OF ST. STEPHEN.

called Abraham out of the land of the Chaldæans, and then traced God's people down to the time of Jesus. He reminded them of Moses' words when he said, "The Lord thy God will raise up unto thee a Prophet from the midst of thee, of thy brethren," and of the many things that had been written concerning the way the Son of God would be treated. And then he told them that many of these things had taken place, and that although they had the law of Moses they did not keep it.

When the judges heard this they became so angry that they gnashed upon Stephen with their teeth. They were like devils, but he was like an angel.

Stephen lifted up his eyes toward heaven and saw the glory of God; for he said, "Behold, I see the heavens opened, and the Son of man standing on the right hand of God."

The angry mob could not stand to hear Stephen talk thus, and they cried out with a loud voice, and stopped their ears that they might not hear his words. Then with one accord they cast Stephen out of the city, and threw stones at him until he died.

But God helped Stephen to bear all this terrible suffering, and he did not speak an unkind word. Instead he said, "Lord, lay not this sin to their charge"; and with these words he breathed his last.

This was the death of the first martyr, but it was not the last. There arose great persecution against the church at Jerusalem. Many of God's people were put in prison, and the believers were scattered far and wide. But although they were suffering so much persecution, they were brave, and spoke boldly the words they had learned of Jesus.

Among those who had consented to have Stephen murdered, was a young man named Saul. This man did much harm to God's people in many ways after that, but you will hear of him later.

When the murderers of Stephen were gone, good men came, took his poor bruised body, and buried it. Many tears were shed, but Stephen did not feel any suffering now. He was happy; he had gone to be with Jesus.

Philip Preaching in Samaria.

—:—

ONE day Philip, who was one of the seven deacons, went up into the country of Samaria to preach to the people there. Many of them were glad when they heard the words of Philip, and saw the many miracles which he did. For unclean spirits, crying out with loud voices, came out of many who were possessed, and many who were sick and lame were healed.

When the people saw what wonders Philip was doing, they believed what he said about Jesus, and many accepted Jesus as their Savior. For this reason there was great joy in that city.

Among those who believed Philip's teaching was a very wicked man, who had made his living by deceiving the people. This man had pretended to be some great person, and by telling lies and playing deceitful tricks, he caused many people to believe that he was what he pretended to be. Although he became to all appearance a believer in Jesus Christ, and was even baptized, yet his heart was not right in God's sight. Perhaps it was the many miracles which Philip did that had caused him to believe. The Bible says he wondered how they had been done, and longed to possess this same power himself. He was no longer considered a great man among the people.

Now, when the apostles heard the good news, that Samaria was full of believers, they sent Peter and John to help Philip teach the people. When these two apostles came to Samaria, they found a great many people who believed in Jesus Christ, and who had been baptized in his name, but none who had received the Holy Ghost.

As soon as these two apostles came, they saw that the Holy Ghost had not been received, and so they prayed, and laid their hands upon some of them, and God sent his gift, the Holy Spirit.

When Simon saw that through the laying on of the apostles' hands the Holy Ghost was given, he thought that was just what he wanted; but he thought that he could buy the power, and that by using it he could soon become very rich. So he offered the apostles money if they would give it to him.

The apostles were grieved when they heard Simon say this, for the gift of God could not be bought with money. Peter's answer was severe. Wanting to show Simon that God understood the hearts of men, he said: "Thy money perish with thee, because thou hast thought that the gift of God may be purchased with money. Thou hast neither part nor lot in this matter: for thy heart is not right in the sight of God. Repent therefore of this thy wickedness, and pray God, if perhaps the thought of thine heart may be forgiven thee. For I perceive that thou art in the gall of bitterness, and in the bond of iniquity.''

When Simon heard the words of Peter, he was frightened, and he said, ''Pray ye to the Lord for me, that none of these things which ye have spoken come upon me.''

Simon asked to be forgiven only that he might not be punished. He had never really repented of his sins. He loved money and the praise of men, and he was really a hypocrite.

Peter and John did not remain long in Samaria, but returned to Jerusalem. Philip did not go with them, neither did he remain in Samaria. God had a great work for Philip, and he sent him toward Gaza. This place was about forty-five miles from Jerusalem, and was on the road which led down to Egypt.

The Stranger Philip Met.

PERHAPS Philip was surprised when an angel spoke to him, saying, ''Arise, and go toward the south unto the way that goeth down from Jerusalem unto Gaza, which is desert.'' But if he was, it did not hinder his obeying; for he arose and went at once.

As he was walking along, he saw at a short distance ahead of him a handsome chariot or carriage. Within it sat a man who was a great lord, from the country of Ethiopia. This country was on the other side of Egypt, in Africa, and was a long distance from Jerusalem.

The man in the chariot was an official in the service of the Queen of Ethiopia. He had charge of all her treasures. He had gone up to Jerusalem to worship God, and he was now returning home.

As he rode along he read from his Bible. The place where he was reading was in the book of Isaiah; but he could not understand the meaning of what he read.

The Spirit said to Philip, ''Go near, and join thyself to this

chariot''; and Philip obeyed. He even ran, and as he came near
the chariot, he heard the treasurer reading aloud. Philip asked him
whether he understood what he was reading, and he answered, "How
can I, except some man should guide me?" The stranger might have
taken this question in a different way if his heart had been full of
pride; but it was not. He was even anxious to have explained what
he had just read.

Something about Philip must have given the treasurer a feeling
that he had found some one who could explain the Scripture, for he
invited Philip to ride with him in the chariot. Philip accepted the
invitation at once, and while sitting there, showed the rich man the
meaning of the words.

The verse that Philip explained was this: "He was led as a
sheep to the slaughter; and like a lamb dumb before his shearer, so
opened he not his mouth. In his humiliation his judgment was taken
away: and who shall declare his generation? for his life is taken from
the earth." Philip told him that the prophet meant Jesus of Nazareth,
who was the Lamb of God, and who had lately been crucified at
Jerusalem.

The treasurer listened quietly to all of Philip's words, and they
made a deep impression upon his heart. Just then they came to a
place where there was water, and he asked Philip what would hinder
his being baptized the same as those he had been hearing about.

Philip answered, "If thou believest with all thine heart, thou
mayest"; and the treasurer said, "I believe that Jesus Christ is the
Son of God." That was enough. They got down out of the chariot,
and Philip baptized him. "And when they were come up out of the
water, the Spirit of the Lord caught away Philip, that the eunuch saw
him no more: and he went on his way rejoicing. But Philip was
found at Azotus: and passing through he preached in all the cities,
till he came to Cæsarea." Acts 8: 39, 40.

The man from Ethiopia must have been sorry to lose his teacher.
Still, he had heard joyful news, and had found out who the Savior
was; and he returned to his home with a happy heart. He was now

able to teach Queen Candace and all her people, and to spread in Africa the news about Jesus.

The Story of Saul.

—:—

ALL the time that Philip was away, the disciples in Jerusalem were suffering terribly. Saul, the young man who had taken part in the death of Stephen, was now doing all he could to destroy the people who loved Jesus.

Saul was really not a bad young man, for he thought he was doing right in ill-treating believers in Jesus. He believed that Jesus was a deceiver, and not the Son of God, and this was his reason for acting as he did.

It was not enough, he thought, to punish only those living in Jerusalem; for he could see that the number of believers were increasing every day in the other cities also. So he decided to go to the high priest and get permission to go into any city he chose, even as far north as Damascus.

The high priest was very glad to give his consent, and Saul started out on his long journey at once. The high priest had given Saul letters, and Saul meant to show them to the rulers among the Jews, to prove his right to bind and punish the believers. It was a long journey, but Saul did not mind that.

As he was traveling along with several other men, such a strange thing happened. All at once there was a bright light from heaven, far brighter than the sun, shining all around Saul.

The travelers were all astonished, and they trembled with fear; but Saul fell upon the ground. Then he heard a voice from heaven, saying, "Saul, Saul, why persecutest thou me?" Saul answered, "Who art thou, Lord?" and the voice replied, "I am Jesus whom thou persecutest: it is hard for thee to kick against the pricks."

Saul was still trembling, but he said, "Lord, what wilt thou have me to do?" The voice replied, "Arise, and go into the city, and it shall be told thee what thou must do."

All this time the men who were with Saul had not spoken a word. They had heard the sound of the voice, but they could not see any one, neither did they understand the words.

When Saul rose from the ground, he was blind. The great light had made him so that he could not see. But those who were with Saul could see, and they took him by the hand, and led him to Damascus to the house of a man named Judas.

What must have been Saul's feelings now? Surely he must have thought of the many cruel and wicked deeds he had committed in causing Jesus and his disciples such suffering.

When Saul arrived at Damascus, he sat down, and for three days he refused to eat or drink. While in this sorrowful and wretched condition, God gave him a dream. He seemed to see a man named Ananias coming toward him. He seemed to come up to Saul, to put his hands upon him, and to say, "Receive thy sight."

Ananias' Dream.

—:—

You have read the story of Ananias and Sapphira, who pretended to give all they had to the work of the Lord, and have read that they could not deceive God's people; but the Ananias that we now wish to talk about was a very different man.

This Ananias loved God with all his heart, and believed that Jesus was the Son of God. He did not believe this simply because some others had said so; but Jesus had really become his Savior, and he loved him sincerely.

God spoke to Ananias in a dream or vision about the same time he gave the dream to Saul. The Lord said to him, "Arise, and go into the street which is called Straight, and inquire in the house of Judas for one called Saul of Tarsus: for, behold, he prayeth."

How surprised Ananias must have been when he learned this! for he had heard much about this Saul of Tarsus, and of the terrible suffering he had brought upon God's people. Perhaps he knew why

THE CONVERSION OF SAUL.

Saul had started to Damascus—but now Saul was praying! Ananias could hardly believe that so great a change had come over Saul. But God continued to talk with him, and said that Saul, also, had dreamed, and had even seen a man named Ananias coming in and putting his hand on his eyes that he might receive his sight. For Saul, the Lord said, had been chosen to tell many people about Jesus, the Savior of the world. He would preach to the Gentiles, to kings, and to the children of Israel; and he would have to suffer many things for the name of Jesus.

Ananias did not wait any longer when he heard all this. He went to Straight Street, and entered the house of Judas; and there sat Saul, as he had seen him in his dream. Saul could not see Ananias, but he heard him say, "Brother Saul, the Lord, even Jesus, that appeared unto thee in the way as thou camest, hath sent me, that thou mightest receive thy sight, and be filled with the Holy Spirit."

Then, when Ananias laid his hands upon Saul's eyes, something like scales fell from them, and Saul could see. As soon as he was baptized, he ate some food, and his strength returned, and he went to stay for a while with the disciples that were in Damascus.

As soon as possible, he went to the synagogues and preached that Jesus was the Son of God.

The news about Saul soon spread, and many came to hear him preach of Jesus. When they heard his words, they were astonished, and said, "Is not this he that destroyed them which called on this name in Jerusalem, and came hither for that intent, that he might bring them bound unto the chief priests?"

Then some tried to kill him; but he was bold, and he continued to preach to them as long as they would listen.

Soldiers Try to Kill Saul.

—:—

SAUL stayed a long time in Damascus, and he was loved by all those in that city who believed in Jesus. The very ones whom he

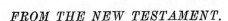

had expected to cast into prison were now his dearest friends.

As Saul continued to preach to the people, they became more and more angry with him, and tried to plan how they might kill him. When they had gained permission from the governor to take Saul's life, soldiers were placed at all the gates of the city.

When Saul learned this, he thought he would leave Damascus, and go back to Jerusalem. He knew how carefully the gates were watched; so the disciples let him down by night through an opening in the wall of the city, letting him down in a basket; and he escaped from the Jews that wished to kill him.

He was soon on his way back to Jerusalem. How differently he felt now from the way he felt the day he came to Damascus. Then his heart was so full of hatred and anger, but now it was full of love and peace. He longed to see the disciples whom he had caused so much suffering in Jerusalem, and to tell them how sorry he was. Then he had hated Jesus, and his best friends were the priests and those who would help him in his wicked ways. Now they were his most bitter enemies, and he loved Jesus more than his own life. How happy and thankful he must have felt as he walked along!

As soon as he reached Jerusalem, he inquired for the disciples. When they heard that Saul had come, they were afraid that he had come to do them harm. They had not heard of the great change that had come into his life, and they remembered his cruel treatment in the past.

One of them, however, had a very kind and loving heart, and he went to Saul and listened carefully to all he had to say. This was Barnabas, of whom we spoke before. He believed that what Saul said was true. After this, it did not take the others long to have confidence in Saul, and they soon saw that what he said was really true.

But Saul's life was now in great danger, and he could not stay long in Jerusalem. He soon left for Cæsarea, and from that place he went to Tarsus, where he was born. But wherever he went, he told the people about Jesus.

Peter at Lydda and Joppa.

—:—

WHILE Saul was taking the good news about Jesus to his old home, the other disciples were all very busy preaching salvation to the people.

At one time Peter visited the town of Lydda. This was a village not very far from Jerusalem. There he found a man that was sick with a disease called the palsy. This man, whose name was Eneas, had not been able to walk any for eight years.

When Peter saw the man in this helpless condition, he went to him, and said, "Eneas, Jesus Christ maketh thee whole: arise, and make thy bed." Eneas rose as soon as Peter said this, and made his bed. Many saw the man, and knew what a miracle had been done, and they turned to the Lord on account of it.

While Peter was still in Lydda, two men came to him with sad news.

They were from the town of Joppa, which was close to Lydda, and had heard of the great work Peter was doing.

The news they brought was that a good woman who had spent all her time in making garments for poor people was dead.

When Peter heard this, he went at once to Joppa. There the saints led him to an upper room, where he found many widows and poor people weeping over the dead body of the woman who had been so good to them.

It was very hard for them to give her up, and they showed Peter many coats and garments that she had made while she was yet with them. They loved Dorcas very much for spending her time in working for them.

Before Peter knelt in prayer, he sent every one out of the room. He wanted to be quiet, and alone with God.

Then when he had prayed, he turned to the body of Dorcas and commanded her to rise. She opened her eyes and saw Peter. Then, at his command, she rose and greeted her friends, who were now allowed to enter the room.

It certainly was a happy time, for God worked it all out to his glory, and it caused many sinners to turn to the Lord.

Peter's Vision.

—:—

PETER remained in Joppa a long time. While there he lived with a man called Simon. This Simon was a tanner by trade; that is, he made his living by making skins into leather. His home was near the seashore.

Peter often went up on the roof of Simon's house to pray. One day while he was up there, he had a very strange vision. He had not, it seems, eaten anything for some time, but he had left orders with the servants to prepare his dinner as soon as possible. It was while he was waiting for his meal that he saw this strange sight.

He thought he saw the sky open, and then a large square sheet seemed to be let down before him. The sheet was full of all kinds of animals and birds and creeping things. How strange they must have looked, all there together in the sheet!

Then Peter heard a voice saying, "Rise, Peter; kill, and eat." Peter was surprised when he heard this command, for God had strictly commanded the Jews to be careful about what they ate. In the sheet were both animals and birds that Peter had never dared to eat, because they were forbidden in the book of laws which governed the Jew.

So in answer, Peter said, "Not so, Lord; for I have never eaten anything that is common or unclean." The voice from heaven replied, "What God hath cleansed, that call not thou common." Three times the voice said these words, and then the sheet of animals was taken up into heaven.

The vision seemed very strange, and Peter could not help thinking about it after he came to himself. But God did not long keep him in doubt as to its meaning.

There was living in Cæsarea a man named Cornelius. This man tried to live just as he thought God would like to have him live; but there were many things that he did not understand, and he longed for some one to come and teach him.

Cornelius was a Roman, and captain over one hundred Italian soldiers that were stationed at Cæsarea. Although he was a Gentile, yet he was a very devout man, and was also a believer in the fact the Jesus was the great Prophet and Messiah of God. He had heard about

PETER'S STRANGE VISION.

Jesus' preaching and healing (Acts 10: 36-38); but there were some things concerning him and his wonderful salvation that he had not yet heard or experienced.

One day as he was praying, an angel told him to send some of his servants to Joppa, and ask Peter to come to his house and teach him about Jesus. The servants were at once called and sent.

Now about the time that Peter was studying over his dream, and trying to understand its meaning, three men came to the gate in front of Simon's house and inquired for Peter. At the same time, the Spirit of the Lord spoke to Peter, saying: "Behold, three men seek thee. Arise therefore, and get thee down, and go with them, doubting nothing: for I have sent them."

Peter needed no further message to go. He went down to the men, and said, "Behold, I am he whom ye seek: what is the cause wherefore ye are come?"

Then the three men replied that their master, Cornelius the centurion, had sent them to him with this message, that a holy angel had told him to send for Peter to come to his house, and Peter would explain to him the things that he could not understand about Jesus.

Peter soon found that the men were servants of Cornelius, and that Cornelius was not a Jew, neither were the servants, but that he was considered a good man by the Jews.

How easy it was now to understand what the vision upon the housetop meant. Peter invited the three men to come into the house and remain until morning.

O✱O✱O✱O

Peter at Caesarea.

VERILY early in the morning Peter invited some of his friends to go with him to Cæsarea. He no doubt told them about the wonderful vision and of all the strange things that had taken place. And perhaps they spoke about some of the things Jesus had said while he was upon the earth—about the Gentiles having the gospel preached to them.

Cæsarea was a beautiful city, for the Roman king had taken much pains to have everything about it as nice as possible. It was quite a long journey from Joppa; and though they started as soon as possible in the morning, yet they did not arrive there until the next day.

They went at once to the home of Cornelius, and found that he was expecting them, and had invited his relatives and nearest friends to come to his house that day.

When Peter entered the city, Cornelius met him, fell down at his feet, and worshiped him. Peter at once stooped down and lifted him up, saying, "Stand up; I myself also am a man."

Then as Peter was led into the house and saw how many people were there, and all of them Gentiles, he could see why God had given him the vision a short time before.

He then told them that to meet with a company of Gentiles like that was something that he would not have dared to do before; but that God had warned him not to call any person common or unclean, for Jesus had shed his blood for all.

Then turning to Cornelius, he asked why he had been sent for Cornelius told what the angel had said to him four days before while he was fasting and praying.

How glad Peter was when he heard the words of Cornelius! He said he now believed that God did not think any more of the Jews than he did of other nations; that the persons whom God loved best were those who would obey him and do his will.

Peter preached to these people who were so eager to hear him, telling them many wonderful things about God and about the plan of salvation. He finished his sermon by telling them that any who would believe that Jesus had died to save them could be saved from their sins.

He explained everything so simply that all these people understood his words. How glad they were they could be saved as well as the Jews!

And then God gave these believing Gentiles the gift of the Holy Ghost, just as he had to the apostles on the day of Pentecost. Many of them spoke in different languages, and praised God for his goodness.

When Peter saw that God had accepted these Gentiles in Cæsarea, he knew that they ought to be baptized. So he had them baptized.

God showed by this event that he makes no difference between Jews and Gentiles, when they believe in Jesus.

Peter remained with Cornelius many days; for there were so many things that the saints needed to be taught; but after a while he returned to Jerusalem.

A Misunderstanding.

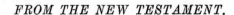

WHEN some of the brethren at Jerusalem heard that Peter had been up to Cæsarea preaching to the Gentiles, they did not understand what it meant. They felt that he had done wrong, and told him so.

But Peter was patient and humble. He told them of the whole matter, beginning at the time when he was in Joppa at Simon's house. He told them all about his vision—how he had seen descending from heaven the sheet full of all kinds of animals, and how that God had said he must not call common or unclean anything that had been cleansed. Peter also told them about the three men who had come for him to go to Cæsarea, and how that, besides all this, the Spirit had said, "Go with them, doubting nothing."

Peter further explained that an angel had spoken to Cornelius, telling him of his coming, and all that had happened afterward.

When those who had been objecting to what Peter had done, heard all these things, they praised God, and said it must be true that salvation was for the Gentiles as well as for the Jews. And ever since that time it has been plain that God makes no difference between them.

It was about this time when people began to call those who believed in Jesus by the name of Christians.

The cruel hatred of the Jews increased so fast that Christians everywhere had to suffer awful persecution. Many were killed because they said that Jesus was God's Son, but they were brave, and endured all suffering for his sake.

And Jesus helped them to bear it, as he does his dear people to-day. O children, it is so precious to have Jesus to help us. We may look around and see those who do not love Jesus as we do, and they may sometimes seem to have an easier time than we do; but, oh! they haven't the sweet comforting peace that fills every Christian's heart.

When they pass through a trial, Jesus does not help them. Why? Because they will not let him. Oh, let all who read these words see that they have accepted Jesus as their Savior!

An Angel Delivers Peter.

—:—

HEROD, the king that had consented to have John the Baptist killed, and the Herod that had mocked Jesus, were dead; but there was still another Herod, who was a great enemy of the church. Many suffered from his cruelty. He even killed the apostle James with the sword; and when he found that it pleased the Jews to see the Christians suffer, he planned to kill Peter also. He sent soldiers, who arrested Peter, and put him into prison.

What sorrow and suffering the church of God must have endured then! Many prayers were offered for Peter, that God would in some way show his power and deliver Peter.

Their prayer was not answered until the very night that Herod had planned to have Peter brought forth.

Peter was lying quietly asleep between two soldiers. He was carefully bound with two chains; and more than this, there were keepers guarding the doors of the prison. Suddenly, while all was so quiet and dark, an angel came into the prison and smote Peter on the side, saying, "Arise up quickly"; and as Peter obeyed, the angel helped him, and the chains fell from his hands. A bright light shone all around, and Peter hardly knew whether he was dreaming or not; but when the angel said, "Gird thyself, and bind on thy sandals, and follow me," Peter obeyed.

As the angel led him past the many soldiers that had been placed there to watch him, past one door and then another, Peter thought he must have seen a vision.

At last they came to the great iron gate that opened into the city. Peter saw it open of its own accord, and they went out. The angel brought him down one street, and then left him.

Peter was now fully awake, and he realized that all these things were truly happening. He said, "Now I know of a surety, that the Lord hath sent his angel, and hath delivered me out of the hand of Herod, and from all the expectation of the people of the Jews."

It did not take him long to decide what to do. He hurried off to a house where the saints were praying for him.

THE DELIVERANCE OF PETER.

As he knocked at the door, a damsel named Rhoda came to see who was rapping at that late hour.   Peter answered.   She knew his voice, but she was so glad that she forgot to open the door and let him in.

She ran at once to tell the others that their prayers had been answered, but they would not believe her.   They thought she must surely be mistaken, but she said it was true.   At last the door was opened, and there stood Peter.   Oh, how astonished they were!   Peter soon told them the story of the angel that had come to him in the prison, and of all that had taken place.

When he had finished telling them, he said to tell the brethren, and he would go away into another place.   Peter knew that Herod would be much surprised and disappointed, and that he would try very hard to find him.

We will now leave Peter, and see what happened when the soldiers awoke in the morning.   How surprised and worried they must have been, for they well knew that their own lives were in danger.   And they were.   When no news could be had of Peter, Herod ordered put to death all the soldiers that had been on guard.

But now what became of Herod?   One day he wished to look very nice in the eyes of the people; so he dressed himself in a beautiful robe, and sat upon his throne.   And the Bible says he made an oration or speech to the people.   He must have used very fine words; for when he had finished speaking, they gave a great shout and said, "It is the voice of a god, and not of a man."

Herod was pleased when he heard this; but God was displeased, and because of Herod's wickedness sent an angel to destroy his life. He became very ill, and his body was eaten by worms.

By Herod's sad death we see how much God hates pride.   Herod's sin was that he enjoyed being called a god, and not giving God the glory.

God used all of these things to advance his work, and his word grew and multiplied among the people.

Saul and Barnabas.

—:—

I wonder if you have forgotten where we left Saul. Perhaps you have, so I will tell you. He had returned to his old home in the city of **Tarsus**.

This was the place where he had spent his boyhood days. Then when he was older had been taught the Jewish customs and laws.

Saul wanted to serve God the very best he knew how; but he thought that the only right way was as the Pharisees taught, and in making cold formal prayers.

He was this sort of man when he consented to the death of Stephen and of other Christians.

But now Saul was a different person. He loved the Christians, for he knew that they were the true people of God. And now he was a Christian himself. God was calling him to go out into the world and preach salvation to the people, to tell them the glad news about his dear Son and his mission to this earth. God had chosen Saul to preach not only to the Jews, but also to the Gentiles.

It was about this time that his name was changed to Paul, which was only another form of the name Saul.

You have not forgotten about Barnabas, the good man, who sold all his possessions, and gave the money he received for them to the apostles, for the good of the church in Jerusalem; and you remember that it was Barnabas who went to see whether Saul had really repented after the trip to Damascus, and who then introduced him to the disciples in Jerusalem.

Well, this same Barnabas now went to Tarsus; and when he had found Saul, they both departed for the church that was at Antioch. There were a number of prophets and teachers in this church who prophesied of the great work God had planned for Barnabas and Saul to do, and said they must prepare themselves for this work.

When the time came for them to go, where do you suppose they went first? They went to the place where Barnabas had lived when he was a little boy. Paul had been to his home in Tarsus, and had

told his old friends about this Savior, and now Barnabas wanted to go to his home.

Barnabas had been born on a beautiful island in the Mediterranean Sea, called Cyprus. It was a long distance to the island from Antioch, so they sailed as soon as possible. They took with them a young man named John Mark, who was a nephew of Barnabas'.

In Paphos.

—:—

PAUL and Barnabas went through all the cities on the island, preaching to the people. In fact, they told every one they could of the wonderful salvation they had found.

In the town of Paphos, at the western end of this island, lived the governor, Sergius Paulus. He was a Roman, but he was much wiser than Pilate had been. He became very anxious to hear more about Jesus, who had given his life for sinners. So when he had called Paul and Barnabas, he asked them to explain to him the word of God.

Now, in this same city was living another very wise man, whose name was Elymas; but Elymas was a very different man from Sergius Paulus.

Elymas had another name, which was Bar-jesus. This last was a Jewish name meaning "the son of Jesus"; but he was really a son of Satan, for he cared only to do the things Satan wanted him to do.

Elymas was a sorcerer, or false prophet; and when he heard Paul and Barnabas trying to teach the governor, he did all he could to turn the governor away, and to prevent him from believing the words.

We do not know what Elymas said; but Paul understood his motive and spirit, and turning toward him, said: "O full of all subtilty and all mischief, thou child of the devil, thou enemy of all righteousness, wilt thou not cease to pervert the right ways of the Lord? Behold, the hand of the Lord is upon thee, and thou shalt be blind, not seeing the sun for a season."

When Paul finished speaking, Elymas found that he was blind,

and he went about seeking some one to lead him by the hand.

How this punishment must have reminded Paul of the time when he was blind! We do not know that Elymas ever had his sight restored to him; but we truly hope so, and hope that he repented of his sinful ways.

When the governor saw what had happened to Elymas, he believed the words of Paul and Barnabas; but that is the last we hear about these two men of Paphos.

Soon after this, Paul, Barnabas, and John Mark returned to Antioch, and from that time they continued to preach the gospel to every one they could.

○✦○✦○✦○

A Lame Man Healed.

—:—

LYSTRA was a small town northeast of Tarsus. The people of this place were heathen, for they worshiped stars instead of God. The name of these stars were Jupiter and Mercurius.

Paul felt the great need of the gospel being preached to these people, so he spent some time among them.

One day as Paul was preaching, he saw a lame man sitting near him. This man had always been lame, and had never walked. Just how old he was we do not know, but he had grown to be a man.

When Paul saw how anxious this poor cripple was to hear the truth, he fixed his eyes upon him, and seeing that he had faith to be healed, said with a loud voice, "Stand upright on thy feet." The man leaped up, and began to walk.

When the people saw what had happened, they began to praise Paul and Barnabas for healing the man, then called them gods. Neither Paul nor Barnabas would have allowed this; but the people spoke in their own language, and the apostles did not understand their meaning.

But when they began to bring oxen to sacrifice, and beautiful garlands of flowers, the apostles realized what the people meant. The apostles were greatly grieved over the matter. They knew that the oxen were to be offered up to show them honor. They tore their

clothes, and ran in among the people, saying, "Sirs, why do ye these things? we also are men of like passions with you, and preach unto you that ye should turn from these vanities unto the living God, which

THE CRIPPLE IS HEALED.

made heaven and earth, and the sea, and all things that are therein."

It was hard to make the people understand, but Paul and Barnabas had not long to endure this thing. For some Jews came over from other cities, and told many things that were untrue. It was not hard to change these poor ignorant people from worshipers into murderers.

Gathering up great stones, they threw them at Paul until they thought they had killed him. They then dragged his body out of their city, and left him there.

How sorrowful the other believers must have felt to see the one whom they loved so much lying upon the ground before them! Suddenly the body began to move, and then it rose and walked into the city. Oh, what joy must have filled their hearts! Paul was with them again, alive and well.

Paul and Barnabas left Lystra early the next morning; but after a while they returned, and there was a precious little church raised up in that wicked place.

Young Timothy.

PAUL and Barnabas were now kept so busy that they needed help, so the apostles sent two brethren to help them in the work among the Gentiles. The names of these brethren were Judas Barsabas and Silas.

Paul and Barnabas were in Antioch at the time, and they received them gladly. Much good resulted from their visit, and Silas decided to remain, but Judas returned to the apostles.

Barnabas decided to go to his old home on the island of Cyprus, and he took John Mark with him; but Paul and Silas went up into the country where Paul was born, near Tarsus.

As soon as possible Paul went up to Lystra, the place where the people had treated him so cruelly by throwing stones at him. The people were not so fierce now, but they did not enjoy hearing about Jesus, so he did remain there long.

But there were a few in this place who really loved God, and liked to hear about God's Son, Jesus. One of these was a young man named Timothy. His mother's name was Eunice, and she was a Jewess. She had taught him carefully from the Bible, so that now he understood a great deal about God for one so young. Then, too, his grandmother, whose name was Lois, had taken a great interest in him, and had taught him many things about the Lord.

Paul soon became greatly interested in Timothy, and saw that he

was going to be very useful in the Lord's work. Paul wished very much to have Timothy as a companion in his work, and as Timothy was anxious to go, the matter was soon decided. These two became like father and son, and later Paul spoke of him as his "dearly beloved son."

Now there were three in the company, Paul, Silas and Timothy. They went from one city to another, visiting and establishing churches; and many believed and were baptized.

Lydia and the Servant Girl.

—:—

THERE was a certain woman whose name was Lydia, who was very kind to the ministers of God. A brother named Luke had joined the company, which made four men to be cared for; but she told them that they were all welcome to come and stay at her house.

They were now away up in the country of Macedonia, for God had shown Paul in a dream that he should go there.

Of course, there were not many people in that place who were favorable to the truth; so they were very thankful to Lydia for her kindness to them.

One day as they were on their way to the house of prayer, they heard some one crying out, "These men are the servants of the most high God, which show us the way of salvation."

They soon found that the words were spoken by a young woman who was possessed by an evil spirit. Satan had come into her, and she said and did many wonderful things. She was a servant girl. Her masters were wicked men, and they sent her out to get money by saying the things Satan told her. She was called a sorceress.

Paul was grieved when he saw her under such a power; and as she continued to cry after them each day when they passed, he at last commanded the spirit to come out of her. And Satan came out of her the same hour.

Truly this deliverance was a great blessing to the poor servant

LOIS, EUNICE AND TIMOTHY.

347

girl. But now there was a great change in her life. She no longer told lies to bring her masters gain, as she had done in the past.

Those wicked men became very angry when they saw that their slave brought them no more money, and they decided to have Paul and Silas arrested. This was not a hard thing to do, for there are always many enemies wherever God's Word is preached. So they were soon sent to prison.

⚬✲⚬✲⚬✲⚬

In Prison.
—:—

It was not a hard matter to gain the consent of the judges to punish Paul and Silas. Their clothing was torn off their bodies, and then they were beaten. After this they were cast into prison, and the jailor was told to keep close watch of them.

The jailor did all in his power to obey these commands. He had their feet made fast in the stocks, so that they could not lie down nor stand up.

But now we are coming to the good side of this story. At midnight Paul and Silas prayed, and sang praises unto God. All the prisoners around them heard the prayers and the songs.

Suddenly there was a great crash. It was an earthquake, which shook the prison terribly, and threw open every door. All the prisoners found that their feet were set loose from the things with which they had been fastened.

When the jailor awoke and saw all the prison doors standing open, he was so frightened that he drew his sword and was about to kill himself, when Paul called to him with a loud voice, "Do thyself no harm; for we are all here."

The jailor had at first supposed that the prisoners were all gone. How great must have been his surprise when he found they were there! He called for a light, and sprang in, and came trembling, and fell down before Paul and Silas.

He brought them up out of the prison, and said, "Sirs, what must I do to be saved?" They answered, "Believe on the Lord Jesus Christ, and thou shalt be saved."

THE PHILIPPIAN JAILOR BEFORE PAUL AND SILAS.

How glad the jailor was when he heard this, and how sorry he was for the cruel treatment these good men had received! He saw their bodies still bruised and bleeding from the terrible beating that they had received the night before. And he thought of the meek and quiet spirit that they had shown through it all, and it seemed almost more than he could bear.

"WHAT SHALL I DO TO BE SAVED."

He took the prisoners out of the dungeon, and carefully washed their stripes, and then he and all his family were baptized. After this, food was prepared; and while they were eating, they praised and thanked God for his wonderful goodness.

The Alarm of the Judges.

—:—

In the morning the rulers of the city sent men to the jailor, saying, "Let those men go."

The jailor must have felt that this was an answer to prayer; for when he told Paul and Silas the message, he seemed to rejoice because they could depart in peace.

But Paul would not go. Do you wonder why? Wait and see what his answer to the jailor was. He said: "They have beaten us openly uncondemned, being Romans, and have cast us into prison, and now do they thrust us out privily? nay verily; but let them come themselves and fetch us out."

Ah, what was this? Was not Paul a Jew, born in Tarsus, and not in Rome? Yes, but the emperor of Rome, as a sort of favor, granted certain people the privilege of being Romans, and no judge could punish them unless they were guilty, and the charges brought against them proved that they deserved punishment.

In our country all enjoy this privilege, but then none could expect it except those who were Romans.

Now, Paul and Silas had been cruelly beaten and thrust into prison without even a trial. So Paul reminded them of what they had done, and said, "Let them come themselves and fetch us out."

The judges were certainly alarmed when they heard that Paul and Silas were Romans and they begged them to leave the city as soon as possible.

The prisoners were willing to do this, but they wanted those cruel men to understand what they had done.

We can almost imagine we see Paul and Silas departing with their hearts full of love and praise to God for his goodness to them.

Before leaving the city, they went to the house of Lydia. There they found Luke and Timothy, and told them about all that had taken place. After a little praise-meeting Paul and Silas left the city, and went into other places preaching that it was necessary for Christ to suffer, to die, and then to rise from the dead, and explaining that Jesus was the Christ.

The hearts of the Jews who would not believe seemed to be filled with bitter envy and jealousy. Some of them went to the rulers of the city, and said that the apostles were working against Cæsar, "saying that there is another king, one Jesus."

In Berea, however, the people were more noble. When they heard the words of Paul, they searched carefully in their Bibles to see if what he said was true. In this way many of them believed and became Christians.

Paul Suffers in Jerusalem.

—:—

THERE is much more about Paul's life that is very interesting, but we will mention only a few more instances.

At one time a prophet whose name was Agabus foretold something that was soon to take place in Jerusalem. He said that the Jews there would bind Paul, and deliver him into the hands of his enemies.

This was sad news to Paul's friends, and they begged him not to go to Jerusalem if such things were to be. Paul answered, "What mean ye to weep and to break mine heart? for I am ready not to be bound only, but also to die at Jerusalem for the name of the Lord Jesus."

When his friends saw that they could not persuade him to stay, they said, "The will of the Lord be done."

Not long after that, Paul went to Jerusalem, and found things as he had been told they would be. One day while he was in the temple, some of the people came and seized him, saying, "Men of Israel, help: this is the man that teacheth all men everywhere against the people, and the law, and this place." And they said that Paul had taken some Gentiles into the temple. Paul had been seen walking on the street with an Ephesian, and these Jews supposed he had brought him into the temple, but Paul had not.

Many of the people heard these things and believed that they were true; so they all ran together, took Paul, and dragged him out of the temple. They then began beating Paul, and they would have killed him had not soldiers taken him out of their hands. The city was in such an uproar that the soldiers had great difficulty in protecting Paul, but they at last bore him away from the cruel mob. The terrible cry of "Away with him" could be heard in the streets.

PAUL SPEAKING TO THE PEOPLE.

As Paul was being taken to the castle, he asked the privilege of speaking to the chief captain, which was soon given. Then Paul asked permission to speak to the people. The chief captain gave his consent. Paul spoke from where he was, standing on the stairs, and all could hear him. Then he began and told them who he was; how he had once treated the Christians just as they were doing now; then how he had been converted, and how he had preached about Jesus

23

in Jerusalem until God said, ''Depart: for I will send thee far hence unto the Gentiles.''

Again the hearts of the people were filled with murder.   They were so determined to kill Paul that the captain commanded his soldiers to bind him, and to take him into the castle.

Once more Paul said that he was a Roman, and that they had no right to treat him as they were doing.

The officer to whom Paul told this went to the chief captain and said, ''Take heed what thou doest: for this man is a Roman.''

The captain told Paul that he had paid a great deal of money to be made a Roman; but Paul said, ''I was free born.''

All were now very much frightened, but it seems that they left Paul bound until the next day, when he was to appear before the council.

In the morning Paul received strength and grace from above to say everything that was necessary for him to say, and the Lord took care of all that was said.

It was truly a terrible day.   There stood the angry mob, longing for a chance to kill Paul; but God was on Paul's side, and he was not going to let him die until he had finished his work.

He must testify of Jesus in Rome after this testimony in Jerusalem. This God showed him in a dream, and it soon came to pass.

○✦○✦○✦○

Paul is Shipwrecked.

AFTER having been brought before the different rulers in Jerusalem, who were not able to decide what had better be done with Paul, it was decided that he should be taken to Italy.

Paul was now a prisoner, so there was placed over him a guard by the name of Julius.   This guard was very kind to Paul; and on the way, when the ship stopped at the different cities, he allowed Paul to go and visit some of his old friends.

How glad these friends must have been to see Paul; but they

must have felt very sad indeed to see him suffering so many things.

We can imagine Paul saying many words of encouragement to them, and telling them not to be sorry for him, but to be sure that they

were prepared to meet him in heaven when all their work and sufferings were ended. On the way to Italy they passed the island of Cyprus and many other dear and familiar places; but it was a long and dangerous journey.

At last they came to the island of Crete, and landed at a place called the Fair Havens. While at this place Paul warned the master of the ship not to go any farther, for there was great danger ahead. He said, "Sirs, I perceive that this voyage will be with hurt and much damage, not only of the lading and ship, but also of our lives."

But they did not listen to Paul's advice, partly because they did not like to change their plans, and partly because winter was fast approaching and they would have to remain a long time. So they decided to try to reach Phenice, and winter there.

COPYRIGHT, 1897 BY PROVIDENCE LITH. CO.

PAUL ENCOURAGES THE SAILORS.

They had gone only a short distance when a terrible wind-storm arose, known as the Euroclydon. The wind blew the ship around so fiercely that they were unable to manage it in the storm, and they were forced to let it go as it would.

The waves continued to toss the ship until it seemed necessary to throw overboard everything that was heavy, and thus lighten the load; but this did not help matters.

The men on board began to give up all hope of being saved from the storm, for the sun or stars had not appeared for many days. But Paul knew that he himself could not be lost, for God had told him that he must appear before the people in Rome.

ST. PAUL'S SHIP-WRECK.

Paul reminded them of his warning before they left the Fair Havens; but he also encouraged them by saying: ''Be of good cheer: for there shall be no loss of any man's life among you, but of the ship. For there stood by me this night the angel of God, whose I am, and whom I serve, saying, Fear not, Paul; thou must be brought before Cæsar: and, lo, God hath given thee all them that sail with thee. Wherefore, sirs, be of good cheer: for I believe God that it shall be even as it was told me. Howbeit we must be cast upon a certain island.''

Paul did not know how all this would happen; but he knew that it was to be, for the angel had told him so. The people on the ship could now see that Paul was a prophet.

THE SHIPWRECK OF PAUL.

Day after day the ship continued to be tossed about in the fierce storm. For fourteen days they ate no food. All this time they had been rolling about on the stormy sea, fearing that they would never see land again.

At last they found that they were nearing land, for the sea was becoming more shallow. Now they were glad and afraid at the same time. They longed to be upon the land again, but they knew that there was great danger of the ship's being thrown upon the rocks and torn to pieces. In such a storm it is very difficult to reach the shore from a ship. But though they were in such danger, they were cheered by the kind and loving words of Paul, and they ate some food.

They soon found that it was as they had feared. Their ship ran aground; and as the front of it caught, the back part was torn away by the violent waves.

Two hundred and seventy-six persons were on the ship; and when they saw what had happened, they knew that the only way to reach land was to jump into the sea and do their best to get to the shore.

The soldiers thought they had better kill the prisoners; but Julius thought of Paul, and said no. Some escaped on boards, and some on broken pieces of the ship; but all reached the land in safety.

The Island of Melita.

—:—

THE name of the island upon which Paul and the rest that had been on the ship found themselves was Melita. Not one of the two hundred and seventy-six were lost in the sea, and no one was hurt; but they were wet and cold.

They found that there were people living on the island. These people may have been ignorant so far as books were concerned; but they all had souls, and Paul felt sorry for them. He knew that Jesus died to save every one.

The people of the island must have had very kind hearts; for when they saw the shipwrecked party in such distress, they did what they could to comfort them. It was now winter and very cold, and to make matters still worse, it was raining. The poor strangers must have looked very pitiful indeed. We can imagine them standing about shivering, and with clothes dripping wet.

A nice warm fire was soon built by these kind-hearted people, and perhaps they brought dry clothing for some. At any rate, they showed them no little kindness.

Paul was very glad to see these people show such kindness, not only for his sake, but for their own. He, too, was anxious to do what he could to help warm his companions; so he went and gathered a bundle of sticks, and laid them on the fire to burn.

Now what do you suppose happened next? The fire began to burn afresh, and Paul must have been holding his hands out, trying to warm them. All at once a viper, which is a very poisonous kind of snake, sprang out of the flame, and fastened itself upon Paul's hand.

Ignorant people are nearly always superstitious; that is, they believe in signs, and think when certain things happen, something else far worse will take place.

So when these people saw the snake hanging to Paul's hand, they thought it must be a punishment sent upon him by some of the gods; for these people were heathen.

They said among themselves that Paul must have murdered some one, and that even though he had escaped being drowned in the sea, he would have to die anyway.

Then they watched the snake upon Paul's hand, to see what would happen. They knew that when people were bitten by a viper, they nearly always died.

But Paul shook off the viper from his hand into the fire, and he felt no harm from the bite.

The barbarians kept on looking at Paul, expecting to see him swell and fall down dead suddenly; but after they had looked a great while, and saw no harm came to him, they changed their minds about him, and said that he was a god.

We are sure that Paul would not let them worship him; for you remember that while he was at Lystra, the people wanted to worship him and Barnabas, and he would not let them. Paul's only desire was to teach people everywhere he went, to worship the true God, and to follow the meek and lowly Jesus.

PAUL BITTEN BY THE VIPER.

361

The Sick are Healed.
—:—

THE experience of Paul with the viper opened the way for him to do much good among the people.

A very rich man by the name of Publius lived upon the island. This man sent for Paul to come and stay at his home for three days.

How kind it was of Publius to do this, and how much Paul must have appreciated this favor, after having passed through such terrible sufferings.

Quite a case of healing took place one day while Paul was visiting at the house of this rich man. The poor old father of Publius lived there, and he was very sick with a fever. When Paul heard of it, he went to the old man's room and prayed. Then, when he had laid his hands upon the man, the Lord raised him up, and he was well.

The news of this healing soon spread among the people; and others who were sick came, and were healed of their diseases.

How welcome Paul must have been after that in all of their houses!

God certainly was very good to show these poor heathen such kindness, and many must have learned to love Jesus, especially when they saw that he loved them well enough to heal them when they were sick.

Jesus is just the same to-day. He not only taught divine healing when he was upon earth, but gave his apostles power to heal the sick.

This power was first given to the Twelve (see Mat. 10: 1), and they exercised the power. Mark 16: 20; Acts 5: 12-16. He then gave this power to the Seventy (Luke 10: 1, 9), and they exercised it. Luke 10: 17-20. Next he gave this power to Stephen, Paul, and others (Acts 6: 8; 14: 8-10; 28: 8); then to some in the church (1 Cor. 12: 9), and to the elders. Jas. 5: 14, 15. And last of all the power was given to us if we believe. Mark 16: 16-18; John 14: 12.

There is something, however, that is required of all who desire healing. That is faith. Mat. 9: 29; Mark 5: 25-34; 5: 36.

Some, however, are healed through the faith of others; but those who pray must have faith, and "all things are possible to him that believeth." Mark 9: 23. We must believe when we pray, and expect that God will answer our prayer. 1 John 5: 15.

Some people think that the day of healing is past, but this is not true. Mark 16: 16-18.

The fifth chapter of James, from the thirteenth verse to the fifteenth, tells us just what to do in case of sickness. And we may be sure that Jesus is still able and willing to heal us when we go to him in prayer. Read Heb. 13: 8 and Eph. 3: 20, 21.

> To all who will believe
> Our Jesus is the same:
> They may his grace receive;
> Oh, bless his holy name!

⭕✹⭕✹⭕✹⭕

Paul in Rome.

—:—

WE will now return to Paul where we left him on the island of Melita. The people on this island must have learned to love him very much.

No doubt they would have liked to keep such a good man with them always, but Paul knew that God wanted him to go to Rome in Italy.

He had spent three months with these people, and the winter was about past. The fierce storms were over for a time, so a ship prepared to sail from the island. Paul was taken on board.

Everything necessary for the long trip was brought by those kind-hearted barbarians, and we are sure God blessed them for their kind and generous offerings.

Many days passed before they landed in Italy. The ship stopped for a short time at several harbors on the way. At one of these places, called Puteoli, Paul found some Christians. How glad he must have been to find some one else who loved the same Jesus that he loved, and who was willing to suffer, if necessary, for Jesus' sake! Julius allowed Paul to visit the brethren for a whole week, and then they went on toward Rome. On the way Paul met other friends, who greatly encouraged him.

PAUL BEFORE CAESAR.

At last Paul arrived in Rome. He was not taken to prison, as were the other prisoners; but he was carefully guarded by a soldier. This would not have been necessary; for Paul knew that God had some good reason for sending him to Rome, and he had no desire to disobey.

Previously to appearing before Cæsar, he sent for some of the chief men among the Jews living at Rome to come and see him. He wanted them to understand why he had been sent to Rome.

Perhaps he thought they might have heard things about him that were untrue, and he wanted them to understand that he had done nothing at all to deserve the chains with which he was still bound.

The Jews told Paul that no one had sent them any word or spoken anything against him. This, they said, was the first that they had heard regarding the matter, and they should be glad to hear more. So a day was set for them to come.

Upon the day appointed, a large company of the Jews came to listen to Paul. He preached to them all day about Jesus and his kingdom, and explained many things the prophets had said about the coming of Christ. Some of them believed that the things Paul said were true; but some did not believe, and became his enemies.

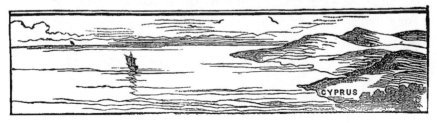

Paul said that the prophet Isaiah had spoken truly concerning them; for their ears were dull of hearing, and their eyes they had closed. For if it had not been so, all would have believed, and received salvation.

As it was, God had taken their portion, and had given it to the Gentiles, for they would hear and accept it. The Jews went home with many new and strange thoughts in their minds, and they had much to say about Paul.

For two whole years Paul remained in Rome, and preached the gospel of Jesus and his kingdom to the people in Rome, and no man forbade him.

The Bible does not tell us much more about Paul; but other books tell us that Paul really died at Rome. It was not, however, before he had fulfilled his mission to the Romans.

Persecution.

—:—

ALL the apostles had to suffer many things because they were brave enough to preach against sin; but Paul, I think, suffered more than any of the rest.

One time, while speaking of his suffering, he said that he had been beaten, stoned, imprisoned, shipwrecked, besides many other things just as bad; but God cared for him, and brought him through every trouble with victory. He was happy because he could suffer for Jesus, for he often remembered how he had persecuted Jesus and the disciples before he himself loved Jesus.

One time he said, "I take pleasure in persecutions for Christ's sake: for when I am weak, then am I strong." God's people are often persecuted to-day; but we have the same Jesus to trust in that Paul had, and we need not be discouraged, even if at times things may seem dark and terrible.

God will not let Satan kill us until our work is finished, for he cares for all who put their trust in him; but if, when our work is

Fear GOD AND KEEP HIS COMMANDMENTS

Eccl: 12. 13.

done, God sees fit to let us die the death that Stephen died, we should be glad that he considers us worthy to suffer and die for Jesus.

Persecution does not always mean death, or to suffer as much as the apostles did. Many things are being done every day against God's people by the enemies of Jesus; but remember, when you have to meet anything like this, the words that Jesus spoke to his disciples upon the mount—"Blessed are ye, when men shall revile you, and persecute you, and shall say all manner of evil against you falsely, for my sake. Rejoice and be exceeding glad: for great is your reward in heaven: for so persecuted they the prophets which were before you."

Oh, how precious were these words! But remember that Jesus said, "For my sake." So when we suffer, we must be sure it is for Jesus' sake, and not because we have done something wrong, and are suffering for that.

We should have to suffer to-day for Jesus just as the apostles did, if the law did not protect us; for the same hatred that was in the hearts of men and women when Jesus was here is in the hearts of some people to-day. Let us praise and thank God for a law of this kind; but let us never shrink from bearing the cross for Jesus, for, remember, without the cross there will be no crown.

My Crown.

—:—

I would wear a crown in heaven,
   A crown of jewels fair,
Which must be gained through suff'ring,
   Yes, I must sorrow share.

For Jesus bore before me
   The cross to Calvary,
And then he died upon it,
   From sin to set me free.

Ah, can I bear for Jesus
   My cross here day by day?

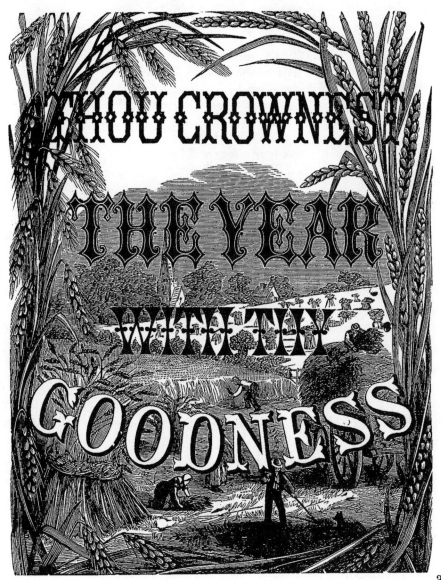

THOU CROWNEST THE YEAR WITH GOODNESS

Yes, Jesus helps me bear it,
   He is my strength and stay.

I'll trust him ev'ry moment,
   His power to keep, believe;
Then when I go to heaven,
   A crown there I'll receive.

My trials will adorn it,
   As jewels they will be;
And I'll see why I suffered,
   I'll solve each mystery.

Paul's Letter to the Romans.

—:—

WE do not read very much more in the Bible about any of the apostles, except their letters which were written to the different churches.

In Paul's letter to the Romans he said, "It is written, There is none righteous, no, not one: there is none that understandeth, . . . there is none that doeth good, no, not one."

Does it seem strange that Paul wrote in this way? Ah, no! You have been told that all have sin born in their hearts, and this was what Paul wanted to tell these Roman brethren—that all the world was guilty before God.

Paul did not stop when he had told them this; but he went on to say that although all had sinned and come short of the glory of God, yet they might be justified freely, or forgiven of all their sins by God's grace, for Jesus had been offered as a sacrifice for every one who would believe.

Oh, how hard it was to explain so that they could understand it, and yet so that it would teach others as long as the world should stand just how they ought to live in order to please God. It took Paul a long time.

When he came to the seventh chapter, he told them some things

HE that walketh Uprightly walketh Surely

PROV. 10.9.

371

that made it look still more as if no one could live without committing sin; for, speaking of his former condition, he said: "What I would, that do I not; but what I hate, that do I. . . . I delight in the law of God after the inward man; but I see another law in my members, warring against the law of my mind, and bringing me into captivity to the law of sin which is in my members. O wretched man that I am! who shall deliver me from the body of this death?"

What a miserable condition for a person to be in!—to want to serve God, yet unable to do so, because of a sinful inborn nature.

But Paul told them there was a way to be delivered from this nature of sin that had been born in them, just as well as a way to be delivered from the sins they had been in the habit of committing every day.

God forgave them of their sins for his Son's sake, and the blood that his Son shed on Mount Calvary was to cleanse them from this sinful nature. God had sent his own Son in the likeness of sinful flesh, that he might condemn sin in the flesh.

Paul's advice was very good. He explained to them that it was the carnal mind which made people want to commit sin.

Paul clearly taught that when a sinner was forgiven of his sins, he was born into the family of God, or justified in God's sight; but that there still remained within him a nature that would sometime cause him to want to commit sin again. This nature, nothing but the blood of Jesus could remove; and when it was removed, the man would be sanctified, or perfectly holy in God's sight.

God loves all the people that he has made, and he longs to see them happy and good. We should be very thankful that he ever permitted his dear Son to die to make them so, and that he gave the apostles wisdom to write down words that would teach us the way to be like God, even in this wicked world.

Paul did not stop when he had written such a long letter to the Romans. Many letters were written by Paul and the other apostles to the brethren at Corinth, Galatia, Ephesus, Philippi, Colosse, Thessalonica, and to the Hebrews, or pure-minded Jews. Letters were also

HAST THOU ENTERED INTO THE TREASURES OF THE SNOW?

Job XXXVIII. 22.

written to Timothy, Titus, and Philemon, who labored much in the gospel work. Then, too, there were special letters that were called by the names of those who wrote them. They all contain the advice and comfort that Christians need.

What John Saw.

—:—

The last book in the Bible gives an account of the wonderful things that John, the beloved disciple, saw in his old age.

Jesus loved John very dearly. He was the youngest of the Twelve We do not know much about John's life after Jesus returned to heaven; but when he became a very old man, he was sent to an island called Patmos.

This was a small rocky island at some distance from the country of Greece. He was sent to this island as a prisoner; but God was with him, and gave him a vision that was indeed glorious.

It was on the Lord's day when suddenly he heard behind him a great voice, as of a trumpet. The voice said that John must write a book, and send it to the seven churches which were in Asia. He turned to see who was talking to him, and saw a very beautiful sight. He saw Jesus standing in the midst of seven candlesticks, clothed with a beautiful garment.

When John saw him, he was frightened, and fell down as one dead. Then the Beautiful One laid his right hand upon him, and said, "Fear not; I am the first and the last: I am he that liveth, and was dead; and, behold, I am alive forevermore."

The Shining One then told him to write, and John did so. A special letter was written to each of the churches in Asia. After these letters were written, John saw angels. These showed him the different kinds of punishment that were to be sent upon the earth to punish the wicked people that did not repent of their sins.

But the beautiful part of his vision was the city which he saw,

SPEAK TO THE EARTH, AND IT SHALL TEACH THEE; AND THE FISHES OF THE SEA SHALL DECLARE UNTO THEE.

and which was prepared for the people of God. This was the new Jerusalem.

The Jews had always expected to see the city of Jerusalem again restored to its former beauty and grandeur; but this was never to be. They had refused to let Jesus reign over them, and now the Jerusalem where Jesus would reign would be entirely new, prepared of God.

John saw it descend out of heaven, and heard a voice saying: "Behold, the tabernacle of God is with men, and he will dwell with them, and they shall be his people, and God himself shall be with them, and be their God. And God shall wipe away all tears from their eyes; and there shall be no more death, neither sorrow, nor crying, neither shall there be any more pain: for the former things are passed away.

"And he that sat upon the throne said, Behold, I make all things new. And he said unto me, Write: for these words are true and faithful. And he said unto me, It is done. I am Alpha and Omega, the beginning and the end. I will give unto him that is athirst of the fountain of the water of life freely. He that overcometh shall inherit all things; and I will be his God, and he shall be my son." Rev. 21: 4-7.

John was then taken up, as it were, in the spirit upon a high mountain, where he could see the city in all its beauty. Oh, how beautiful it was! The walls and streets shone as precious stones, and the gates were as pearls.

In writing about it, John said: "And I saw no temple therein: for the Lord God Almighty and the Lamb are the temple of it. And the city had no need of the sun, neither of the moon to shine in it: for the glory of God did lighten it, and the Lamb is the light thereof. And the nations of them which are saved shall walk in the light of it: and the kings of the earth do bring their glory and honor into it. And the gates of it shall not be shut at all by day: for there shall be no night there. And they shall bring the glory and honor of the nations into it. And there shall in no wise enter into it anything that defileth, neither whatsoever worketh abomination, or maketh a

Therefore being justified by faith we have peace with GOD through our LORD JESUS CHRIST.

WHICH HOPE WE HAVE AS AN ANCHOR OF THE SOUL BOTH SURE & STEDFAST.

HEBREWS VI 18

lie: but they which are written in the Lamb's book of life." Rev. 21: 22-27.

And John saw the river and tree of life. The fruit of this tree was for the healing of the nations.

When John had seen and heard such wonderful things, he fell down and was about to worship the angel that had shown him these things. But the angel said, "See thou do it not, for I am thy fellow servant, and of thy brethren the prophets, and them that keep the sayings of this book: worship God."

In the closing of the book, are these words, spoken by Jesus: "Surely I come quickly." And John answers, "Even so, come, Lord Jesus."

Thus ends our New Testament, and we should all see to it that we are ready to meet Jesus when he comes; for he is coming, and all who are not ready will be left behind.

THE GRACE OF OUR LORD JESUS CHRIST BE WITH YOU ALL. AMEN. — Rev. xxii. 21.

The Voice of Jesus.

—:—

What voice is this I hear,
  That's warning souls to flee;
  That tells of misery,
  As well as mystery;
That says the time is near?

'Tis Jesus, God's dear Son,
  The One who years ago
  Endured death below,
  To save mankind from woe,
Who claims the vict'ry's won.

Let's say with John of old,
  "Lord Jesus, haste the time
  When we shall leave this clime
  To hear the happy chime
Of angels' praise oft told."

How welcome is this voice!
  We hear it when we pray,
  It guides us on our way,
  And teaches us each day:
We'll ne'er regret our choice